D0271706

SCOTTISH BORDERS LIBRARY SERVICES	
007768068	
Bertrams	16/09/2009
941.009	£14.99

BESIDE THE SEASIDE

EDITED BY RUTH PETRIE

guardianbooks

Published by Guardian Books 2009

2 4 6 8 10 9 7 5 3 1

Copyright © Guardian News and Media Ltd 2009

This book is sold subject to the condition that it shall not, by way of trade or otherwise, be lent, resold, hired out, or otherwise circulated without the publisher's prior consent in any form of binding or cover other than that in which it is published and without a similar condition, including this condition, being imposed on the subsequent purchaser.

Every effort has been made to contact copyright holders. The publishers will be pleased to make good any omissions or rectify any mistakes brought to their attention at the earliest opportunity.

'Pulpits in the Sand' by Fiona MacCarthy from the *Guardian* (© Fiona MacCarthy 1966) is reproduced by permission of PFD (www.pfd.co.uk) on behalf of Fiona MacCarthy.

First published in Great Britain in 2009 by
Guardian Books
Kings Place, 90 York Way
London N1 9GU

www.guardianbooks.co.uk

A CIP catalogue record for this book
is available from the British Library

ISBN 978-0-85265-137-7

Typeset by www.carrstudio.co.uk

Printed and bound in Great Britain by Clays Ltd, St Ives PLC

Contents

SCOTTISH BORDERS COUNCIL

LIBRARY &

INFORMATION SERVICES

Introduction

'Oh, I do like to be beside...' conjures up for each of us the intense pleasure, recalled or imagined, of the seaside. Sifting through many thousands of articles from the *Guardian's* digital archive using keywords such as 'beachcombers' and 'beach huts', 'Wakes Week' and 'wading birds', the messages in the bottle lapping at the shore were all about pleasure, pure and simple – but of course never quite pure and never simple, as these more than 130 pieces show. In 1822 an anxious letter-writer worries about mixed bathing at Southport; another writer in 1916, clearly a man who would brook no contradiction, suggests that children, instead of building sandcastles, contribute to the war effort by collecting seaweed for its potash and iron ...

Then and now, everything was different and many things much the same: the competing virtues and vices of the resorts – Blackpool or Llandudno, Bournemouth or the Isle of Wight – vied with each other, as they still do: then, special trains were laid on at bank holidays as crowds invaded the fronts and piers; now cars clog the main arteries to the coast; seaside landladies ruled with an iron hand with bath regulations and indifferent food in their own Fawlty Towers. Now second homes and beach huts cost a bomb and posh nosh is everywhere.

Through the decades changes in holiday habits and enthusiasms are charted: in 1922 Rhyl was 'sufficiently summerlike to warrant the wearing of flannels by both sexes'; swimsuits took on bold colours in the 30s; campers deserted boarding houses for canvas; Butlins opened its first resort in Skegness in 1936, Brighton was declared off-limits in 1941; in the 50s music struck up at Aldeburgh and art galleries opened at St Ives. Getting away from it all meant that caravans lumbered through country lanes, while the remoter pleasures of coastal path walks, the drama of Welsh cliffs and Shetland islands, offered up the glories of seabirds, seals, sea holly and other fauna and flora.

By the 1970s, with the advent of cheap package holidays, home-grown seaside pleasures took a dip, and struggled to stay afloat. Basking under an overcast sky meant a longing for the always-sunny Med, not for the Naples of the North, as Llandudno had been known.

Nowadays we're inundated with columns of advice about the best beaches/best restaurants/best loos/ best ice cream ... But the pastimes of the seaside are much the same: sandcastles and sculptures ingeniously erected to be erased by incoming tides; beach cricket still played; rockpool discoveries that induce squeals of delight; bacon and egg butties from rackety beach kiosks are as delicious as Padstow lobsters; nude bathing continues to upset sensibilities; coastal birds rise up in front of delighted walkers. And the infinite variety of Britain's coast continues to thrill and delight us all.

What, if anything, is missing then in Paradise-by-Sea? Possibly just the sun over the Easter bank holiday? But still we do love to be...

Where to Go – Blackpool or Llandudno?: 1821–1899

Court Of King's Bench, November 7:
right of bathing on the sea shore
November 17 1821

Blundell v. Catteral. – When the judges took their seats this morning, a decision was given upon a question of considerable interest to the public. It arose out of an action of trespass tried before Mr Justice Bayley at Lancaster.

The plaintiff, who is lord of a manor, and owner of soil on the banks of the Mersey, where he claims the exclusive right of fishing with stake nets, sought to deprive the defendant, who keeps an hotel on the spot, of the power of passing machines below high and low water-mark, for the purpose of sea bathing. The defendant insisted upon the common-law right of all the subjects of the king to bathe on the sea shore.

The jury found for the plaintiff, subject to the opinion of the court.

Letter to the editor from a visitor
August 24 1822

Sir – Impressed with the hope, that by your indulging me with the insertion in your paper, of a few remarks on the bathing at Southport, I may have an opportunity of promoting my own wishes, and, perhaps, the satisfaction of contributing in some degree towards public benefit, I venture thus to address you on this subject. – It is well known, that at most of the watering places in England, but on the eastern coast in particular, the bathing is conducted with the strictest attention to the feelings of the visitors. It is not the custom for men to bathe near the ladies, and females have the office of attending the ladies in the water instead of men, and in general the bathing machines have awnings. I should be sorry to make any remark on the very different mood of bathing at present adopted at Southport. My only motive for troubling you on this subject is, to point out to the parties, who conduct the bathing at that place, that it is their duty and interest to pay the utmost attention to the feelings of the company who patronise them, and, no doubt can for one moment exist, as to the nature of those feelings. I beg to add, that my influence can avail but very little; however, should my remarks be considered worthy of the notice of those, who can easily effect this desirable alternation, or point out to the parties, whose support depends on their attention to the wishes of the public, my family will be sincerely indebted to the one, for the benefits to be derived from sea-bathing, and I will insure to the other my warmest support and interest. – I beg to subscribe myself, sir, your obedient servant;

A. Visitor

Shark caught in the Firth of Forth
September 26 1838

On Wednesday last week, the boat's crew of Mr James Kelly, of Cantabay (a few miles east of the town of North Berwick), when fishing for herrings in Dunbar bay, were much surprised in finding a shark of great size entangled in their nets, which they with great difficulty succeeded in getting into their boat, where they accomplished his destruction, but not before one of the crew had his arm slightly lacerated. The monster was upwards of seven feet in length, three feet nine inches in circumference, twenty-three inches across the tail, had three rows of formidable teeth, and was supposed to weigh from ten to twelve cwt. The fishing village of Cantabay has been in a state of commotion ever since the monster was brought to land. The news of his capture having soon spread around, every one able to walk has repaired to the spot to see the much-dreaded creature. Mr Kelly intends preserving the skeleton for the inspection of future visitors of the Bass Rock, of which he is the tacksman.

Domestic and miscellaneous
May 20 1840

A large shoal of porpoises passed Brighton on Wednesday last, and by their sportive gambols attracted much attention. At Kemptown they approached the shore very closely, affording much amusement to the children, and others on the spot.

– Brighton Herald

Herm and Jethou
August 31 1842

Herm and Jethou!! Ninety-nine persons out of a hundred will say, 'I never heard of them: what are they: places, or people, or what?' Let it be my task to tell what they are. If the Right Honourable Secretary for the Home Department were asked to name 'the Channel Islands,' he would certainly say, 'Jersey, Guernsey, and Alderney;' possibly he might add 'Sark,' for Sark is named in the orders of council affecting the Channel Islands: but Herm and Jethou he certainly would not name. The reader will, therefore, have gathered by this time, that Herm and Jethou are the two smallest of the Channel Islands. Let us spend a summer's day together at Herm.

Herm possesses one peculiar distinction – an attraction which, during the summer, is the frequent cause of picnic parties from Guernsey – its shell beach. I have been told by competent judges, that the little island of Herm is richer in shells than all the shores of all the rest of the British Islands; and that the shells found there may be considered miniatures of the shells found in most other parts of the world. The divisions of the order testacea in this little island extend to upwards of forty genera, embracing upwards of two hundred varieties; and in sponges, corals, and corallines, Herm is as rich as in shell.

The shell beach of Herm, which extends from half a mile to three quarters of a mile, is one mass of shells, unintermixed with either pebbles or sand. Dig with your arm deep as you may, there is still nothing but shells – minute perfect shells, and fragments of larger shells. The minute shells are extremely pretty, and may be gathered in millions; and although I am myself no conchologist, and might probably commit so great a heresy as to estimate the value of shells by their beauty, I spent a long summer's noon much to my mind in Herm, wandering on the shell beach; lying upon it; digging my hands an arm's length down, and sifting, and examining, and pocketing.

As I returned along the rocks, I observed that several boats with shrimpers had arrived from Guernsey. This amusement is in fact a passion, and is indulged in by persons of all ranks; and so various are tastes, in the matter of recreation, that I have seen individuals, who found quite as much pleasure in wading knee-deep for half a day among the rocks, to make capture of some handfuls of shrimps, as has ever been afforded to others in the pursuit of the deer or the fox.

It was almost sunset when I had finished my rasher and egg in the little inn; and dusk was beginning to settle over the sea when I entered the harbour of Guernsey.

– Correspondent of Saturday Magazine

A whale stranded
March 23 1842

On Wednesday week, a strange-looking craft was descried in the sound between the Isle of Puffins and Penmon, steering wildly, evidently a stranger to the locality. The great unknown was eventually cast upon the rocks by the violence of the sea, and turned out to be a regular Greenland whale – a prize to the lord of the manor, Sir Richard W. Bulkeley, who relinquished his claim in favour of the captors. It fetched £10, and was towed up to the Menai Bridge, and beached on the Anglesey side, where the body corporate is exhibited at a trifling charge. The visitors are very numerous to the illustrious stranger, which is of colossean proportions. Lower jaw, 8 feet; full length, 44 feet; girth, 5 feet; weight, about 12 tons.

– Chester Chronicle

Blackpool
September 2 1848

There can be no question that Blackpool is the bathing place, par excellence, of the Lancashire coast. Bootle and Crosby can scarcely be called sea-bathing places: their proximity to Liverpool is their chief recommendation. Southport is an arid, sandy desert; its inhabitants have one perpetual struggle against the encroachments of their arenaceous enemy, which chokes up their very doors, if not continually driven back by shovel and broom. The sea, too, at Southport is less the sea proper than the ebb and flow at its estuary of the Ribble, upon the south bank of which river Southport is in reality placed. Nearly opposite, on the northern bank of the Ribble, is another so-called sea-bathing place – Lytham; but it has still smaller right to the name, for it lies somewhat higher up the river. True, the estuary of this river is at high water some eight miles across, and the water is salt; but it is very different from 'the wide, the open sea.' The temperature of both Southport and Lytham is considerably higher than that of Blackpool; and for one class of invalids, who need a soft and balmy, rather than a strong and bracing, air, the two bathing places on the Ribble may have advantages over their northern rival.

But in this age of close application to business, of long, unremitting toil, a bathing-place is sought by the worn and weary Liverpool merchant, or Manchester manufacturer, to restore the lost tone, to brace up the system to renewed vigour, and to repair the waste of physical strength by a change of scene and a strong fresh sea air – to which may be added, in many cases, the beneficial effects of sea bathing. For this purpose, Blackpool is really an invaluable possession to a large manufacturing and industrial county like Lancashire. Within two hours' distance of Liverpool or Manchester, its accessibility is not the least of its recommendations to men in business, who can thus, with a small expenditure of time, pass a day and a half or two days a week at the sea, without materially deducting from the hours due to the warehouse or the counting-house. Nay, it is accessible to another large class – those employés who enjoy the half-holiday – for a day and a-half-a-week – and there are few more wise uses of this time for them than to give themselves the healthful benefits of sea air and water at Blackpool. Since the opening of the railway throughout, it is known that this privilege has been extensively enjoyed by the class referred to; and in a season of commercial prosperity, Blackpool has become so full of visitors, that instances are numerous in which 'fresh arrivals,' who have not taken the precaution of securing apartments beforehand, have had to sleep in their carriages, no better dormitory being procurable throughout the place.

Blackpool appears to owe its chief advantages to its position on the coast. It faces the open sea, with an aspect nearly W and this is a matter of more importance than might be at first supposed. When Dr Dalton, many years ago, was asked to point out the best site for a botanical garden near Manchester, he first ascertained the proportion in which different winds blew throughout the year, in this part of England, and finding that westerly winds (including, of course, NW and SW) prevailed here nearly 300 days out of the 365, he urgently recommended that the gardens should be placed on the W side of the town, thus securing them an immunity, during the greatest part of the year, from the smoke of Manchester. Now, the same prevalence of the westerly winds secures to Blackpool an almost constant seabreeze: and this circumstance alone makes Blackpool not only a more desirable bathing place than the others named above, but also greatly preferable to those on the Yorkshire coast. At Scarborough, for instance, the seabreezes must be an E wind, and in later autumn, these easterly winds are piercingly cold, and, so far from bracing the frame, are really injurious to health. Then it is another advantage to Blackpool to stand on a sort of clay cliff, considerably elevated above the beach. In front of the range of houses next the sea, there is, at all times of the tide, a pleasant esplanade, or terraced walk. In Southport, the want of this has been supplied, at great cost, by the construction of the 'marine esplanade.' Then, at Blackpool, the beach is an exceedingly good one in most places for bathing, and there is a good supply of bathing machines. There is also an ample stock of vehicles, and especially of donkey chases, &c., for invalids, and donkeys for children. Within the last two or three years, a very neat and commodious market-house has been built, which is well ventilated, and very fairly supplied with poultry, vegetables, fruit, &c. Near it is a fish-market, also duly supplied with 'the usual delicacies of the season.'

From what has been said, it will be seen that the writer can have no desire to depreciate Blackpool; but it must nevertheless be confessed that there are one or two offensive nuisances tolerated there, to an extent which must astonish the visitor, and which greatly detract from the comfort and pleasure of an occasional sojourn there. It is chiefly with the object of calling the attention of the respectable residents to these, with a view to their remedy, that this notice has been written. Probably, the nuisances referred to may all be the result of a want of good local government; but on this point a stranger cannot be expected to be well informed, and it is only thrown out as a hint or conjecture.

Few visitors remain a day or two in Blackpool without complaining of an exceedingly offensive smell, especially perceptible to the inmates of the houses fronting the sea. This proceeds from the effluvia of the house drains, which find vent both into the houses themselves and occasionally through outlets and openings near the cliff. It is, of course, a continual nuisance; but necessarily worst during the Blackpool season, from the heat of the weather, and the greater quantities of putrefying matter which find their way into the drains. With an active and vigilant local government, enforcing certain obviously necessary sanitary regulations – as a due attention to the amount of fall, the placing of stench traps, &c – a great nuisance might be very speedily remedied.

Another nuisance, and, it may be said, the worst that can afflict any sea-bathing place, is the total absence of any regulations respecting bathing, and the consequent improprieties that are of daily occurrence on the shore. It is unnecessary to describe these: it is sufficient to mention them; for they must be matter of notoriety to every one who has visited Blackpool. This nuisance, which has grown more and more extensive of late years, as Blackpool has been more extensively resorted to, is of very easy cure. Let separate bathing grounds be assigned to the two sexes, a quarter or half a mile apart, clearly marked out by stakes or poles, and a heavy penalty imposed on any keeper or driver of a bathing machine who disregards these boundaries, and the thing is done. It is really a disgrace to Blackpool, that indiscriminate bathing should have so long existed there, when so simple a remedy would effectually put an end to it.

There are several other things which might be named; but this writer has no desire to prolong this part of his strictures. A good public news-room is much wanted. The market needs a few good regulations; and especially should the two entrance doors be kept clear of the vendors of fruit, butter, &c who prevent ready ingress and egress.

If some public body would apply themselves vigorously to the remedy of these evils, Blackpool would become more and more the favourite resort, for sea-bathing, of the vast town constituencies of both Lancashire and the West Riding of Yorkshire.

Value of seabirds to mariners
April 27 1850

'This coast (the South Stack, near Holyhead) is the resort, in the breeding season, of innumerable seabirds – especially gulls, razor bills, cormorants, and guillemots, but there are no puffins; peregrine falcons breed in the loftiest crags. No one, by order of government, is allowed to shoot the seabirds, as in foggy weather they are invaluable to steamers and shipping, being instantly attracted round a vessel, or induced to fly up screaming, by the firing of a gun; poor Captain Skinner's mail packet was once saved in this way. The late Bishop of Norwich, in his work on birds, states that the gulls instinctively assemble here on the same night, on or about the 10th of February, when they make a great noise; and nearly all retire on the same day, about the 12th of August.'

– Cliffe's Book of North Wales

Llandudno
July 28 1857

This agreeable bathing place is not so much known to, or frequented by, Manchester families as it deserves to be. To all who have become wearied of the places of resort on the Lancashire coast; to all who would find a milder air than that of Blackpool; a fresher and cooler than that of Lytham; or something less suggestive of a hot, sandy desert than Southport; nay, to all who would have something more than sea to look at, who love the scenery of hill and crag, no less than shingly beach, or sandy bay, or sea dotted with white sails flashing in the sunlight – to all these Llandudno offers attractions numerous and varied. It has about it all the charm of novelty and of youth, scarcely emerging indeed from childhood; for it dates its rise from the sales of land here, part of the estates of the Mostyn family, in August, 1849. A few years ago and the little peninsular was a sort of marsh, and all that then bore the name of Llandudno, was a poor village of scattered cottages along the mountain slopes and fisher-huts upon the shore. Its rapid rise is due less to judicious fostering (of which it has had a fair share), than to three great natural advantages, which it cannot lose – its good sea bathing, its salubrious air, and its admirable and beautiful situation. A glance at a map of Wales will show that the Llandudno of today nestles snugly at the foot of that huge promontory which on its north-easterly faces bears the name of the Great Orme's Head, and on its south-westerly that of Llandudno Mountain. The watering place stretches in interrupted crescents and terraces along the margin of a semi-circular bay from the Great to the Little Orme's Head, and at present consists of only four or five streets; but others are planned and need only time to convert rough and newly formed roadways into peopled avenues. The most remarkable feature about the place is that the narrow neck of land on which it stands possesses within a thousand yards two sea fronts, in two different bays – that nearest the village looking northerly and easterly to Llandudno or Orme's Bay, bounded by its two bold headlands, and presenting an open sea; while the other, looking west and south, opens upon Conway Bay, whose headlands are Llandudno Mountain and Penmaenmawr; and still more to the west are seen Puffins' Island, Anglesea, Beaumaris, the Menai Strait, and when the atmosphere is clear even the memorial pillar at Plas Newydd and the piers of the Menai suspension bridge.

Along the further shore, at the foot of Penmaenmawr, runs the Chester and Holyhead Railway; and by the white puffing steam, seen against the dark hue of the hill, the trains may be discerned from Llandudno. This frontage to Conway Bay is almost wholly neglected; though anywhere on the Lancashire coast, it would speedily become our first bathing place. Across this thousand yards of reedy flat a great drain has just been carried, to take the sewage of Llandudno. Three streets are commenced next the village, which will hereafter, in direct line, traverse this land from bay to bay – named Gloddaeth, Lloyd, and Clonmel streets; but at present the chief communication is near the hillside of the town by two irregular and nearly parallel streets, Church Walks and Tudno-street, both converging to, and continued in, Abbey-street, to Conway Bay. If to these the reader adds the Crescent along the long line of Llandudno Bay, and parallel to and in rear of it, the equally curved Mostyn-street, he will have a fair notion of this bathing-place. But neither verbal description, plan or map, can convey any idea of the beauty of the place, or of the delightful way in which every view, whether from sea or land, plain or eminence, blends the two great natural beauties of marine and mountain scenery. There is a complete panorama of these, finer than that of the landlocked straits of Menai. The place, as we have hinted, has been carefully fostered in its growth. There are good roads; others are being formed; drainage has been specially cared for; a waterworks company has been formed, to bring water from the Great Orme's Head; gasworks are also in contemplation; a railway is being carried from Conway (distant four miles) over the level land near the river; and buildings of uniform character, with spacious rooms and every convenience, are rapidly rising and filling up the vacant places. There is a church, several dissenting chapels, public baths, news room, and libraries; a new market hall has just been opened; and the place has already become one of great resort from Liverpool and Birmingham, especially the latter town, notwithstanding its distance. Public affairs are administered by a body of commissioners, under an act of parliament; and if these, and the landowners, and inhabitants generally, pursue a judicious course, Llandudno will speedily become the queen of Welsh bathing places.

Rural notes
August 19 1884

A correspondent, a competent and keen naturalist, who visited the Farne Islands, off the Northumbrian coast, in the height of the nesting season, informs me that all the seabirds had bred well. He writes:

'On the 1st July I visited the Farne Islands, now happily no longer the yearly scene of wanton plunder and cruel slaughter during the breeding season. The Association for the protection of the seabirds is certainly doing a good work, and is deserving of all support from every lover of nature. Those who have never visited the Farnes cannot have the faintest idea of the bird-life there; and, doubtless, without some such protection as the birds now have, they would soon have disappeared to other breeding haunts. The water around the rocks seemed alive with birds, and the continual screams of the various species of gulls, terns, &c., was bewildering. The following list represents the birds which nest occasionally or regularly on the islands: rested cormorant (shag), common cormorant, roseate tern, Arctic tern, Sandwich tern, common tern, lesser black-backed gull, herring gull, kittiwake, shieldrake, razorbill, oyster catcher, eider duck, guillemot, ringed guillemot, puffin, ring dotterel, redshank, rock pipit, starling, skylark, wagtail, titlark, and jackdaw. The king duck (king eider) was seen on the islands this season, but there is a fear of its having been shot. I did not see it. On the Longstone Island there was a pair of wagtails breeding, and, curiously enough, the male was a pied and the female a grey. Their nest was among some wood on the top of a small outhouse. The birds, it is believed, got stranded in making for the mainland, and settled down. Another strange freak brought under my notice was an eider duck sitting on the eggs of lesser black-backed gull. The jackdaws create great havoc among the eggs of the seabirds whenever they get a chance. I saw two or three fine broods of shieldrakes. Oyster catchers are now numerous. When these shier birds are unmolested for a season or two, as they are now, they will no doubt soon increase again. Young black-backed gulls, terns, puffins, and other species were very plentiful. How strange to hear, amid 'the myriad cry of wheeling ocean fowl', the cheering strains of the skylark, which was nesting near the lighthouse on the Inner Farne.'

The Royal National Lifeboat Institution: a letter
August 20 1891

Sir – I have followed with much interest and sympathy the correspondence in your columns on this subject. My two youthful sons during their stay at South Shore, in conjunction with their companions, by building sandcastles and decorating them with flags, spent their time pleasantly in making collections for this fund. Fortified with official badges on their arms and the well-known boat-shaped collecting-boxes of the Institution (both supplied by the courteous local hon. secretary), they enlisted the sympathy of all passers-by, with the gratifying result that probably about £20 was collected during the month. If this can be accomplished on one portion of the shore only and within a limited period, I don't see why at least £100 could not be collected during the season at each watering place. These youthful helpers would be a great accessory to a powerful sermon delivered in mid-season to the visitors. – Yours, &c.,

Maurice Cowen
Gordon House, Rusholme

Heading Round the Coast: 1900-1919

Safe in Sark
September 26 1901

If anyone wants to get away from the din and dust of the city, let him take a late train from London and the midnight boat to Guernsey, and he will wake up, like Bottom, translated. If then, after having a good wash and breakfast, he will go on board the little steamer at 10 for Sark, he will soon be safe for a time from that world that 'is too much with us.' In Sark there is no telephone, no telegraph, no gas, no railway, no shops or streets, no anything – except Nature in her grandest and loveliest moods, and abundant human kindness. The post arrives once a day, with the Guernsey steamer at 11. Letters are despatched when the steamer returns at 5pm; that is all. There is a little harbour in Creux Bay where the hand of man has somewhat improved a natural landing place. But there is no house near by of any kind. There are two comfortable hotels, but, like nearly every other house in the island, they stand detached and in the midst of fields and lanes. There is no village; the whole island is one scattered, rural parish, and the church bell rings the scholars to the day schools each morning before nine. Only in one corner of the isle is there a small cluster of cottages, and this is proudly called La Ville.

What is the charm of Sark? Partly its rural quiet, its absolute repose. It is as Nature left it. This, in days when even the Lakes and Snowdon are not safe from the improver or the speculator, is no little recommendation. But even more the endless variety and grandeur of sea and cliff and caves. The island is small – indeed insignificant in size. It is a mere rock, three or four miles long and very much less in breadth. You are never out of sight of the sea. But Sark is shaped like a starfish, with I know not how many rays. Each ray is a mass of granite crags of every conceivable outline, and these rugged cliffs, that rise to 200 or 300 feet, enclose as many little bays, many of which reveal little or no beach even at low tide, so deep is the water close to the shore and so steep and jagged the cliffs.

Down to these bays generations of fishermen have found or made steep paths down grass and rock, sometimes cutting rough steps in the cliff, and sometimes fixing rings and ladders to help themselves down its face. These cliff paths are many, and vary in ease and safety. One of the amusements of the place is to find or make new tracks up and down, and no one should come to Sark who is not a bit of a climber. The young and nimble expert will find it quite worthy of his skill to scale Les Autelets, the fine rocks off the western shore – so dear to the man with the camera or the pencil – the highest of which rises to 90 feet sheer out of the sea. If when he descends he finds the tide coming up, he can cool himself with a swim to shore. Ordinary folk, however, will find full satisfaction for their energies in climbing down to the Gouliots, Les Boutigues, and other caves, wading through their vast halls in a foot or two of water amid limpets, anemones, and rocks, and then climbing up the cliff again by another route. In a word, Sark is all cliff, and every bit of cliff a marvel of grandeur and beauty. Round the tall, dark brown crags the sea comes playfully in, splashing at their feet at the ebb of the tide and on a calm day, but with a rising wind and a tide of 50 feet the scene is changed. There being no sands and the cliffs all of granite, the water is perfectly clear, and often as blue almost as the Mediterranean. Is there anywhere such a paradise for bathers? There is not in the island a bathing tent or bathing house, far less anything so vulgar or conventional as – but I am ashamed to speak of bathing-machines in such a connection. Yet everybody bathes, and you can bathe anywhere. The Dixcart bay affords shore-bathing at most states of the tide, and there are everywhere rocks and caves that shelter the bathers while they undress and dry themselves and dress again. It is always a nice question where to bathe in Sark; you have the embarrassment of riches. You take note of the slope of the sun, the direction of the wind, and the state of the tide; and the endless bays and caves and rocks afford to those who know the island well a plentiful choice of spots whence you can see the stones and rocks far down below, and presently can bask at leisure in the sun upon the rocky ledge. Then the boating and the fishing! I do not know that our amateur fishermen make great hauls. But they find ample sport, with bass and brill and bream, and mullet grey or red, and mackerel and rock-fish of famous colour and size, if not taste.

We learn to speak of the Channel Islands as four in number. It is an absurd mistake. Victor Hugo is never tired of telling us they are an archipelago. I have not counted them; I should not like to try. For the Channel Islands are an endless group of rocks and isles varying in size from considerable islands like Jersey and Guernsey down to tiny rocks that only appear at ebb tide and are a constant peril to the mariner. Wherever an island is large enough to grow grass it is made use of. Often there is a solitary little farm and one small household. How they live I wonder. Herm is inhabited by Prince Blucher and his household; he is a descendant of the famous general. Jetou belongs to Mr Austin Leigh, of the Paris embassy, and has one nice residence on it. There is a farm and homestead on Brecqhou, close to Sark, and plenty of rabbits. Even the little rock called Le Tas de Sark grazes a few sheep; but they soon grow so wild, from being left to themselves, that when one is wanted for the market you land and shoot it as you might a chamois. I repeat, these islands are an archipelago, and a perilous one for the ships. There seems to be hardly a passenger boat plying in these waters that has not been on the rocks. Sometimes the consequences are terrible, as in the case of the Stella. Yet I am assured by the sailor folk that there is no danger, except in fog, if only reasonable care is taken by captains and pilots. They know these seas well, so well that at times they have been careless. For fear of losing their harvest of visitors, they are now redoubling their care.

Of all the archipelago, Sark is the gem. Jersey, being nearest France, has caught most of French culture. It has two small railways, it has some towns of note; the French visitors, as well as English, are many. It exports enormous quantities of cabbages and potatoes, besides fruit. Alderney – despite her famous cows – may be left out of account. The scenery is comparatively tame, and the chief thing that strikes the visitor is the number of empty houses and the perilous ruin of the abortive breakwater. The breakwater was one of the many costly blunders of our Admiralty, and the empty houses once held the workpeople employed to make it. One thinks of the taxpayers, and wonders whether the Alderney blunder is being repeated at Gibraltar. Guernsey has a mild climate, several flourishing towns, and some fine scenery. The fish market is a wonderful sight on a Saturday morning. But the chief business of the island is to feed the insatiable appetite of the English for grapes and tomatoes. To this end the whole island is fast being put under glass, and firms from Covent Garden and elsewhere have their offices on the spot. By one boat last week 76 large 'cases' and 9,000 'baskets' of fruit were sent to England. You see the carts bringing them in to St Peter Port, where piles of them await the Southampton or Weymouth boats. Sark is quite subordinate to Guernsey. It has no registered boats of its own.

Its supplies of every kind come from Guernsey. On Saturday the morning boat starts early, and carries the Sark folk at cheaper fares to do their marketing at St Peter Port and so return. It is like driving into the market town, only the cart is a little steamer and the road is by water.

But Sark is Sark after all. Its natives are rightly and amply proud of it. 'There is only one Sark in the world,' one said to me, as soon as I landed. Its people have their marked qualities. They are very thrifty, very industrious, very independent, very loyal. They dislike the French; they are very Protestant, but they are thoughtful and well-read. They love the English monarchy, for was it not Queen Elizabeth who founded the Sark that is today? But they love the British flag the more because they have home rule, and because they were never conquered. One of the residents in Sark had an English gardener, and he was boasting of the military greatness of his country, saying that England had conquered France and had annexed the Channel Islands. The Cereguois immediately had him at his mercy. 'No, no,' said he. 'We are the Normans; we conquered you, and that is why Sark is part of Great Britain.' Queen Elizabeth's hand is still felt everywhere; her date marks the older buildings; you read 1571 on the old mill, 1572 on the cannon in the Seigneurie grounds, 1588 on the old 'Creux' in the harbour. The laws are still as she gave them. The name of De Carteret is not extinct. The land is still parcelled out into forty holdings, no more and no less. All sorts of old laws and usages survive.

You live under the government of a seigneur, a seneschal, and two connétables. The forty 'tenants,' or copyholders, have an exclusive franchise. The inhabitants pay but one tax, which is expended by the islanders themselves; there are no paupers, and the jail is never used. The navigation of the boats is not under the jurisdiction of Trinity House. Yet the islanders love Great Britain, and if there is a cotton famine, or a war fund, they give, in proportion to their numbers, twice or thrice as much as England. You are everywhere told that the French language is giving way to the English in the islands; there is no movement as yet on foot, as in Wales, to maintain the ancient native tongue. Yet it is pleasant on Sunday to hear the service of our prayer book so earnestly conducted in old French. Outside, at the church door, you pause to read the notices upon the board. You are told that such a farmer will kill *une bete grasse* on Wednesday, and such another on Thursday, and you are advised to bespeak a joint. It is easy here for a house to run short of provisions, for there are no shops, except such as become a tiny village.

Such is Sark; and how beautiful in the bright September days, when the bracken on the slopes above the sea grows brown and red under the westering sun! But if Sark is fair in autumn, what is she like in May, when the flowers are out and the grass is green, and the birds are singing their loudest, and sea-fowl are nesting in thousands on the cliffs? No one, they say, ever visits Sark without coming again and again. I accept the omen.

Puffin Island and its inhabitants
June 28 1902

Willughby, speaking 'of some remarkable isles, cliffs, and rocks about England where sea-fowl do yearly build and breed in great numbers,' says that Priestholm is 'a small uninhabited island near Beaumaris, in the Isle of Anglesey, belonging to my Lord Bulkley. On this island build the Anates Arcticae of Clussius (here called puffins), razorbills, guilliams, cormorants, and divers sorts of gulls.' On the Ordnance map the island is called Puffin Island, and below, in brackets, are the names Priestholm and St Seiriol's Island. Giraldus calls it Ynys Lenach, or Priest's Island, 'because many bodies of saints are deposited there and no woman is suffered to enter it.' Other early writers spoke about it as Glannauch or Glanach, but said it was more generally known as Puffins' Island; now the possessive is dropped, and the place is seldom spoken of by any other name than Puffin.

Everybody knows Puffin Island; it is visible from so many well-known seaside resorts along the North Wales coast. During the holiday season it is a regular show-place, sailing-boats constantly crossing to it from Llandudno, Beaumaris, and Llanfairfechan. The island is a private property, belonging to Sir Richard Bulkeley, and visitors are not supposed to land upon it and wander where they will. No objection would be made if people would only have the sense to recognise that property is property, and would not wilfully break the law because the island is uninhabited. It is no unusual thing for visitors to land with guns and shoot the rabbits and seabirds, even killing the latter during the breeding season; while the eggs of the seafowl are robbed without any regard for law or morality. Every now and then the keeper from the mainland pays a visit to his charges, and frequently finds that during his absence damage has been done. It was my privilege recently to accompany the keeper on one of these trips, for I wished to see what birds still bred upon Puffin.

In size the island is about five-eighths of a mile long by a quarter broad, and everywhere, except at the southern end, nearest to Anglesey, it rises steeply from the sea, weathered limestone cliffs providing ledges and cracks on which the birds can nest. These crags are not actually very high, but above the rocks the steep grass slope rises to 100 or 160 feet. It is on this grass slope, not on the rocks, that the puffins nest. The whole of the top of the island resembles a great rabbit warren, being honeycombed with burrows; but it is by no means certain that all these are rabbit holes, for certainly in some cases puffins excavate their own tunnels.

Pennant, Bingley, and other writers at the end of the 18th and beginning of the 19th centuries describe Puffin Island as being thickly populated with puffins, but many years ago the birds forsook the island for some time. It was said that they were driven away by rats, the descendants of some that escaped to the island from a wreck, and that now there are few, if any, rats left. This may be true, for we saw no signs of rats, but there were a fair number of the birds. Every few minutes one would dart out of a hole and fly straight down to the water, and there were a large number swimming about at a safe distance, but they were evidently shy. The eggs too were not within reach, being perhaps eight or ten feet below the entrance. There can be little doubt that constant persecution has made the birds wary, and also accounts for the comparative fewness of their numbers. The puffins all breed on the western side, and where the holes are thickest the turf is covered with thrift, which, when we saw it, was one mass of purple-pink flowers.

On the ledges of the steep cliffs the guillemots were sitting on their single eggs; it was amusing to see them alight upon a ledge and poke the big green or white mottled egg between their legs with their long bills. Razorbills were crouching in cracks, not in such open ledges as the guillemots; and in one place there was a fair-sized colony of kittiwakes. These pretty little gulls nest in most impossible-looking spots, their weed-built nests apparently stuck against the rock face. The larger herring gull was nesting in considerable numbers all round the island, but the nests were placed upon the turf in much more secure positions – secure in one way, but easily accessible sometimes, and consequently robbed by visitors. There was a large colony of lesser black-backed gulls on the eastern side, and the deeper, fiercer call of the birds was easily distinguishable from the wild, shrill 'hehoh' of the lighter-backed gulls. In one spot half-a-dozen or more pairs of sheld-ducks were nesting in the rabbit burrows. We saw 16 of these beautiful black, white, and chestnut ducks, and probably many of them were nesting. We only managed to find one nest, which contained fresh eggs; but there were sure signs that many of the other burrows were in use. I was a little surprised to find sheld-ducks breeding on the island, for the bird usually frequents low sand-hills, but these nests were fully 100 feet above the sea. The peregrine falcon bred on Puffin last year, but the young were taken and the female bird shot. I think I am safe in saying that the birds have not entirely deserted the neighbourhood, for on a cliff not very far away we spent two happy hours watching a pair of these noble birds, the finest of our resident falcons. The tiercel had obtained another mate, as hawks so easily do, and though we did not see the eggs or young I have little doubt where they were. I hope they may continue to rear their young in this spot and forsake the tripper-haunted Puffin. On the island we saw a young carrion crow sitting at the mouth of a rabbit hole; it could only just fly, and so must have been bred on the island. Several lesser black-backed gulls swooped at it with angry cries, well knowing the evil egg-stealing habits of the carrion.

Besides these larger birds there are a few others that make Puffin their home during the breeding season. We saw two pairs of oyster-catchers which, from their behaviour, had got young hidden away in the thrift; there were also a few rock pipits breeding on the cliff face, and a pair of meadow pipits on the top; and a young blackbird and some anxious hedge-sparrows proved that the stunted bushes had not been untenanted. Starlings nest in the ruins and wheatears in the burrows, and we also saw one song-thrush and heard a skylark. The last two may have been visitors from the mainland. Pennant says that 'the Smyrnium olusatrum of Alexanders almost covers the south-west of the island, and is greedily eaten (boiled) by the sailors who are just arrived from long voyages.' The umbelliferous plant still grows in profusion, but it is now more on the south-east than south-west, but it was pleasant to find that in this respect Puffin is as it was a hundred years ago. If only visitors will let the birds and the plants alone it will be much the same in a hundred years from now.

Let me close with an extract from Giraldus Cambrensis, written more than 700 years ago, probably the earliest description of Puffin: 'There is a small island, almost adjoining Anglesey, which is inhabited by hermits, living by manual labour and serving God. It is remarkable that when, by the influence of human passions, any discord arises among them all their provisions are devoured by a species of small mice with which the island abounds, and when the discord ceases they are no longer molested.' We are yet seeking for the 'species of small mice.'

TAC

Arran in September
November 10 1902

It is perhaps too much to say that Arran is Goatfell and Goatfell Arran, for there are soft rounded masses of rolling hillside dyed to green and purple and russet. There are glens grey with rock and rugged with boulders or sheltered by fir forest and gleaming with heather. But still, dominating all is Goatfell, grey and sharp, recording the weather – an unfailing register. The clouds cling about it, and the trailing mists, on many of these autumn days, when the east wind blows and blots out the opposite shores of Bute and Ayr. Then there comes a day of Indian summer, and sharp and clear, a spire of silver, Goatfell shines above the heathery sides of Glen Ross or the rock-grey shadows of Sannox. From the sea, it towers and dominates the island. On shore, it constantly rises into view, changing a hundred times a day in the changing lights, never alike two days together – the glory and the crown of Arran. September has its special value here, even the capricious September of such a travesty of summer as this year's. There is a cold sting in the air by day. The large moon rises over Ayrshire and fills the night with glory, and sets in her rising a golden pathway across the sea, seen from the stony shores of Corrie. The visitors are few in number, and if the regular service of steamers to the Lochs is no longer available, the days are made for walking and the colour in the woods and hills is richer than any summer can show.

Goatfell and Holy Island! Sleeping there in Lamlash Bay with the whispering sea about it, full of old stories of the devotion of St

Molios and the monks and the hard faring of those who counted
not their lives dear unto them in the good cause, the island rises – a
place of dream and story for those who can forget the city and dream
still. There, at the end of the long coastline it towers, now just a
dark shape in the mist, now sharply rising from a placid sea – green
and grey and weather-stained. Resting here at Corrie, the changing
lights on sea and shore renew the sense of beauty; the cloud-shapes
sweeping across the sky bring a fugitive delight. It is only when
we get back to the sea and the mountains and the wild wind-filled
glens that we know how hungry we had grown for the life of our
forefathers, and the ways of a simpler folk, and the recreation given
by a world where no trains run and no 'works' or machinery exist.
It is never the wrong time to see the hills; the days of sweeping rain
and drifting mist, broken now and again by the sunshine that hung
glittering in the wet air, had a strange beauty, not less than that of
the tranquil days of soft air and unruffled sea. Up over the hill and
through the glens of Shurig and Suidhe to Shiskine and the west
coast at Blackwater and Laag, the skies were blue and the hills bright
at one moment, and the next they were dark with sudden showers
and blurred with driving mist.

On one day of tempest, when the steamer rocked and rolled in
Brodick Bay, the water was at rest under the lee of Holy isle, and
there were intervals when its high perpendicular shores glowed
softly, a restful grey green in the afternoon sunshine. On this day
the landing at Corrie in the ferry boat, heaving and rolling at the
steamer's side, was an experience with just enough risk in it to
give excitement and an edge to the day, to make it live in memory.
One tourist asked the ship's officer if there was anything in the
landing in such a sea to alarm a lady. 'Aw weel, that depends on the
alarmabeelity of the leddy, just,' was the dry and safe answer. It was
a fine sight to see the stalwart, motionless boatmen, unmoved and
self-controlled, holding on to a cable laid alongside the paddle-box,
while the sailors with the utmost care got the passengers on to the

tossing craft. Then, with the gleam of her electric lights flying and dancing over the heaving water, the big ship drew away from us and left us in the darkness pulling for Landing Rock.

Arran has its sturdy characters, and at Corrie, at any rate, one notices the prevalence of spinsters. There is a distinct type – the good-hearted, bustling, middle-aged woman whose housewifely qualities are considerable and who has lacked either time or inclination to find a mate. Indeed at Corrie spinsters and bachelors abound, and wise old collie dogs who have that placid and benign expression which old dogs possess. As one shepherd said to us, 'Ye canna easily mak' an end o' a dog when it's followed ye 14 year.'

The Cowes week: Meteor's day
August 5 1903

Although the King and Queen are here, and all manner of great folk are to be seen on the sacred lawn of the Royal Yacht Squadron, everyone is of opinion that 'Cowes is flat.' As you pass through its crooked old streets, where London West End tradesmen have hoisted their signs and everything breathes of Bond street, you see notices that many delectable apartments and houses are to be let. If you question the shopkeepers about the part of the world in which they are most concerned you will hear a tale of dolorous happenings – how the death of Queen Victoria has ruined Cowes, how such a baker loses £2,000 and such a barber £50 a year now that the court has gone from Osborne and the convalescent home is being prepared there. But for all this there is to the outsider every sign of bustle and pleasure-making. More yachts have combined to make the forest of masts which is so obvious a sign of the Cowes week, but never yachts of more grandeur. The *Victoria and Albert*, on which the King and Queen are taking their leisure after their Irish journeys, and the *Osborne*, on which the Royal grandchildren are supposed, erroneously, to live, are there. The *Osborne*, with its old paddle boxes, was sent round to Cowes because the Prince and Princess of Wales were expected to spend some hours there before the royal yacht arrived; but, reaching Cowes at the right time, they went at once to the *Victoria and Albert*.

There are more Americans here than an active man can count. The most prominent Americans are the Drexels, mother and son, and their amazing steam yacht *Margarita*, which, after Mr Gordon-Bennett's *Lynstrata*, is the finest private yacht in the world. Besides her, flying the stars and stripes, are Mrs Goelet's *Nahma*, a vessel which has gained some notoriety among yachtsmen and Americans from the fact that its owner flew the German standard from the mainmast when the Emperor lunched on board it a few weeks ago at Travemünde. It is difficult to convey to non-yachting people how epoch-making the act was, but it may be set on record that if a yachtsman wishes to do special honour to a guest on his boat he flies the guest's flag at the mizen. The main flag proclaims the nation and club of the person whose castle the yacht is understood to be. Beside the American yachts, there was a wintry forest of yachts under bare poles, among which one could discern German, Spanish, and French as well as English yachting club flags of many colours.

The presence of the King, of course, brought crowds across from the mainland round the old stone pillars which guard the pier on which only officers of the navy and yachtsmen of the Royal Yacht Squadron are allowed to land. Minstrels came and ultimately went, motor-cars plunged through, the most wonderful tailor-made yachting dresses passed and repassed, lunch became cold, but still the crowd lingered, their camera (for everyone who goes to Cowes has either a yacht or a camera) loaded and ready, and a letter to America as good as written – but the King did not come.

The yachting today was full of excitement. In the early morning the wind was from the south-south-west, and as the day wore on it increased until it blew at the velocity of 12 knots an hour. At sunset it slackened, and night fell upon quiet gilded waters. It was *Meteor's* day. Yesterday she won the Royal London Handicap, and today she won the King's Cup with 13min 12 sec to spare. The course was a very flat one, so flat, indeed, that with the wind in the present quarter spinnakers were not available during the whole race. A schooner's best point is in reaching, when every bit of her long canvas tells, and with a steady course her great weight will carry her in the long run past anything. The test of the schooner is her beating, for she takes longer to turn than a craft of any other rig. Today's conditions were the best possible for a schooner. In the fifty miles there was only ten miles beating, and the other courses were a fore-reach and a close-reach. There was no running. The entry was:

> *Meteor*, schooner, 412, German Emperor.
> *Brynhild*, yawl, 153, Sir James Pender.
> *Fiona*, yawl, 151, Marquis of Camden.
> *Glory*, yawl, 205, Sir H. Seymour King.
> *Cetonia*, schooner, 203, Lord Iveagh.
> *Cariad*, ketch, 152, Earl of Dunraven.

Meteor allowed *Brynhild* 9min 56sec, *Glory* 18min 31sec, *Cariad* 30min 25sec, *Cetonia* 38min 43sec, and *Fiona* 45min 46 sec.

The boats went on at the end of a drizzle, all carrying jibheaders except *Brynhild* and *Glory*, which had small jackyarders. When they came round on the starboard *Meteor* had a small lead from *Fiona*. After the thrash to windward down the west channel *Brynhild* closed up and took second place. They gybed round Lymington spit, and, reaching the winning post at Cowes, *Brynhild* was five minutes behind *Meteor*. After rounding Old Castle point sheets were hauled in. At Bullock Patch *Glory* was only a minute behind *Brynhild*. They came back close-hauled on a port tack, and, the wind having slightly quietened, they stole along and finished without weakening their tack. There was great excitement to see if the German boat would work in with her full time allowance ahead of the rest. The long slants were very

favourable for the schooner, and when the gun boomed out from the
Castle she had won the King's Cup by 13 minutes 12 seconds, which
nullified her time allowances. The finishing times were:

Meteor (winner)	2hr. 17min. 49sec.
Brynhild	2hr. 40min. 57sec.
Glory	2hr. 48min. 56sec.
Cariad	2hr. 55min. 31sec.
Fiona	3hr. 12min. 29sec.
Cetonia	3hr. 24min. 45sec.

The second race, from a yachtsman's point of view, was even more
interesting. It was one of the class races, and now that these races
have been revived it has been a peculiar interest because of all the
old class fixtures it is the only one which has not been abandoned.
Class racing is racing where the first requisite is speed. You have
certain measurements, and it lies with your designer to sacrifice
comfort, sleeping room – everything, in short, that connects a racing
yacht with an ordinary citizen, to procure a frame which will hold
an extremity of sail area. The race was for yachts exceeding 52 tons
and not exceeding 52 linear rating. There was no time allowance.
The entry was:

    Camellia, cutter, 52, Mr A Coats.
    Moyana, cutter, 51.9, Mr J W Leachars.
    Viola, cutter, 52, Mr W B Paget.
    Lucida, cutter, 52, Mr W P Barton.

The race was a hard one, the yachts carrying all the sail they could
stagger under. The result was a win for *Moyana* by nearly 4min,
Lucida, *Camellia*, and *Viola* arriving in the order named.

Tomorrow the Emperor's Cup, initiated by the German Emperor
ten years ago, is the great race. It is open to all yachts of 40 tons
and upwards built in Europe. It is a cruisers' race, and is regarded
by practical yachtsmen as a much more important fixture than the

America Cup, as it is in every sense the great race for yachts and not for racing machines.

'The island' in autumn
September 7 1904

It is small wonder that the Isle of Man is such a favourite resort to the toilers on our coal beds. Wherever the wind comes from, you get the purest of sea breezes. Nothing picks you up like that, after your eleven months of monotony and hard work. Then there is the little variety of travel in getting there. The trip in the train, the crossing of Liverpool, the sea journey with all its variety and perils. Nothing is more amusing than to notice the way certain bad sailors settle themselves down to a supposed and certain calamity. This reconciliation to necessity has its mildly heroic side. These people are of that numerous frightened band whose one remedy against sea-sickness – staying ashore – is never taken. You can see them with their various remedies – worse, probably, than the disease. However, they brave it, and are, no doubt, all the better for it.

We cross with the 'Owdham Wakes' folk. We have not seen them for 30 years under these circumstances. One wonders what has come over them, this well-dressed, orderly crowd. It is not at all what we saw before, in the old rude, pre-school board days. No rowdiness, no rudeness, not one of us drunk. Has the school done all this? one wonders, for the transformation from bad to better is complete. In fact we were decidedly and most respectably dull. Everybody seemed to be on their good behaviour, with 'Beg your pardon!' at every turn as you threaded the crowd to see if anything was toward to relieve the monotony. The three and a half hours' sea journey was all it should be; everybody was freshened up, and not a soul sick.

Douglas, of course, was the destination of most of us. It is wonderfully improved, and is evidently a prosperous place. Its style is the obvious one – something of Blackpool with better scenery, or of Llandudno with less style. Scarborough beats them all even yet in both, barring the sunsets, which foolishly occur behind you. That is an east coast calamity, save at Felixstowe, where, by some special magic, you see both sunrise and sunset at this time of the year.

The pastimes at all these places run on the same lines – promenading, bathing, bands, pierrots, some driving, less golf, and no end of harmless gossiping. The tone, so to speak, has advanced all along the line, and here at Douglas you see no evidences of a declining physique in the people or of the poorness of the times we hear so much of. The times are bad, though – so everybody says. The boat was only two-thirds full, lodgings are not scarce, hotels not over-full, and all the exuberant expenditure on driving and the rest is curbed. Yet at Oldham alone there was no less than a hundred thousand pounds paid out of the saving clubs for the annual wakes festival that we all remember of yore as a rather vulgar carnival.

Ramsey ranks second in the island, but it is rather a compromise after all, being neither so quiet as other spots nor so holiday busy or interesting as Douglas. The bathing everywhere is perfect, for the sea is as clear as crystal wherever you go. The boating too is universally excellent, and the accidents few and far between. There are terrible storms in the Irish Sea westward, and only the other day we heard near Port Erin a pathetic story of four men from that hillside, all belonging to one parish, who had just been lost and never more heard from, save by evidence from floating spars and bits of obviously wrecked boats. The island is full of such episodes, recent and long remembered from past times.

The Manx people are peculiarly bright minded, with beautiful voices, especially among the women. They have not the singing notes of the Welsh, but their spoken notes are more beautiful. We fear that all romance has gone out of them, and no wonder, from the crowd of prosaic visitors flooding them year after year. Everything under such conditions inclines to the morbid or the mercenary. We come across nobody who has so much as heard of TE Brown, their one genuine and true if somewhat minor poet. It is sad to relate also that references to their successful novelist results in their own chaff of his long hair and somewhat forlorn and affected appearance as shown in his portraits, which are in all the shops. They are busy with other matters – farming, boating, keeping lodging-houses. Here at Port Erin we get the highest picturesqueness on the island. The bay is small, but framed in with hills and flanked with a high promenade in a perfect way. The magnificent open-air bath is a delight daily both to bathers and spectators. Above this, to the north, is the charming bungalow of our own Alderman Jennison, most hospitable of men. His lovely grounds extend right along the breast of Bradda, with low woods at the shore end and the loveliest of heather sward. Below are fascinating caves, coves, and haunts of seabirds. But the coast hereabout is truly noble. Quite near we have the Calf of Man, with the find sound between it and the mainland. Near by, again, is the famous Spanish Head, from wrecked Armada days so called. This, along with the splendid rocks at South Stack, near Holyhead, is among the very finest headlands of our islands. Nothing can be finer than its rugged sheer splendour of dip to the clear sea. Its purple colour, its noble form, make a combination of dignified beauty hard to beat.

Charles Rowley

Fleetwood regatta
August 14 1905

The 11th annual regatta promoted by the Fleetwood sailing club was held under favourable conditions on Saturday afternoon. In addition to an exhibition of high diving by Professor Norris and several local swimmers there was a launch of the lifeboat Maude Pickup, while in the evening a grand cycle parade in fancy and comic costumes afforded a good deal of amusement. The following are the different events:

Rowing match for deep-sea trawlers' punts, two men and no coxswain.

Rowing match, double sculls and coxswain.

Obstacle race, two men in each boat.

Open swimming handicap for men (amateurs).

Swimming match for local boys.

Horizontal greasy pole.

Horizontal greasy pole (in costume).

Tug-of-war for men (10 a side).

Tug-of-war for ladies (10 a side).

Jingling match.

Sack race.

Sandcastle competition (for girls under 14).

Sandcastle competition (for boys under 14).

Cycle parade – most grotesque costume and best-decorated cycle (gentlemen).

Prettiest costume and best-decorated cycle (ladies).

Best costume and decorated cycle (gentlemen).

The October tide
October 12 1909

The gulls were drifting up the main when we crossed the wet sands towards the beacon-crowed islet, the smallest of the three islands of Hilbre, but the tide had not yet begun to fill the two shallow gutters which are seldom emptied of water. Away seaward a line of foam marked the advancing waters which were breaking on the East Hoyle, and the red and black buoys began to lean over towards the land in Hilbre Swash; the big tide was coming, but there was time to cross comfortably from the mainland. Bare-footed amateur cocklers trudged back to West Kirby, and two visitors to the little colony on Hilbre raced, knee deep, through the rapidly filling gutter between the two larger islands, and we were left in sole possession of the turf-grown sandstone rock of the Eye. Then the sport began.

Our weapons, no deadlier than field-glasses and telescope, were at hand; our coats, fortunately unnecessary, were spread below a sandy rampart. Then we peeped over the bank and levelled glasses on the noisy crowds which were lining the ever-swelling Swash. The oyster-catcher, better known to Dee fishermen as the sea-pie, has a single note described as 'peep' or 'keep' in books, which is shortened to a sharp angry 'pic' when the bird is disturbed on its breeding ground. When 20 or 30 of these beautiful black and white birds fly past, calling in harmony, the combined peeps are very musical, but feeble and of little interest compared with the concert of three or four hundred individuals singing together over their meal on the edge of the tide. No word-picture can adequately describe the thrilling music of the sand-banks; the curlew's wild clear call, the triple note of the whimbrel, the sharp bark of the godwit, the liquid whistle of the grey plover, the purr of the dunlin, and the call of the redshank were mingled continually with the music of the sea-pies, whilst the laugh of herring gulls and the rook-like complaints of black-heads introduced harsher though not discordant notes. Hour after hour the sounds swelled or died down, but the birds were never silent; the difficulty was to pick out the cries of individuals.

High tides in October are perhaps the best of the year from the bird watcher's point of view, for the hosts from the north have arrived, and the majority of the birds, though many come for the winter, are of double passages, here for a few weeks in autumn and spring, but in winter far away to the south, and in summer on remote breeding grounds in the far north. Many of the various species – countless thousands of individuals – only arrived late in September, and some had not been noticed before in the district, but a greater tide than that which was fast surrounding us was steadily flowing south; the tide of migrants sweeps along our shores, marked by a marvellous increase in October of birds which seldom or never nest within the limits of our islands.

A few yards away, on the red rock, a single knot, grey-backed, black-billed, and olive-legged, was dozing unconcernedly, and shortly fifty or sixty of these birds, which puzzled the zoologist for so many years, swept past, a grey party. Then a small army, how many hundreds who can tell? alighted on the sand and ran in a close grey little cloud along the edge of the water, calling their sharp little note 'knut, knut.' Fanciful writers connected the bird, which wades and runs back from the advancing waves, with the tradition of Canute, but the longshoremen who first gave the knot its name knew more about its note than Camden or Drayton, and perhaps had never heard of King Canute. The knots, fresh from the north, were in great force, though not so plentiful as the pies. Curlews, easily distinguished by their note and size from the whimbrels, constantly passed in parties, their long, curved bills outlined against the skies; as the water covered bank after bank they gathered on the grass of Little Hilbre, until at high water the top of the island was grey with their crowded masses. From the Eye it looked as if the grass was occupied by a flock of diminutive brown sheep, or as if some volcanic upheaval had strewn the island with brown stones.

When the sand-browned water lapped the red rocks below us the sea-pies began to settle; first a single bird and then a score, then a hundred or more would alight upon the rocks, crowding the others into the inflowing waves. Then nearly all, nervous because of our presence, would take wing and wheel round the islet, only to alight again with much clamour a few moments later, or be joined by a fresh lot which had been swept off the fast-vanishing Red Noses. With them came the bar-tailed godwits, barking as they flew, looking like straight-billed whimbrels until they passed near by. Then one could see the slightly upturned bills of those which came near or settled with the pies, and note how they jump out of the waves on to the dry rock; the sea-pies often allowed themselves to be washed off and swam easily, though we read that the bird only swims when wounded. Party after party of these northern birds, which though common last autumn and winter were hardly seen two years ago, so capricious are their visits, swung round the Eye and passed on up the river or crossed to Little Hilbre. With one lot came five much rarer birds, which by their larger size and longer, darker legs, as well as by their note and the colour of their tails, were easily distinguishable as the very occasional visitors, black-tailed godwits. This is one of the species which is known as a lost British bird, for little more than fifty years ago it nested in small numbers in the eastern counties; now it is only known as a rare visitor on migration. The five birds separated from their more abundant relatives, and swung round and round us, but unfortunately did not settle. On the same day, I learnt later, a keen observer was watching one feeding on the beach at Hoylake.

Few wader notes are more beautiful than the liquid 'tluieh' of the grey plover, known to the coastwise gunners by the more expressive name of silver plover, distinguishing it from the golden plover and the lapwing, which to them is always the green plover. Far up on the marshes green and golden plovers are abundant, but here the silver plover is the representative of this group. One or two small 'wings' passed, but no bird settled; the silver plover, even in winter dress, is one of the most beautiful of our many waders.

Away over Little Hilbre great flocks of dunlins and other small waders – 'little birds' the shooters call them – flashed in the sun as they wheeled and exposed their silver breasts, but only a few dunlins and no sanderlings, though there are many in the river, came near the Eye. Now and then a cormorant, going as if on business bent, flew by on strong wing, and when the Red Noses were lapped by the full tide the gulls, six different species, left the flooded rocks and flew up the river or took refuge among the pies and curlews on Little Hilbre.

At high tide there was a lull; the last bank of empty cockle shells was covered in the tiny mud inlets between the red rocks; the last sea-pie deserted the refuge below us, and we were left birdless except for one active little rock pipit which was engaged in fly-catching almost at our feet. Then we rose and looked seaward. The tide had turned, and with it common, herring, black-backed, and black-headed gulls were drifting seaward, and the telescope revealed in the main a scoter and a guillemot, birds of the open sea which had come up with the tide. As the water fell, leaving patches of mud, full of animal life that had been stirred to activity or left by the tide, a few noisy redshanks came to feed, and stood bowing in little jerks with bright eyes upon us. Then the gulls came down the river and settled on the wet sand to hunt for cockles or lob-worms, and little parties of dunlins spread themselves over each drying bank, wading until the water lapped their breasts in their pursuit of crustaceans. But the sea-pies, curlews, whimbrels, godwits, knots, and many other waders distributed themselves over the freshly exposed banks in the estuary and left the island until the next tide should drive them once more to seek refuge on the rocks.

TAC

Along the shores of Cardigan bay
May 4 1912

In a day's walk we may reach Pwllheli, the capital of this part of Wales. There are two Pwllhelis. There is the old market town at the head of the harbour, with its narrow winding streets, and there is the modern seaside resort half a mile away, on the shores of the open bay. Separating them is the Gimlet rock, and the sandy isthmus that leads to it. While you are in the old town it is worth while to have a meal at one of the old-fashioned commercial hotels, and be sure to order a dish of Pwllheli soles. They are small soles, caught in the waters near by, but very fresh and very delicate, and quite a speciality of Pwllheli.

The new town or watering place is one of the pleasantest in North Wales. It has two short parades, both broad and very handsomely designed; and because they are not of endless length, both of them always well filled and animated. There is splendid bathing on the beach, and though there are bathing vans for those who like them, it is quite the thing to walk down from your rooms to the shore in bathing costume, and plunge into the water without any more ado. There are the usual entertainments at Pwllheli – pierrots and the like – and it is a great place for golf.

One pleasant and characteristically Welsh institution would be sadly missed by the visitors if it were to be given up. On a Sunday evening after church or chapel all the Pwllelhi lads and lasses who have any pretence to voices gather at a particular place on one of the promenades to sing in chorus the plaintive Welsh hymns. As soon as a hymn is finished somebody will start another one, and the whole gathering promptly joins in, putting in all the parts, for Welsh folk understand choral singing.

In easy reach by walking, driving, or cycling from Pwllheli are some of the most delightful seaside villages in all Wales. Abersoch is a romantic little inlet which has been discovered by the open-air young man. It is a great place for easy clothing and for boating, bathing, and fishing all day long. During the season it is populous with stalwart young figures and bronzed faces. It has been discovered by men of the undergraduate type, and so far they hold it as their own preserve.

War work for young seaside visitors
June 15 1916

Mr James F. Butterworth writes from 24, Linden Gardens, London, W: It occurs to me that really useful work might be done by the children at the seaside during the coming holidays by gathering seaweed instead of digging and making sandcastles all the time. Potash and iodine are very scarce and are urgent necessaries. The weeds when stacked above high water mark, dried, and burnt will yield these and other valuable residues. If local authorities or committees would organise such collecting parties, and make the other required arrangements, they would be rendering their country material service at little or no cost to anybody.

The sunny south
June 16 1915

Hove
This seaside health resort adjoining Brighton is pleasantly sheltered under the South Downs. Famous for its 2 ¼ miles of seaside lawns and promenades on which regimental band concerts are given. In the delightfully wooded gardens, spacious parks, and recreation grounds are public tennis courts, bowling greens, etc. Six golf courses. Mixed bathing from tents. Ample hotel and boarding-house accommodation.

Littlehampton
The lovely summer weather enjoyed lately has given a decided impetus to bathing, for which the coast here is so admirably adapted. The increased facilities for family bathing are much appreciated. The excellence of the golf course, too, appeals to many of the visitors. Evening amusements just now are mostly confined to the al fresco concerts at the Shelter hall on the Common.

Southsea
The perfect weather conditions continue day by day, and in consequence a much earlier season is being experienced. The safety of the resort is realised, and its sheltered position on the silvery

Solent is largely responsible for its growing popularity. Excellent entertainment is offered at the piers, theatres, halls, and cinemas, whilst the golfing, tennis, croquet, bowls, fishing, boating, and bathing facilities provided are much used and thoroughly enjoyed.

Brighton

Bathing is now well under way, notably from the tents that have become such features of the sea shore. It is noteworthy, too, that there is a great deal of boating, an eloquent testimony to the sense of security that prevails, On Saturday and Sunday the water was dotted with small craft, and there were many ships in the offing. With the bands playing to large audiences, with entertainers on the beach, and the crowds on beach and esplanade the scene was suggestive of that of holiday in normal times.

Eastbourne

The town's hygienic repute is confirmed by the medical officer's report, which shows the death rate for the past year is the lowest ever recorded, it being only fractionally above 9 per thousand of the population. The public and private sanitary system is maintained on a high scientific level, and is believed to be as nearly perfect as possible. The town is looking its best, the Parade gardens and slopes being a picture of artistic ornamentation.

Isle of Wight

No resort in England provides more opportunities for rest and recreation, health and pleasure than the Isle of Wight. Soft yet bracing air. Magnificent coast and inland scenery. Lofty, sloping Downs. Charming health resorts at Ryde, Newport, Sandown, Shanklin, Ventnor, &c. Yachting, boating, bathing, and coaching facilities. Excellent golf links. Inexpensive weekly island railway tickets.

The Bucket and Spade Brigade: 1920-1939

Lines from coast resorts
June 5 1922

Southport

The town is comfortably crowded. The five specials from Manchester, Bolton, Wigan, East Lancashire, Todmorden, and Rochdale, at Chapel Street, and the specials from Manchester and Liverpool in the Cheshire Lines Railways were all well filled. Thousands came from the Merseyside for Saturday afternoon and evening, the electric trains during the morning being taxed to the utmost. Ainsdale and Freshfield claimed many Southport residents, who took advantage of a good tide for bathing. The tennis courts in the parks and gardens were occupied until well after dusk, and 'woods' have rolled merrily on all the greens. The open-air bathing pool has been crowded. Lord Street in the evening presents its old animated scene. The band played operatic selections on Saturday evening, and for yesterday's church parade the promenade was thronged. If the weather holds,

Southport will experience a record Whit Monday. Over 50 specials are due on the L. and N.-W. and Cheshire Lines systems.

Morecambe

There were heavy arrivals of weekend visitors at Morecambe, and the town has regained pre-war season appearance. Especially beautiful at present are the adjacent areas of Lakeland. The new motor launches on the bay are proving a big attraction, and considerable developments in regard to conditions and style of craft on the water are suggested now that the corporation has purchased the rights of control from the Duchy of Lancaster. Yesterday promenades were crowded. The band of the Seaforth Highlanders played at the Tower.

Scarborough

As a result of the arrival on Saturday of ten specials from Leeds and three long-distance excursions, Scarborough was very busy over the weekend. Many people also travelled by road. While there is much reason for satisfaction at the prospects, holidaymakers are not here in quite the usual numbers for Whitsun. The weather over the weekend was ideal.

Bridlington

Saturday and yesterday were days of sunshine at Bridlington, and an unusually large number of visitors have been living on the sea front. They all go in for sun baths, and yesterday morning from 500 people enjoyed the sea-bathing. There has been a large increase in the motor traffic to the town. The number of visitors staying in Flamborough is about the average, but the day traffic on Saturday and yesterday was abnormally large. Although motors abounded, there was an unusual number of horse-drawn vehicles from neighbouring centres, and the crowds throughout yesterday were far in excess of those of previous Whit Sundays.

Aberystwyth

Aberystwyth is well filled. Special train and road traffic on Saturday was heavy, and the full programme of the season's entertainments began on Saturday night. The prospects for the remainder of the season are very promising.

Barmouth

Barmouth has had a record Whitsun weekend, somewhat to the surprise of the residents. Motor garages were packed, and a large number of cars had to be stored in mews and in a field near the Great Western railway station. Three large motor-charabancs arrived from Leeds in addition to the special trains. There is firm sand on the beach, and visitors have taken to beach cricket, which is a new feature here.

Criccieth

It is many years since Criccieth experienced such a crowd of Whitsuntide visitors as on Saturday. There was the double attraction of the Premier laying the foundation stone of the memorial hall and the singing festival by the Methodist choirs of south Carnarvonshire. Better weather could not have been desired, and the countryside is at the height of its summer beauty.

Rhyl

It has been an ideal weekend at Rhyl, not too warm, but sufficiently summerlike to warrant the wearing of flannels by both sexes. The greatest attraction was the new miniature lake, which was freely used for boat-sailing and paddling. There was a tremendous muster of motors, and a new fleet of charabancs was put on. The regular service of motor vehicles from Lancashire and the Midlands brought full loads. The marine gardens were crowded for the band concerts, and a sacred concert was given in the pavilion yesterday. Several camps from the Manchester district are in the neighbourhood, and the Cheshire Yeomanry are encamped at Foryd, just over the river.

From our correspondents

Those lost buckets and spades
May 27 1925

Many little tragedies of the summer holidays are foreshadowed by the arrival of the first bucket and spade at the Euston lost property office yesterday. It was found at Crewe. 'Every year,' stated a BMS official, 'hundreds of buckets and spades, together with dead and living souvenirs of the beach, reach us throughout the holiday season – treasures that, guarded with much patient care throughout a long train journey, are forgotten in the excitement of being home again.

'Such tragedies are not very serious and are easily rectified, although perhaps not before copious tears are shed. But forgetfulness does sometimes lead to more serious heart burnings, as was instanced by a distraught young mother who once found herself plus a bucket and spade but minus a baby. We found it here.'

Lobsters and crabs: supper from the rock pools
June 23 1925

Three or four times at least on our holiday we sit down to a delicious supper from the rock pools. Lobsters make a 'run' in and out of their lair below the rocks that lie in about knee-deep water at low tide. It is not as conspicuous, of course, as a rabbit ashore, but you will soon learn to recognise the slight trough in the sand that looks as though someone had drawn his heel along. Now your willow wand, with an iron hook at the end, comes into play, and you gently probe about in the seaweedy crevices underwater until, at last, he grips the hook. You must pull him out very slowly and gently, lest he take alarm; use your left arm, so that your right hand will be free to catch hold of him behind the claws as soon as he appears. Lobsters and crabs, remember, sleep in the daytime. A good catch is often to be made by fishing in a deep pool, on a calm, starry evening, with a cod's head tied on a line: you pull up very gently, and your friend must be prompt with his flash lamp and landing-net the moment Mr Lobster, clutching his bait, comes to the surface.

Crabs, too, are to be obtained in the same way, but also, unlike lobsters, on the verge of low-water pools from which the tide has entirely receded, snuggling down in the wet sand with only a patch of their dull red back showing. There are many sorts of crab, but none but the well-known 'eater' is worth cooking.

For seaside residents: the ideal beach-hut
August 3 1925

Nowadays a beach-hut for those living near the sea is a necessity, if only to provide shelter from the rain. But it must provide a great deal more than that. It must be a cosy dressing-room for bathers, an open-air dining room, and a kitchen and pantry all rolled in one.

The ideal beach hut has large doors, folding outwards, to admit sunshine and sea breezes, and has a window at each side. At bathing time, curtains hung midway are drawn together, and the back half of the hut is then secluded for bathers to undress in. A built-in locker runs the whole length of the back wall, forming a delightful seat as well as a useful receptacle for bathing suits, buckets and spades, needlework, and magazines. Above the locker are hooks on which to hang clothes and towels. Two little shelves, to be used as dressing-tables, are fixed to the wall, and a small looking glass hangs over each shelf.

The dressing room is also the kitchen. Folding tables are fitted to each side wall. The primus stove lives in a large tin biscuit box, with one side taken down, upon one table. Above it are shelves for china. A saucepan, a frying pan, an enamel basin for washing up, and a most necessary broom and dustpan hang upon this wall. Upon the opposite side is the servingtable, and above it is a cupboard in which food is kept. It is most convenient to store such things as tea and coffee, salt, sugar, and biscuits in the beach hut, but only in small quantities, and always in tins.

The rest of the hut is the sitting-room. The floors and walls are stained brown. The former are covered with rush mats, and the latter are decorated with coloured prints cut from magazines. There are plenty of ordinary deck-chairs; each is covered with chintz cut the same size as the original cover and tacked over it on to the wooden bars with drawing-pins. Two canvas camp chairs are thoughtfully provided for stout or elderly friends, who often have strong objections to the ordinary deck-chair.

The chintz coverings of the chairs match the long curtains in the middle of the hut and the short curtains in the windows. In the ideal hut the chintz is patterned with golden oranges and lavender-blue birds nesting in a soft green foliage. The tea service is painted with big yellow oranges and picked out with lines of soft blue and green. The cushions of which there are many, are orange, blue, and green. The oblong table is covered with a reversible cloth of green and blue.

Blue-grey ginger jars are kept filled with yellow or blue flowers and green foliage, and give a finishing and distinctive touch to the colour scheme of this delightful hut, which even on the greyest and dullest of days imparts a welcoming impression of sunshine and warmth to all who enter it.

Toy ships: naval manoevres in the bath
September 2 1927

In early years the toy ship was quite as indispensable on our holiday to the sea as the bucket and spade. I think that we should probably have a new one each year because of the difficulty of transport.

There was something extraordinarily fascinating in the ownership of a brand-new vessel, immaculate in paint and snowy canvas. The maiden voyage would be treated with proper solemnity. I fancy that the rough caress of the sea was too violent for our tiny craft. It would be certain to sail broadside on to an approaching wave, and with equal certainty it would heel under the rebuff and have to be dragged out with great loss of dignity and a drenched sail. We might, however, be fortunate in finding one of those shallow lakes which are the true paradise of all nautically minded children.

In a park behind the promenade of the place where my first holidays were spent there was just such a pond. All day long it would be covered with bird-like yachts speeding gracefully to the further margins. Those holidays caught one between the charm of the lake and the lure of the sea. One wanted to be in both places at once. There also were seen the clockwork motorboats, which made their owners independent of the vagaries of a passing breeze. They were indeed the aristocrats among all the vessels of the lake, but they enjoyed no greater liberty than the rest. The democracy of our state made that small ocean as free to the tiniest pea-green boat as for the passage of nobler craft.

When the holiday had ended we used always to bring home our newest boat. Thus, in the course of years, a small navy accumulated. With special permission we could sail them in the bath. It is somewhat surprising in retrospect to see what tremendous events could occur within each narrow compass. The most peaceable journeys of our fleet were when they carried cargoes or passengers from port to port. With some little ingenuity a landing stage and crane could be erected. But even the sanctity of commerce was not always undisturbed. On occasion a ship would be ravaged by a rakish pirate sloop which would have been lying at anchor in a lagoon formed by tying two scrubbing brushes together. Such of the victim's crew as could not be taken prisoner would be compelled to walk the plank.

Sometimes our ships would be divided into opposing fleets. They would manoeuvre and ram each other in a most convincing manner.

A remarkable effect of heavy firing could be obtained if a friend were continually employed in throwing pebbles or pieces of coal into the water. The smooth floor of our sea made the conventional type of anchor absolutely useless. Instead, we should have to use a piece of lead fastened by a string. The operation of heaving the anchor required a certain delicacy in handling or the ship would capsize. Additional security, of course, could be given by mooring the vessel to a tap.

A storm could be evoked as and when desired simply by stirring the sea vigorously with a stick or by inserting a cork mat. Gales could be produced by blowing or, better still, by wafting strongly with a stout sheet of cardboard or folded newspaper. One was conscious of a delicious thrill of excitement in watching the boats so bravely battling against the elements or in listening to the hungry lapping of waves at the narrow end. The storm brought a double peril: for besides putting the ships in considerable danger, it frequently recoiled upon our own heads. The fury of its approach, accompanied by a great deal of noise and splashing, usually attracted the attention of someone downstairs, with the result that our sea epic would be ended, at least for that day.

The romance of ships may be alive in us today. We see a little boat bobbing on the water and a flood tide of memory opens somewhere inside; or we visit a seaport, and along the quay we come upon the old dreaming ships lying at anchor. We sense again the unforgettable, unforgotten smell, and in an instant we are a thousand miles away, 'slung atween the round shot' or piping a stave with Long John Silver. Such stuff, they say, is a part of our national heritage, but may not one suggest that it is rather an echo of our own toy ship adventures?

A woman in Manchester: the yellow sands
June 8 1929

All the Manchester shops that can reasonably do so are filling their windows with the paraphernalia of bathing. This has now become one of the most important parts of the holiday outfit and is correspondingly expensive. In our mothers' time a navy blue serge bathing suit, trimmed with braid and having a sailor collar and frilled legs, was bought at the end of school days and lasted until the young matron of 25 or so decided that her time for such frivolity was over. Probably even then the serge was as good as ever, as this unexciting material has a way of being, and out of its voluminous breadth a pair of knickers, faintly scented with salt and seaweed, were made for the matron's little boy. In these days, if a bathing suit lasts for two summers – the second spent in a very quiet place – its owner regards it as an interesting relic. Then there are bathing shoes, trimmed caps, rubber earrings and bracelets, beach wraps, and the fantastic rubber beasts which have to be inflated by the strong man of the party. The suggestions that Manchester makes for this summer are not, on the whole, very different from those that went to Abersoch or Nice a year ago. There is a fancy for low-cut suits that allow for a sunburnt back, but these are not likely to be very popular. Perhaps the newest idea is the detachable skirt which, if it has also a little coat to correspond, converts the bathing suit into a costume that can be worn on the beach or even taken to the shops on the esplanade.

Oil pollution and seabirds
July 12 1929

The Royal Society for the Protection of Birds is issuing adhesive stamps depicting a seabird in trouble crying for help, and bearing the words 'Urge the shipowners to install oil separators, and so save the seabirds.' The society is issuing these in English, Italian, French and German, and will be glad to supply them to bird lovers who will turn them to useful account.

Skegness is so bracing: vigour imparted even to correspondence
September 19 1929

The surveyor of Skegness council reported to the monthly meeting yesterday that he had written to a woman shop-keeper drawing attention to the fact that bathing costumes displayed outside her premises were suspended in such a fashion as to impede the progress of passersby.

The following reply has been received: 'I have a right as a ratepayer to know why you should write to me, and not my neighbour re the bathing display under my verandah. But what can I expect from a despicable, brainless, uncultivated crowd. Such an action has not been known by any other council in this country.'

Blackpool's bank holiday: happiness on the sands
April 22 1930

There is an old lady in Blackpool who sits on a stool and sells matches. She wears a blue sun-bonnet and a pink shawl, and occasionally she looks down into her basket in a friendly way to see if her stock is getting any lower. She was out at her pitch early this morning, for the sun shone brightly. Like the rest of us she felt that this was going to be a successful bank holiday.

By 10 o'clock the happy business of scattering orange-peel over the promenade was well started. People had begun eating within half an hour of finishing breakfast. Down on the sands it was uncomfortably easy to blunder into some classic system of fortification, or find yourself lighting your pipe in the middle of a family cricket pitch. At one moment everyone appeared to be wildly throwing balls about with no sense of direction and a polite desire that you should stoop down and return them. At another moment Blackpool seemed to be nothing but sandcastles.

You discover, when you try to make your peaceful, non-interfering way across Blackpool sands on a bank holiday morning, that sand castles arouse a strong sense of proprietorship. A family dumps itself down on the sands, spreads the perambulator, the newspaper, the lunch basket, and the overcoats all around, and then, with a sweep of his arms the son of the house makes a pile of sand, and the estate comes into being. From that moment the place is inviolate. If a strange foot grazes a tower, or a strange spade digs in the well – ''Ere, that's our 'ole, we dug it ourselves.'

Nine out of ten castles are in the jelly-mould tradition. We are not an artistic race. But people are very happy playing with sand. There is something about sand that destroys their sense of what is proper to their station, and quite elderly ladies may be seen to roll in it hysterically. It even affects dogs. One little white dog discovered this morning the joy of digging in sand. He dug at first rather contemptuously. Then, as he made good progress, his success went to his head, and he dug madly. His paws went like pistons, and he was stopped from losing himself completely only by an irritable gentleman with a bald head who looked up from his slumbers to see what caused the sandstorm.

The morning had not advanced far before the air was rent by the howls of the donkey men. No men and fewer donkeys work harder than these at holiday time. All day long the men run behind groups of trotting donkeys, urging them with stick and voice to jolt their riders into renewed states of hysteria. They seem determined to create a donkey stampede. The donkey, however, is not an animal to lose its head. It is a sight apparently fascinating to young men, who find themselves possessed of a zeal to display their donkeymanship. This zeal is sometimes complicated by the causal absence of a stirrup, which nearly always happens when they bet the donkey man 10 shillings they can race his daughter. But donkey men must live.

Ventriloquists abounded. They sat, with their dolls, in little boxes on the top of step-ladders, and gathered an audience by means of groans and shouts and invitations bawled through megaphones. They kept an eye on the Punch and Judy shows, and by careful arrangement one entertainment would start up just as its rival was stopping, so that the same audience would be passed up the line from one pitch to another. This was a good scheme for getting the maximum audience, but the seaside showmen's life still appeared vexatious. Their hearers had a wonderful instinct for sensing the approaching end of the performance and so choosing the right moment for trickling away before the collecting bag came round. Punch and the shivering Toby have earned few coppers this day.

The motorboats and sailing boats drew good custom. For a shilling you can sail almost out of sight, which is a consideration. Going aboard is something of an adventure to the elderly, since you are packed like miller's sacks in a horse-drawn cart, and the ride across the crowded sands is reminiscent of the tumbril. A fair number of those who so rashly went to sea would not have minded if the simile had become the fact. Beneath the blue and glittering surface of the sea was a deceptive swell, and ices and chocolates are no diet for sailors.

As yesterday, the weather became disappointing at midday, when clouds obscured the sun and the full effect of a chilly breeze was felt. People walked about with the collars of their coats turned up, or rode up and down the promenade inside the tramcars. The low temperature did much to dispel bank holiday zest. But undoubtedly another big factor was a shortage of money. All along the sands, from the pleasure beach to the north pier, were the oyster, lemonade, and sweet stalls quite unpatronised. In most cases the proprietors resentfully went to sleep. The promenade shops, too, lacked custom, although there were plenty of people passing to and fro. Another sign of poverty was in the deserted halls given over to slot machines. Disconsolate attendants had little to do beyond warning irresponsible small boys. Even the pleasure beach, with all its extraordinary structures for jolts and thrills, was crowded chiefly by people who had come to look on at those who paid out. It has not been a successful bank holiday.

This bathing business: then and now
August 15 1930

Those of us who do not help to decorate the beach at popular seaside resorts, either because we go inland for our holidays or because we stay at home, naturally gather our impressions of seaside scenes from the photographs in the papers. Judging by these, our shores must be presenting a gay spectacle at the moment. The weather forecast may prophesy, and the news columns' report, wet or cold weather, but according to the pictures it is sunshine, sunshine all the day at Shrimpton-on-Sea. Sun-bathing and sea bathing seem to be universal full-time occupations this summer, and the sands and shingle appear to be always covered with heaps (rather than groups) of sprawling youth, very bare of leg and back, dressed in – or partly in – very scanty bathing costumes of startling design. Everyone seems to have caught the Lido spirit.

Musing over these studies of massed youth and beauty and grace (for all three are undoubtedly well represented), one recalls the beach scenes and the attitude to bathing of yesteryear – or, to be accurate, of 20 odd years ago. Nowadays, the bathe seems to last intermittently all day – sun-bathing, in the same costume, filling up the gaps between dips. In pre-war days, when parents had a say in the affairs of youth, it was a more or less solemn ritual. The pre-breakfast bathe was allowed to those hardy spirits who cared to indulge it, but one might not bathe within two hours of a heavy meal. Twenty minutes was the regulation period to spend in the water; if one overstayed the time an unwary glance toward the shore would be certain to reveal a figure gesticulating wildly and issuing shrill orders to come out.

The bather, when suitably clad, joined the family group on the sands – father and mother firmly planted in deck chairs, the one with a newspaper, the other with sunshade and sewing, and the younger fry in well pinned-up garments (with a predominance of flannel petticoat) busy with bucket and spade. In the bosom of the family party, the bather then ate a biscuit or bun, and attempted to dry long hair and so wring superfluous sea out of sodden bathing costumes. A 'good brisk walk' along the shingle and back completed the ritual ... and so to midday dinner at the lodgings, with 'this bathing business' over for the day. Some energetic young folk might bathe again, or it might be that the tide was too low in the morning, but an afternoon bathe was never the same and seemed to overthrow the day's programme.

The sea, to be sure, was the same then as now, and, once in, there was no doubt the same enjoyment; but what a thicket of small discomforts hedged round the pre-war bath! Clothes, vans, hair ... the very bathing suit was often of scratchy serge or alpaca, often hampered with a little skirt, and when sodden with water was of a considerable weight. From the comfort and convenience of modern feminine dress one can look back with belated pity on the beach clothes of twenty odd years ago. There was the long, cumbersome skirt, the shirt blouse, up to the neck and down to the wrists; the belt, well pulled in which was supposed to establish discreet relations between skirt and blouse, but often failed in its aim, allowing edges of blouse to escape above or skirt bands to gape below, to the constant distraction of its wearer. Cotton dresses were made on much the same lines, and the full skirts were apt to behave treacherously in a high wind, needing one hand to keep them under control while the other endeavoured to restrain the hat from breaking away from the painful anchor of a couple of long and deadly hatpins. Black woollen stockings and black or brown canvas shoes were usual for beach wear, and freedom was further restricted by flounced petticoats that twined round the legs and corsets that reduced – or were expected to reduce – the waist to elegant proportions.

Of this complicated outfit the bather had to disencumber – and in it again to encumber – herself, her fingers and limbs sticky with salt, tapes refusing to be tied, stockings refusing to be pulled on without disaster; all in the confined interior of a bathing van lighted only by a few pierced holes over the door. With a towel over her shoulders, seaweed-like tresses hanging loose, nose shiny and blue and unsolaced by powder, she then emerged to meet the coldly accusing gaze of an impatient queue of successors to occupation of the van.

The bathing machine itself was a source of discomfort to some of us. Always damp and smelling of stale seaweed, it was a depressing introduction to the waves and warranted to inspire the timid beginner with unpleasant apprehensions. On some inhospitable shores it was necessary to have the van drawn, jolting and swaying, down the uneven shore to the water by a plunging horse, which added to the victim's sensations that of being in a tumbril on the way to execution. For it might happen, as once it did indeed, that the horse might refuse to face the widening expanse of water between van and shore when the time came for the return journey, and the risk be run of the van's floating off like Noah's Ark. Long ago one bather came to the conclusion that bathing from the house, from the rocks, even from a tent, could be sheer delight, but bathing from a van was a game not worth the candle.

Do bathing machines still exist? One cannot imagine the bright young people of the photographs using them, any more than one can imagine them clad (for I suppose they do more or less clothe themselves for some part of the time) in the black woollen stockings, the petticoats, the 10-inch hatpins, of 20 or so years ago.

B. Noel Saxelby

The dam: a warning to holiday makers
August 26 1930

There seemed fewer children in sight than usual on the beach when I glanced up from my book. True, the tide was going down, and it is not much fun building sandcastles on an ebb tide. But there were shrimping and messing about in rock pools to be done, kites and cricket, rounders, shell-collecting, and so on.

Looking round, I saw the counter-attraction. The rough sou'-wester of the previous day or two had scooped a big lagoon in the sand, up near highwater mark, and the collective juvenile energy of the beach was combining to prevent its outflow down to the sea by constructing a dam. It was a very workmanlike dam, a wall such as Roman Balbus, at the age of 11, would have felt proud to have sponsored. A flock of infant Balbuses and Balbas were as busy as beavers on it. They shouted indignantly at such amateur dammers as showed ignorance of the elements of this ancient and noble craft by omitting to pack into the wall alternate layers of long streamers of seaweed or by excavating sand within five feet of it and thus tempting it presently to slither down into the waterlogged moat, as a jelly subsides into its dish when the hot sun shines on it. They stopped the wall sagging, as it grew higher, by reinforcing it with triangular buttresses of big stones, and they saw that the leakage in the moat behind it was led away by a nice neat little traverse canal. They forbade anyone to paddle in the pool or to sail boats, and shooed away dogs, once the water along the wall was a foot deep, for that's the sort of thing that plays Old Harry with even the best-built dam.

The water continued to soak into the lagoon from the steep top of the beach. The pool grew deeper and deeper. The spades worked harder and harder. The dam rose higher and higher. Anxious engineers screamed SOSs as bits of it suddenly became waterlogged

DB

and began to slither. Distraught small girls rushed up with bucketfuls of shingle or large cake-like slabs of fresh sand; red-faced small boys, bent-backed, short of breath, staggered up with rocks as big as their heads, and dropped them at just the psychological spot at just the psychological moment.

At last, up among the scattered bungalows in the windswept marram grass above the beach, dinner bells tinkled, drawing off two or three of the greediest dammers. Then daddies and mummies, here and there, called from the porch and waved towels, to indicate that the potatoes were getting cold. A nannie or two came down to the shore, to scold and drag away a young fellow to whom the exacting job in hand was more important than even the fruit salad quoted from the menu as a lure normally certain to hasten the homeward trek to lunch.

Louise and Roland, who didn't lunch, I gathered from the shouted discussion, until half-past one, were exhorted to hold the forces of nature at bay for the next half-hour. But Louise, running up to the house for a handkerchief, met Michael, who, she shouted, said that he and Arthur would be coming down in a minute or two, and on that understanding Ronald agreed to come along to dinner. Michael and Arthur, however, would appear to have changed their minds or lost count of time, for they did not appear in two minutes – or 10.

Engrossed though I was in my book, sitting in a deck-chair a hundred yards to the left of the pent-up lagoon, the kindly gods caused me to glance up at the moment when, about a yard of the dam having given way, a swift, silent wall of water sped down the beach and on to a man who lay prone on the sand, fully dressed, having a nap. It carried him several feet before he woke up and got up.

I myself was obviously fast asleep in my chair as he came up the beach.

Wouldn't you have been?

Next week's carnival
September 6 1930

Morecambe

Morecambe continues to have a very satisfactory season, for the glorious weather has attracted many latecomers to the resort. It was described by one tradesman as being the best Oldham wakes that Morecambe has experienced for a long time, and the town, on some days, has appeared to be nearly as crowded as it was on August bank holiday. Certainly Oldham people have flocked to Morecambe this year, and their dialect mingles with that of hundreds of Yorkshire folks, who, during the Spen Valley holiday, are enjoying a respite from work on the shores of the bay.

Up to Thursday afternoon, when rain fell heavily for a time, the weather this week could not have been improved. Blazing hot sunshine was experienced every day, and the large crowds have revelled in the summer-like conditions. The sun-bathing cult has received a great impetus at Morecambe this week, and bathers have lounged on the sands for hours, making the most of the ideal conditions. Some bathing parties have taken portable gramophones to the beach, and after a swim have enjoyed dancing.

Preparations are now actively in hand for the Carnival, which will start on Saturday next. Throughout the week electricians have been busy stringing the promenade with wires for the illuminations, and, judging by the novel designs being prepared by many of the shopkeepers, it will be a gorgeous spectacle. Thousands of visitors are expected to arrive in the town next weekend.

Bournemouth

The brightening effect of the present vogue for colour in beach wear has been particularly noticeable during the brilliant if late spell of real summer weather now being experienced. The bathing costumes of both sexes are of every conceivable colour, while the bathing cloaks and pyjama suits and brilliant wraps provide an unceasing variety. Bournemouth sea front has, indeed, this season provided a bright and joyful aspect. Its many hundreds of beach huts and tents nestling snugly against the base of the cliffs provide ideal shelter for the holiday makers. Night bathing has been a favourite occupation during the warm nights recently, and often supper parties in the beach huts and tents follow the bathe.

The number of visitors is still very great, although September has arrived, and there is still plenty of amusement available. Few resorts are so well equipped for evening entertainment at first-class kinemas, the Theatre, the Hippodrome, up-to-date dance halls, and the municipal pavilion. In the daytime the two municipal golf courses attract large numbers, while the municipal bowling greens and tennis courts in all parts of the town are extremely popular. The corporation is now considering the establishment of a midget golf course at the winter gardens, and an ice rink is being erected by private enterprise.

Besides the concerts on the piers at Bournemouth and Boscombe this week the municipal orchestra programmes at the pavilion are being supplemented by performances by the June Dancers.

Sea shanties by old sailors
April 23 1931

According to Sir James Sexton MP, who broadcast last night from London Regional, there are sea shanties and sea shanties, and, in any case, he prefers to call them 'sea chanties'. Before giving us his idea of the real thing Sir James asked his listeners to imagine themselves on the deck of a windjammer as they listened to the singers, and, indeed, it needed little imagination for the veriest landlubber of us to imagine the ship and its sailors even as he was speaking to us.

His introductory remarks were full of the lore of the sea, and what romantic scenes his yarns brought to our mind's eye! Both his voice and delivery were ideal for his task.

When it came to the singing of the shanties they proved to be as far removed from the sea shanties we have heard previously from the beautifully modulated voice of a radio tenor or a mixed choir as pseudo-Oriental music is removed from true Oriental music. Certain of the shanties were aided by 'effects,' but never did a broadcast need 'effects' less. The singers created their own atmosphere, and dull must have been the imagination of the listener who could not feel the roll of the ship and taste the salt on his lips as he listened. The choruses were fine and rolling, and though we appreciated the 'Rio Grande', 'rendered,' as Sir James himself put it, by Mr Frank Lowe, it was when Sir James himself took the lead that our enjoyment was at its highest. We think this is the first time he has broadcast; we hope that he will take us aboard his windjammer many a time again.

Who stole the sunshine?
January 28 1932

The Rev LC Roberts, Prestatyn's meteorological officer, thinks he has discovered the identity of the sunshine thief. At the monthly meeting of Prestatyn council yesterday it was alleged that somebody had been deliberately tampering with the sunshine recorder on top of the Beach café, and had caused all the recent meteorological reports sent to the Air Ministry to be inaccurate.

Mr Roberts said today he was almost sure that the 'miscreant' was a seagull, which had possibly alighted on the glass bowl covering the instrument and then given it a slight kick as it flew away. That, he said, would be sufficient to move the sensitive crystal out of position.

Miscellany: Beachcombing in Britain
January 3 1933

It is reported that, as a result of the enhanced value of gold, many beachcombers are now washing the auriterous sands of New Zealand's shores. English beaches also yield gold on occasion, since about £100m worth of treasure is sunk around our coastlines. More than once in the past crowds have swarmed over a beach to seek – with shovels and sieves – the coins which a welcome gale had borne up and buried in the sands. A beachcomber who finds gold probably tells a mate, or maybe two, and somehow the news leaks out. A minor gold rush is then inevitable.

In addition to increasing the possibilities of a big find, storms shift the sands, and so uncover small change, bracelets, rings, and other trinkets dropped by summer holiday makers. On the east coast pieces of amber are often found, and all shores receive occasional boxes of apples, kegs of butter or even of brandy, and other largess from the ocean's stories. Driftwood, too, is worth gathering, even if it be only good for firing.

A fortnight's holiday: Yolverton v The Rest
May 20 1933

Now is the time of the year when through our letterboxes plop richly those elegant brochures, dispatched by hopeful hotel keepers in response to our timid inquiries as to accommodation 'from the 14th to the 28th' at Downlands View or Courtlands or Grosvenor House. Eagerly we pour over 'View of a portion of the dining-room,' with its neatly arrayed and invitingly vacant tables, and 'A corner of the lounge,' with a wicker settee and a couple of palms. 'We've had an answer from Maplestoke,' you inform the friend who has recommended it. 'They can take us in, but we should have to sleep in the annexe.' She draws the booklet from your reluctant grasp. 'That's the room we had, the one with the balcony. And this is a corner of the cliff; if you go along there, past the trees, you get right down on to the beach at the dearest little cove…' In the muddy monochrome the whole scene looks uniformly drear, but you try to envisage it with an enthusiastic eye.

The correct disposition of that previous 14 days is a matter of vital importance. We grow out of our belief in Santa Claus and Tinker Bell, but we can never surrender our castle in Spain. Deep in our inmost hearts lingers the conviction that somewhere, if only we could find it, exists the ideal seaside resort. We have more than a suspicion that the Xs found it last year: 'A lovely, unspoilt spot. Yes, not far away from A. [But we have never discovered exactly where.] The bathing is perfect and George got some excellent golf. The food at the hotel was marvellous, too. Quite as good as anything you get abroad.' True, you recall the farm – 'such a sweet, old place' – near T which Mrs X praised in such glowing terms. Five miles from anywhere, across muddy fields and down deep-holed lanes. The car has never been the same since. But, then, the X's did not like Yolverton. And really of all the places you have been to Yolverton … Only you have been there so often it's really time for a change.

So you turn your attention to seeking fresh scenes, but your quest is sadly impeded by the fact that in your memory is limned an idealised spot (scene of childhood's holidays) where the summer sun shone ever in a cloudless sky. In this most happy land agreement was unanimous that the most desirable pursuit of the moment was beach cricket or prawning or sailing. Unheard was that unseemly wrangling which attends too many a holiday breakfast table as to how the day should be spent. 'What about a good long walk round the point to Z bay?' 'Well, if we do that the tide will be too low to bathe in the afternoon, and if we bathe before we start we shall never get there and back in time for lunch.' 'Can't we ask for sandwiches then? It's such a lovely day.' 'Oh, you have to order them at the office the night before. Anyway, I told the Ms we'd see them on the beach this morning.' 'I'm not going down there. I don't feel a bit like sitting in a hot, stuffy tent. Why not?'

But this will not settle the pressing problem. Perhaps, after all, it would be safer to go back to Yolverton. You do know the worst of it – and the best. Of course, that dreadful Smith family may be at the hotel again … But on the whole … It will be nice to take that lovely walk again up the valley. And there's that jolly spot you only found last year where you can dive right off the rock into clear, deep, green water. You may as well write at once: 'The Manageress, Fir Point Hotel, Yolverton. Dear Madam, I shall be glad if you will let me know whether you can reserve us the same rooms as we had last year for a fortnight from the 14th…'

Easter in North Wales: coast bids for the camper
March 29 1934

For the time of year the weather already shows unaccustomed geniality. The sunshine has a warming power in advance of the calendar, and the whole countryside, down to the sea's edge, shows the signs of spring – all before a March Easter! If this will only continue a glorious holiday will be placed on record.

From the Sands of Dee to the Great Orme at Llandudno were sunlit shores today, but shores peopled only by seagulls feeding at the tide line and here and there, along 30 miles of coast, by men who loaded squat steamers at quarry jetties, or applied paint to wood and ironwork, hammered at pavilions in the making, and tested the riveting of skeleton structures designed for the dizzy transports of a bank holiday crowd.

In a dozen years on the North Wales coast I do not recall a more optimistic 'spring cleaning.' There is a feeling here – it is articulate in the larger towns and in the smaller places along the coast – that the season will be better than last year, which, in its turn, was better than the previous year.

Perhaps the most notable development on the coast is the bid for the camper. Opinions are divided as to his value. Boarding and apartment-house keepers, of course, dislike his preference for canvas or hutment over bricks and mortar. But it is being realised that the camper has come to stay, and at least some order is being made out of the camping chaos which has prevailed, to the considerable detriment of some places. West of Rhyl, for instance, there has arisen a small township of wood holiday dwellings with properly organised central facilities for cooking hot meals and for recreation. If it rains a loud-speaker announces a whist drive or a dance. There is cricket or football, according to the temperature or collective inclination, on communal pitches. Where municipal enterprise has provided beach huts for hiring by visitors, electric lighting and provision for cooking by electricity are among the amenities. There are such buildings on the green below the embankment at Colwyn Bay, and at Penmaenmawr, where the structures are of concrete with flat roofs for sun-bathing, conveniently reached by outside flights of steps.

In the way of special entertainments and attractions each resort has made ample arrangements, and in this respect the customary high standard promises to be reached. At Colwyn Bay on Easter Sunday a concert will be held in Arcadia in aid of the Manchester Evening News White Heather Fund. A capital programme has been arranged by Mr W John Parry. It is expected that Sir J Mathewson Watson will attend the concert.

Holiday habits: cold dip
July 28 1934

The idea of jumping into cold water for fun is generally supposed to have existed in England for some 200 years. The indefatigable and discursive traveller Celia Fiennes, thought to avoid a cold by immersion in cold springs. These, she averred, 'shutt up the pores of the body.' To our notions that would seem fatal to the discharge of a fever; it is commonly supposed to have brought Alexander the Great to his demise, and we are all warned against sudden closure of the pores. But Celia believed that she cured herself of colds by this therapy. Health moves in a mysterious way.

With the arrival of the 18th century there was almost a rush to the sea. Indoor spas equipped themselves with cold pools. A considerable literature on Bath waters was composed by medicos and social philosophers of all kinds. The sands of Scarborough, which had been much employed for the galloping of horses, were now invaded by bathers. Early in the century a letter writer from the spa announces: 'It is the Custome, for not only the gentlemen but the ladies also, to bath in the Sea; the gentlemen go out a little way to Sea in Boats (call'd here Cobbles) and jump in naked directly. The Ladies have the Conveniency of Gowns and Guides. There are two little Houses on the Shore, to retire to for Dressing in.' Later on there were 26 bathing machines; but 'the Practick' was now a ceremonial and needed equipage. 'Two women attend each lady who bathes, as guides; and one man every gentleman who required it.' The bathing machines, whose lumbering cavalcade went splashing to an ankle depth of water, are now almost all out of commission; they still haunt the beaches like Martello towers. Perhaps they are sometimes chartered, like the few vagrant hansoms of nocturnal London, by sentimental codgers in search of their youth. Or do the irreverent chop them up for firewood? One has gay memories of the excited scramble up the rickety steps, the young felicity when, horse attached, the wagon lurched towards the ocean, the sand on the floor, the chipped and dirty mirror on the wall, the less than tactful advertisements of insecticide preparations.

They had their history. They rattled and rumbled across two centuries as well as over sands where minstrels dragged their shrill piano and passed the expectant hat. They had housed the austere in quest of vigour as well as the young in search of fun. We can well understand the reluctance of Shadwell's knight to pass beyond a speculative participation. When Smollett's Matt Bramble adventured in the sea at Scarborough he set out at six in the morning. 'The wind blowing from the north and the weather being hazy, the water proved so chill that, when I rose from my first plunge, I could not help sobbing and bawling out, from the effects of the cold.' Whereupon, it will be remembered, Clinker made an unwanted rescue on the assumption that his master was a-drowning and dragged the poor man shorewards by the ear so that the latter could not walk the street without being pointed at as 'the monster that was hauled naked ashore upon the beach.'

So, even from the machines upon the sand, gentlemen still bathed in 'the absolutely.' Rowlandson's cartoon of 'The Pleasures of Margate' suggests that the Kentish ladies also dipped in their skins only, but that may have been his notion of a joke. The right to nudity, so strongly asserted in certain quarters nowadays, was stoutly maintained in 1809 when a Mr Crunden, of Brighton, fought a case against the crown in order to vindicate the freeborn Briton's right to enter the sea in his natural state. It was Brighton under the Regency, a hopeful time and place for such a litigation, But the raffishness of those days preferred silken vices to uncovered virtues. He lost. The new ideas of respectability were coming in. Yet, for a long time, a pair of drawers would suffice the masculine dipper. The 'university costume,' so rigorously insisted upon a few years ago, was quite a recent invention. And now that has been severely cut about, rather to let in the sun than to give water further scope. The history of the bath has seen many changes; now Phoebus is more sovereign than Neptune, and the cold dip seems less important than the hot repose.

Ivor Brown

Cowes: visitors fashionable and unfashionable
August 3 1935

No other yacht-racing centre on this side of the Atlantic appeals to the average man or woman with the strength that Cowes does. For 51 weeks in the year it is a quiet little town, down whose high street – if it were straighter – you might fire a gun without hitting anybody. Tradespeople come and go quietly about their business; workers across the Medina at the shipyard ply their crafts a little less noisily now that electric welding is superseding riveting; and a few aristocratic ladies and gentlemen take life lazily on the lawn at the Squadron Castle. Only when the small yachts of the international or Solent classes are reaching, running, or tacking through the roads – as they are sometimes during the summer months – does the interest of the inhabitants in the pastime rise above the average. They think a lot of the little racing yachts in the Solent. Shamrocks, Endeavours, Velshedas, and Britannias are all very well in their way, but for real yachting, they say, 'give us the six-metre and eight-metre boats.'

During one week of the year's 52 weeks Cowes is another place altogether. The fashionable world, having tired of the attractions of Ascot, Wimbledon, Henley, and Lord's, and having spent a little of its time, and probably some of its money, at Goodwood, joins its yachts, large and little, in Portsmouth harbour or Southampton water, and leisurely proceeds to crowd the historic roads which stretch from Norris Castle in the east across the mouth of the Medina down the west channel as far as Egypt point. The fleet of pleasure craft thus assembled is always notable, not only because of its numerical strength but also because of the quality of the units composing it.

Motor yachts are nowadays more numerous than steam yachts; even cruising yachts with respectable sail spreads have auxiliary power, although in the 90s hardy pleasure sailors were heard to declare that if they had all the wealth in the world they would never own a yacht 'with a kettle.' The cream of the racing fleet also finds moorings or anchorages, and cruising craft flying less familiar burgees than those of the Squadron, Royal Victoria, Royal Albert, Royal Southampton, or Royal Southern are also to be seen. And in the midst of the assembly there is the Victoria and Albert with the King and Queen on board and a large war vessel – usually a battleship – keeping guard over everything and everybody.

The fashionable world is not, of course, in exclusive possession of Cowes during the week, although there is not the least doubt that it would like to be. The people who compose it honestly believe that trippers – especially August bank holiday trippers – are sent by Providence to the Isle of Wight for the special purpose of trying them. The tradespeople are not very fond of the trippers either. The custom of people who are over, or in, for the day is not to be compared in respect of its value with that of yachtsmen and yachtswomen. The shopkeepers, in fact, do pretty well during the carnival, which they no doubt wish came oftener than once a year.

The men and women of the world of fashion and the day trippers are not the only regular visitors during Cowes Week. Scores of ladies, some of them temporary residents and others on holiday for the day from the mainland, take up positions outside the side entrance to the Squadron lawn, from which they can see the distinguished folk arriving at or departing from the Castle jetty. They know everybody by sight, and judging from the conversation have been diligent students of Debrett and similar publications. Most of them bring little camp stools, on which they sit all day, devoting the quieter minutes of their daylight vigil – these occur when the fashionable world is at lunch ashore and afloat – to study of the pictures and gossip in favourite newspapers. The objects of their scrutiny naturally do not care for the publicity thrust upon them, but that seems to be a matter of small account to the observers.

When the racing is in progress the local experts congregate in the road-way in front of the Castle – most of them with their backs to the historic wall. They know the game, of course, and appear to be on familiar terms, so to say, with the principal owners. In their allusions to them, at any rate, they generally use only Christian names. The royal owner of Britannia may, for all I know, never have been alluded to as George, but Teddy was their affectionate loyal way of describing his predecessor on the throne. Their knowledge of the technicalities of fore-and-aft sailing is profound; most of them, indeed, are themselves capable handlers of boats. The palm for proficiency in the difficult art of 'reading' a yacht race belongs, however, elsewhere. Being a Scot, I should like to award it to Largs on the Clyde, but it really belongs to Harwich when the men, women, and children of Rowhedge, Wivenhoe, and Brightlingsea are assembled there for the local club's annual regatta.

The quality of the yachts which race, the numerical strength of the assembled cruising fleet, and the number of well-known people who are present afloat and ashore entitle Cowes week to be regarded as the yachting festival of the year.

Shetland crofters: their fish dishes
September 13 1935

In Shetland the housewives are expert in treating the fish caught by their menfolk. The average Shetlander need never be 'ill-off' for a good dinner. The sea around the isles teems with fish of all kinds. Small boats are plentiful in Shetland, almost every crofter owning one, or more, and with lines, rods, or nets, a sail of a half mile or so brings the fishing grounds within reach. Out-jutting stones, or 'craigs,' by the shore, are noted fishing places, and with a wand, or long rod and thin line and hooks, with some crushed shell-fish for bait, large baskets full of 'sillicks' and 'pilticks' are obtained in the course of an hour's sport.

The fishing is also the isles' principal industry, more than 3,000 men being employed. The herring fishing alone has yielded a catch this season of over 200m fish, valued at more than £200,000. The herring are gutted and treated with salt, in barrels, which are exported to Germany and the USSR.

The Shetlanders, however, know the body-building properties of the herring and 'salt herrin' an' potatoes' boiled form a favourite diet. Fresh herring are fried or roasted, and the early fish, fat and tender, are considered a luxury. Kippers, red herrings, and lightly salted herring are also used with bread or potatoes, the bones having no terror for the Shetland people. It has been said that some people in the course of a hasty meal eat 'bones an' all' with no harmful results!

It is with the white fish, however, that Shetlanders excel in the many different dishes they cook, with almost every particle of the fish, 'head an' rig an' tail an' a'. 'Stap', for instance, can be so prepared as to take in the most knowing fisherman! Cod fish, skate, tusk, flounder, turbot, haddock, whiting, mackerel, are all caught in abundance.

Cod fish swarm on the banks near Shetland, the shoals giving the trawlers good catches. The Shetland men, up to about 1890, used to set long lines from their small open boats, selling their catches to the local landowners, who were the sole merchants in the place. This period was known as the 'haaf fishing' and by reason of their monopoly the merchants gave the men as low a price as possible for their catches, which were salt cured for export to Spain. The 'haaf' period is now an unpleasant memory in Shetland, but it is from this time of oppression and poverty that many of the unique fish diets have their origin, or the old recipes were improved upon. The people were forced to live frugally, often going without a square meal for days on end. Not a particle of the produce from croft or sea was ever allowed to be wasted.

'Stap' is the name of one of the most succulent dishes made. It is made up of pieces of fish, either cod, ling, or tusk, 'stapped' or mixed up with the crushed liver, all the bones being carefully removed, with salt, pepper, and other seasoning added. An old saying tells of the devil being afraid to set foot on Shetland soil because the islanders would catch him and 'lay him in stap.'

Sillicks are the small fish who feed inshore in dense shoals, particularly about harvest-time. They are the young of the saith, or coal-fish, and are caught, like trout, on rods, or in 'pokks,' or rough, small-meshed nets made like a bag and weighted at the narrow, lower end. Pilticks, or coal fish a year old, are also caught on rods, usually 'off at the eela,' or inshore grounds. The boats go off to 'da eela' after teatime and the men sail for two or five miles to the tide streams where the fish feed. The eela provides great sport. The pilticks when boiled are as white as snow and are often compared with the curd of buttermilk. With new potatoes freshly delved from the croft fields and boiled the pilticks form a supper fit for the gods.

The one fish not much in favour among Shetlanders is the trout, although the burns, lochs, and voes (creeks) are full of them. Youngsters go to the burns or off in boats in the voes for a night's trout fishing for sport; but the flesh of the trout seems to be rather strong-tasting even to the palate of the people who eat hard salt pilticks 'down out of the roof-beams' without so much as a tremor! Trout, in consequence, are left to the tourists from 'the south', whose number is increasing yearly.

Mugildens are pilticks or sillicks roasted with the livers inside. Liver kroos is the name given to a lump of dough shaped like a cruse. It is filled with fish livers and baked on the hearth to make a wholesome, if plain, diet. It is not now so common, like much of the fish diet, as all kinds of tinned and other foodstuffs are easily obtained from the shops and vans, but 'kroos wi' livers' are a cheap and body-building food. Liver flakki, two dried pilticks laid together with livers between them and roasted on the hearth, and liver muggi, the stomach of a cod filled with livers and boiled, are two more hunger-killing foods.

All these dishes are famed for their health-giving qualities, being composed mainly of livers, which are full of vitamins. Doctors give the old dishes high praise and are astonished at some of the people who will not bother to cook them. Often at the mention of the old foods laughter is provoked among the young people, whose interest in fish is limited to the universal supper of fish and chips. It can be said, however, that the pure ingredients of the oily, mealy, fish foods did much to keep the Shetland crofter-fishermen strong and healthy, even under the rigorous conditions when hard, wet work on land and sea, with little chance of regular mealtimes, was their lot.

Miscellany: firewood free
February 18 1936

It is after gales like those of last week (writes a correspondent in Cornwall) that beachcombers are reported to have shovelled up bucketsful of sovereigns and pieces of eight – released by the battery of the waves from ancient wrecks. To few people, however, does the wind bring such good luck as that. But here, near Land's End, we must not grumble, for many of us owe all our firewood to the gales.

The variety of the driftwood thrown up by the waves is always interesting. Portions of apple, onion, orange, and bully beef boxes are most plentiful: the Californian fruit-growers and one or two Argentine meat companies are now regarded as old friends. Condensed milk firms and margarine factories (the other day I burnt a board stamped 'Margarinfabrik, Vejle') also help to fill the wood basket. The legends on the wood are in many strange languages. Yesterday I found a board whose origin was attested by the word Holland, but that was all we could understand. Sometimes the box ends carry only Chinese or Japanese characters, so no word is comprehensible. The heavier firewood has recently consisted mainly of new pit-props, which have been washed up in great numbers all along this stretch of coast.

This bounty seems to keep alive some of the same spirit with which the old wreckers were imbued. There could be no doubting the satisfaction in the voice of a neighbour when he remarked to me yesterday, 'I hear there's a French ship sunk and another on the rocks along the coast; soon there'll be plenty of wood and maybe summat else for us, too.'

Beachcombing: Cornish stones
June 23 1938

Already we have solved the 1938 Christmas present problem! The pebbles which we have picked up on the Cornish beach a few weeks ago are now at Penzance waiting to be transformed into souvenirs of our summer holiday. Some of the pebbles are as small as pigeons' eggs; others are as large as an ostrich's. All are sea-worn smooth and white, and it was only by the dim colouring showing through the hard outer casing that we were able to recognise semi-precious stones as, day after day, we searched for them among the shingle at Downderry and Looe.

At Penzance factory workers have their hands fully occupied cutting, polishing, and setting the pebbles gathered by Cornish holiday makers possessing infinite patience and keen eyesight. And patience is truly necessary for the finding of cornelians and amethysts. Chalcedony is comparatively easy to find. That may be the reason why, as a gem, it is underrated, though its opalescent lapis lazuli blue is magical. Charming, too, is the delicately flushed rose quartz, but for magnificent colouring commend me to the blue agate, the watered marking of which shades from the intense electric blue of the night sky in summer to a dazzling jade.

There is a wide choice of articles to be made from these pebbles and the cost is low. A chalcedony, for example, is polished and mounted in a silver bar brooch for half a crown. Topaz-tipped thimbles, blue agate paper-weights, box covers, and knife handles, crystal cuff links and dress studs, rose quartz rings, amethyst pendants, and necklaces in which assorted stones are carefully graded are all skilfully made by Cornish lapidaries, though formerly the pebbles had to be sent to France to be worked.

Just as anglers are reported to buy fish at the local fishmongers rather than confess that they have failed to hook a salmon, so Cornish holiday makers can avoid the humiliation of returning home empty-handed. At the small shops which act as depots for the factory at Penzance pebbles can be bought. Who would grudge a shilling for a chalcedony or three and sixpence for a cornelian? And yet how much more thrilling it is for us, who were successful treasure-seekers, to be able to say next Christmas, 'Just a little gift made from a stone we picked up on the shore last summer'! The recipient, gazing at the honey-coloured topaz quartz or the gleaming crystal, will immediately visualise a beach which scintillates with rainbow colouring like the picture in a child's fairy story book ... We shall not spoil their mental picture by telling them how sober are these Cornish gems in their natural state.

Letter to the editor: birds of the Norfolk coast
February 13 1939

Sir, – Snow, frost, and ice made me hope for something a little out of the ordinary when I went to the Norfolk coast during the recent cold weather. Each day of my stay both high tides took place when it was dark, so I did not see any of the sea duck, grebes, and divers which come close inshore at high tide. Two harbour channels, however, well repaid a visit. One sheltered a gaggle of some two hundred brent geese, six mergansers, and a dozen goldeneye, most of which were drakes. 'Rattlewings,' the name given goldeneye by Norfolk fowlers, suits them better than 'whistlers,' for the sound made by their swiftly beating wings is not a whistle but a loud, metallic rattle. The other harbour channel was tenanted by about 50 scaup, six widgeon, and 50 or so more brent geese. Few paintings of drake scaup depict them as they look in the field, for at the distance from which they are usually seen the delicate grey vermiculations on their backs which bird artists take pains to emphasise are not visible and their backs look almost as white as their flanks.

Most of the small lagoons which lie between the shingle banks or the sand dunes and the marshes were frozen and contained nothing but coots, which seemed to spend most of their time ploughing ways through the thin ice. One large lagoon, however, where there was a considerable area of open water, harboured 40 or so more scaup, seven more brent-geese, three black-necked grebes, and a herd of ten Bewick's swans, five of which were adults. A few days before my visit there had been more than 30 Bewick's swans on this lagoon, one of the many large herds which have been seen in widely separated parts of the country since the first spell of very hard weather began. Several of them are probably herds which had been wintering on the Zuider Zee and were forced to seek new quarters when it froze.

The largest congregations of birds I was watching were those gathered on the flats at low tide. Waders, of which there were at least 13 species, predominated. They were, perhaps owing to the cold, not as active and alert as usual and allowed me to approach very near to them, flying only a few yards farther along the shore when disturbed. One snow-white sanderling excelled all its fellows in tameness. I caught sight of it running towards me, its little feet twinkling over the sand, when I was watching some dunlin, so I stood quite still, and it ran up so close to me that I could almost have touched it with a stick. Only once did I see anything of the manoeuvres one expects of waders, and that from a large party of knots, which flew slowly downwind past me in a long, undulating line, looking like some enormous sea serpent translated to the sky.

One does not often see large numbers of passerine birds feeding with waders. But here, thanks to the cold, which had made it impossible for them to get their normal food, were redwings, fieldfares, greenfinches, chaffinches, and skylarks all flying out from the frozen marshes to hobnob with such aristocrats of the shore as godwits and curlew. Every now and then a hooded crow would fly out over the flats, reconnoitre for a while, and then wheel round and fly back again. It had not struck me before how flat hoodies look in flight. The grey of their backs seems to sink in between the black of their wings in a way that makes their backs look almost hollow.

Some distance from where I saw the hooded crows I came across a party of some 40 snow-buntings which, as if to justify their name 'snowflakes,' drifted over me with dancing flight and dropped down on to a patch of frozen snow. But for shorelarks I searched in vain. There had been some in the neighbourhood before my visit, but as soon as the cold weather set in they had gone, presumably to seek unfrozen feeding grounds farther south.

One always hopes to see one or two birds of prey on a visit to the Norfolk coast in winter, but this year my hopes were exceeded. A female merlin flew over me and a hen-harrier quartered a reed bed in front of me as I lay on a bank enclosing a small lagoon; another hen-harrier flew over to the mainland from Scolt Head Island, and, coming upon a party of shooters, at once turned round and flew back again; and no fewer than nine short-eared owls rose before me as I walked across some rough ground. Most of the owls had probably only just arrived, for they looked tired, and three of them did no more than fly 50 yards or so, wheeling this way and that like nightjars, with their disproportionately long wings first beating regularly and then held motionless, down to the shore, where they sat on the sand and rolled their big yellow eyes in anger at him who had disturbed their piece. – Yours, &c.

JKA

Oxford, February 8

A Country Diary: Cornwall, April 14
April 21 1939

Yesterday we went down to a quiet, rocky spot on the coast. So still was the air and sea that the loudest sound was the faint but unmistakable 'click, click, click' caused by the fan-like mechanism in the gill chambers of the crabs and lobsters hidden in the rock crevices. The only other peculiar sound was the faint hissing – with which is mingled a scratching sound – caused by the movement of the limpets on the rocks (they call them 'limpots' locally).

There is one of the most beautiful rock pools in Cornwall right amongst the higher rocks of the shore; a most unlikely spot only attainable by a tough scramble which brings one to the very base of the towering cliffs; but the tide only falls to the base of the cliff feet and rises well up the cliff face and so pours its refreshing water into this pool of clear, lovely liquid that seems so different in hue to either fresh or sea water as to belong to neither.

The young hermit crabs are always our favourite actors; there are always plenty of the smallest sizes in the pool, and they go lumbering about with their shells like small tanks; they and the shannies (locally 'bull cats') are the life of the pool; its beauty is made up of the coral lines, the little gem pimplet anemones, and the beadlets – which vary in hue from buff to orange-brown, green, and dark-red spotted with green. The whole pool has a most hypnotic effect, and the eye is ever finding something fresh; the antics of the bull cats as they slip out of the crevices, cling to the rock, dart after prey, or find a limpet loosening his hold and catch him before he can apply his sucker and so drag him off are always amusing. Usually they drop the limpet after banging his shell against the sides a time or two as a thrush bangs a shell snail on a stone. It would take a stronger fish then a bull cat to break that tough shell.

Roughly clad: towelling for the seaside
July 18 1939

The question of beach wear for little girls is a problem which none of the passing fashions has really solved for us. The half-dozen or so frocks which at home take turns in the wash and see a daughter through the summer at the seaside are soiled and crumpled too quickly when the wearer discards them in haste in a beach hut. Washing, starching, and ironing are impossible. The problem can be halved by investing in shorts, but even so a number of blouses are needed which still need laundering and which, in term time, make an appearance only at weekends. The beach frock is continually proving inadequate protection against (a) the strong breeze and (b) the strong sun, until one feels that the holiday would be much more restful if it involved less supervision of garments.

This year the perennial problem is solved. When Michael came to lunch, his small form completely clad in towelling, the mother of daughters quickly registered the virtues of this material. Easy to pack, quickly washed and dried, no ironing required! Last year the adult male sex seemed to have the monopoly of shirts in towelling, but this year, so Michael's mother told us, she had found a complete suit for the two-year-old. In blue and white, with a cord to tie at the neck, Michael had the nautical look necessary for the seaside.

The happy housewife had only to visit the sales and return with lengths of towelling to be turned into shorts, shirts, and, in order not to be left out of it, a length for herself. This was made into a lining to be clipped into a beach coat at bathing times. It will be so satisfactory to have all the family going down to the sea roughly clad in towelling. Next year garments which have been outgrown can be passed on to a younger person, until eventually they end their days as excellent floor cloths.

Evacuation to the seaside
September 4 1939

The children who had been sent from Manchester to safer homes along the Fylde coast on Friday were well settled down at the weekend, and showed every sign of enjoyment as if they were on holiday in the normal way. The holiday makers welcomed them enthusiastically, and normally shy children grew accustomed to giving a full account of themselves to people who stopped them in the streets. The main burden of keeping the children in order during the day falls on the teacher, but early on Saturday morning quite a number of children were to be seen walking out with their new 'mothers,' helping to carry home the morning shopping.

One woman who had lost both her own children when they were young had taken in two girls from Hulme and announced her intention of 'rigging them out' with new clothes, keeping them in pocket money, and, in general, treating them as her own family. Some of the evacuees were sent to houses where there were already visitors staying – though, of course, many holiday makers were leaving the coast over the weekend and few coming to replace them – and they received an extra welcome. On Saturday evening, before bedtime, some of these visitors were to been shepherding their new young friends around, giving them pennies to put in slot machines, and explaining to passers-by, 'They're from Manchester. We're just giving them a bit of a treat.'

On Saturday morning the sands were dotted with little parties of children, some of them under the care of teachers, some on their own. They were busy doing all the things that should be done by the sea – building sandcastles, writing their names in the sand, looking for jellyfish, and basking in the sun. Some of the older boys were playing football on an improvised pitch, and some were making piles of stones and knocking them down with other stones.

A few conversations with housewives who had adapted themselves suddenly to the billeting arrangements gave the impression that, so far, the children had behaved themselves admirably – as they did throughout the journey down. There had been a few tears at bedtime when the young ones missed their mothers, but they seemed to have gone off to sleep soon. One boy, when asked if he had slept well, gave the somewhat cryptic reply, 'I don't know whether I slept well, but I slept all night,' and another said he had never gone to sleep so quickly, attributing it to the fact that there were no trams rumbling past his door. In the smaller centres the children were equally happy and well looked after and it did not occur to those who were housed some distance from the sea to envy those who were in view of it.

A policeman on duty at a church hall where dinners were being served said that he had seen hundreds of children coming and going and had not heard more than three crying. Those who have had to deal with the reception and billeting, though they had to work hard under tremendous pressure, seemed delighted to find the children so easy to deal with, and praised the teachers who had managed to impose such general discipline without any apparent strictness.

On the way back to Manchester there were the same crowds of children on the smaller stations, the same trains, their windows crowded with smiling faces and waving hands; and, introducing a new note, there were on one station dozens of perambulators waiting for the mothers who were coming with babies. There were, on the whole, many more adults travelling with children on Saturday, for some of them had been unable to leave on Friday and were going down to join their children, who had been sent to homes where there was room for mothers as well. Food arrangements were running smoothly, and there seems no doubt that within a few days the organisation of schools for the evacuated children will be well in hand, the enormous task of moving them will be finished, and they will be pursuing their normal lives in healthy, safe surroundings.

Rock Pools and Sandcastles:
1940-1959

Brighton's 'last Sunday'
March 25 1941

A cherry tree in one of the old Regency squares at Hove was beginning to break into blossom; there was spring in the air and summer seemed not far away. Yet neither Brighton nor Hove was preparing for the summer season. I went down to Brighton for the day on Sunday – Brighton's 'last Sunday'; for from tomorrow onward Brighton will be included in the banned area. No visits may be paid any more to Brighton, in the words of a Home Office statement, 'for the purposes of holiday, recreation, or pleasure.'

The ban did not come as a complete surprise – in fact, the local people were expecting it – but it came as a disappointment none the less. However, as a Brighton bus-driver remarked, 'The military know what they are doing, and they know best.' A good many people in London must have been sorry to hear of the ban, and they were determined to have another look at Brighton before it came into force. On Sunday morning all the trains for Brighton were packed and long before the trains left Victoria the third class had overflowed into the first class and the Pullmans. Even so, many of the young people – soldiers and RAF boys among them – had to stand in the corridors during the one and a half hour journey. And as the train drove into Brighton Station there was an explosion of loud laughter, for at that moment the familiar London tune of the air-raid warning sounded. 'I thought they'd play a prettier tune than that in Brighton,' one girl remarked.

The procession of passengers streamed down the shopping street running from the station to the sea. Before getting as far many disappeared in public-houses, and many more in souvenir shops. The same old batons of Brighton rock, the same old selection of 'seaside' postcards – hundreds, thousands of them. All the old jokes about the lovesick old spinster and the henpecked, red-nosed dipsomaniac, and the couples in cars and on the seashore; their excess of crudeness makes them almost funny – or, rather, the thought that anyone can think them funny. Probably very few people think them genuinely funny, but they think it highly funny that anyone should. That, no doubt, accounts for the great success of seaside postcards.

Some of the larger hotels at Brighton have been closed for some time past, but those that were open and the restaurants certainly did a roaring trade on that 'last Sunday.' It was an adventure to get lunch. At the Old Ship not a hope. No more luck at another famous place. At last at Jimmy's with its pleasant 'Regency' murals in the lounge, the diligent head waiter firmly promised a table 'in half an hour.' To fill the time we went for another long walk along the promenade, but the Tussaud waxworks were too tempting. So bang went sevenpence for the privilege of seeing a gentle Hitler and a slim Göring and a genteel Mussolini, and another sevenpence for seeing the chamber of horrors and the distorting mirrors. And at the door 'Mr Tussaud' gave one his views on the ban on Brighton. 'Rather a smack in the eye,' he said. He didn't know whether he'd keep open.

He would see. He wasn't sure whether regular Brighton and Hove residents were really interested in waxworks. It was the London public that mattered most.

Back to Jimmy's. The head waiter had kept his word: at neighbouring tables, a startling sight, several parties were drinking champagne or, at any rate, some kind of fizz. 'A wedding?' 'No,' said the waiter; 'just remembering old days and saying goodbye to Brighton.'

As one walked along the promenade and looked down on to the blue sea amidst this crowd of normal-looking London trippers, one could hardly imagine that Hitler's fellows, treading on French soil, were just a little beyond the line dividing sky and sea. And there was a great deal of animation all around the Pavilion. Looking at its odd oriental domes, a London girl uttered a cri de coeur – 'Oh, look, just like onions.' And a local worthy, showing some trippers round, sadly remarked that in peace time the Pavilion was floodlit and there were fairy lights on the trees around. In the Pavilion itself a Methodist service was in progress, and at the other end a notice said that the state apartments could be visited every morning. Another notice on the same door gave directions concerning the local food control.

Trolleybuses in the streets were numerous, and there were also taxis, one of which took me round the older residential parts of Brighton and Hove. The regency houses were calm and serene, and, unlike so many of the houses round Regent's Park in London, undamaged and inhabited. There were still many people living in the smaller residential hotels; probably they will stay on as regular residents. There were signs of bomb damage in only a very few places, but children had been evacuated from Brighton none the less. Before the fall of France it had been an evacuation area. The favourite Brighton story was that in one of their communiqués the Germans had boasted of having heavily bombed and severely damaged 'the port of Brighton.'

The return journey was much the same as the journey there. The train was even more crowded. 'Well, goodbye, Brighton,' many of the passengers said, as they looked out of the window. And perhaps they wondered what Brighton would look like on their next visit. And at least one young pair vowed that they would 'celebrate the end of the war at Brighton; and a jolly good holiday we'll have.'

Alexander Werth

Rights of drift
January 22 1946

Thin snow covers the beach down to the high-tide mark, but there it ends. Below this the shingle has been licked bare by the sea and millions of coloured pebbles gleam in the weak sunshine. The wind has dropped and the small waves break with little noise, though it was only two days ago that the roar of the rolling shingle could be heard far inland whenever there was a momentary pause in the yell of the storm. The beach at this season of the year is always steeper than it is in summer, for these on-shore gales drive some of the shingle hard against the low cliffs and pull the rest of it away into deep water; the harder the wind hurls breakers against the shore the stronger grows the undertow, pulling any loose objects out to sea. It seems curious, but it is the off-shore winds and light airs of summer that will bring the missing beach back again.

We are gathering driftwood. The only other people down here are a few cold men casting lines for bass. Driftwood is here in plenty, lying scattered on the beach or buried in the rampart of tangled seaweed built by the last high tide. Some of it, however, is beyond our powers; one piece in particular has for years defied all wood-gatherers. Sometimes after storms this huge baulk of timber disappears for a while under the stones, but when calmer weather returns it always emerges again like some ponderous hibernating tortoise. Fifteen feet long and three feet square at the ends, it must weigh tons. It is an enigmatic object, vast, black, and unexplained.

Our pieces are lesser ones. Burdened, we trudge up the sliding beach and cast our loads down on firm earth. Lightened, we recross the snow for more.

There is room in the cottage fireplace for logs and we seldom need to use the saw; when a big piece breaks in the middle one pushes the ends together. Stacks of wood, faintly steaming, stand on either side of the fire, giving off as they dry the queer, pungent smell of timber long pickled in brine. On the hearth bright pointed flames are dancing round a pit-prop that already has an hour-glass waist. It burns fast this battered bit of spruce, for teredo, the shipworm, has been at it, and the fire penetrates deep along teredo's burrows. In these latitudes timber is not attacked like this until it has been in the sea at least a year; we do not have the terrible six-foot teredos of the tropics, which attack with a much greater promptness and appalled the early navigators. Some ship was lost a year ago or more and this pit prop was probably part of a deck cargo. It is not only worms that have attacked it; the ends are frayed like old rope; it looks as if it has been battered for weeks with heavy mauls. As a matter of fact, it has: the power of the storm waves is terrific.

The fiery caverns pulsate gently. In the depths the colour turns from red to blue, an exquisite hovering blueness, meconopsis and speedwell, blackbirds' eggs and a mandrill's cheeks, but the final and most astonishing revelation of blue must be a two-inch copper nail in a piece of burning teak. Teak and copper nails! I wonder where she was lost. And when. Far away and long ago perhaps; driftwood travels for thousands of miles across the oceans and teak will float indefinitely. This plank may have crossed the Atlantic like those nuts from West Indian trees that are sometimes found on Hebridean strands and are said to have helped in persuading Columbus that the western ocean was not the world's end. Then there was the wreck of the *Jeanette* that drifted across the North Pole, inspiring Nansen to emulate it with his *Fram*, and there were the Greenland Eskimos who build driftwood kayaks, but had no idea of what trees could be. But, as the plank falls in ruin and the blue glow fades, a dim and ancient superstition stirs. This teak plank was once a treasured boat that had no doubt done good service. In the fishing villages a boat that is no longer of use lies on the mud and rots quietly, blackened and weedy ribs emerging from the ebb. Fishermen do not burn old boats to boil kettles.

This next bit was never meant to get into the sea. It is an oak fencing post. Along the whole Channel coast the sea is eating the land, especially where natural resistance is as weak as it is here. Once there was a right of way along the cliff top, but the sea ate it, and now there are barbed wire fences and threatening notice boards. And the sea eats them.

It will go on eating. The shore is buttressed and groynes are built, but the sea is working round the ends of the sea wall before the cement is hard, and if the groynes anchor the shingle here for a while it only means that places up the Channel will be deprived of it and lose their best defence. If the sea could be prevented from deepening inshore waters the battle would be won, say experts; for then the great waves would break far out and only small and harmless ones would reach the land. We should strive to defend the sea bottom a mile out, but we seem no nearer knowing how to do this than the people of vanished Selsey and Dunwich and Ravenspur. Lyonesse has gone, and Gwaelod – the lost land of Wales, – and their fate has made them countries of romance. Will romances be spun round our seaside bungalows that are going the same way?

The wind is getting up. Tomorrow this cold, still interval will have ended and the snow on the shore will give way to a blanket of quivering foam as the gales begin again. At last the kettle is boiling. We'll go after more driftwood tomorrow. From lost ships and lost lands.

Stephen Bone

Dunromin
March 8 1949

At last that flatly fictitious house-name Dunromin may be used with propriety. For an advertiser offers for sale as a seaside bungalow 'a large private railway saloon coach.' The price of this potential pied-a-terre is not stated, but the offer is sure to draw many inquiries. Which of us does not fancy the idea of living – if only for a change – in a barge, a Martello tower, or even a converted LCT [landing craft tank]? So we may imagine this saloon coach anchored hard by our favourite saltings, completely at home amid the foreshore derelicts, the ancient craft that will sail the seas no more. Improving the property would be our fondest care. We would not rest until our visitors would say, as the Water Rat said of Mole End, 'This is the jolliest little place I ever was in.'

Sodalis

Those seaside postcards: Blackpool's watchdog
October 31 1951

The newly formed postcard censorship committee at Blackpool will examine about two thousand comic postcards next week – the first batch for next season. The board was formed after several shopkeepers had been prosecuted for selling allegedly indecent postcards, some of which, it was stated in court, had been passed by the Isle of Man censor. The local authorities were unable, or unwilling, to say which card could be sold without fear of prosecution and the traders decided to form their own censorship board. The watch committee and the chief constable (Mr H Barnes) were invited to send representatives but both refused.

Leading publishers of comic postcards have been approached by the board and have offered to send their cards for inspection.

A transit camp for mislaid children
August 19 1953

Whitley Bay, where everybody looks reassuringly like everybody else, is a good place for observing that remunerative abstraction the Average Holidaymaker. Who, but the abstraction himself, is to deny the figures? He buys a 'science' novel, two Sunday papers, three postcards (one scenic, two comic), large quantities of ice cream and strong tea, a packet of indigestion tablets, and anything up to half a stone of fish and chips. He wins a doll or an alarm clock at some skilful game of chance, plays a dozen games of beach cricket for the sake of the family but also because he likes it, and has one-third of a swim (up to his knees) between the green flags. He is accompanied by one wife and one-decimal-six children.

Here, surely, the facts beat the figures, for never was there a beach so swarming with children. Just as you can wildly guess at the number of fish in the sea by the number that come out of it, so the imagination can stretch towards how many children there may be at Whitley Bay from how many get lost. They run to 50 or 60 a day in fair weather – hundreds on a bank holiday – and are collected into a special clearing-house or transit camp with the help of three loudspeakers.

The strays range from one year to 14, but mostly look to be adventurous four-year-olds. 'People bring them in from miles away, sometimes as far as the lighthouse,' says Mrs E Davidson, who looks after them. They are brought in smeared with sand, ice cream, and tears, but are swiftly put at their ease in a kind of juvenile club provided with miniature deck chairs, books, and comic papers. Here the more spirited ones compare notes on their adventures, and eventually greet their harassed parents with composure.

Older children sometimes come here of their own accord: 'They get tired, and give themselves up,' says Mrs Davidson. She has observed that young Tynesiders are more likely to stray than the young Scots who also come to Whitley Bay in large numbers. Among the national statistics that still do not exist, those of lost children at seaside resorts would be particularly formidable.

Near the lost children's shelter is the ambulance station, which brings us to a more sombre side of Average Holidaymaking. Apart from traffic hazards – I have myself seen three accidents, two of them serious, at seaside towns within a week – there appears to be a daily risk which might be estimated at a thousand to one of getting your feet cut on glass. Here the beach ambulance men handle 16 or 20 casualties a day, mostly cases of cut feet, some of them severe. 'Don't leave bottles on the beach,' the loudspeakers implore. The appeal might be made still more pointed, on the lines of the railway notice to train spotters: 'Don't jump on the mailbags; there may be a present for *you* inside.'

There are also broken ribs and ankles from falls, but the most remarkable casualty that has happened here is known to the ambulance men as 'The Case of the Two Shilling Piece'. Determined to plunge deeper than the customary knee level, a visitor left his clothes on the beach but decided that the two shillings in his trousers might put too much temptation in the way of his fellows. He popped the coin in his mouth, and struck out. Soon he was back, this man of little faith, frightened and – to all practical purposes – penniless. He had swallowed it.

Such misadventures apart, the beach is gay; far more animated than most. The ponies pulling small carts, the flags and swings and roundabouts, the perambulating salesmen ploughing through the sand with crisps or 'lovely Sweet William toffee pears, sixpence,' bring a touch of Epsom Downs to the scene.

Up on the promenade, in powerful contrast, are two elderly men playing open-air draughts. They face each other on benches, between which is a large paved platform, perhaps eight feet square. The pieces, pink against white, are wooden hexagons with staples knocked in the middle, and they are moved with long spiked poles. Amid flower-beds the players sit, intent and silent through the hours, and the fifty spectators clustering round them are silent too. On they go, the strange draughts players, until the day-tripping crowds are surging past them, homeward bound for Newcastle.

The electric trains go chuntering off, packed to the sliding doors; it might be the Paris Metro in the rush-hour, except that the floor is littered with shells. The endless stream flows up the Esplanade, and the hump where it becomes Station Road is the point where the holiday is over. Look back from there, and the sands are gone; the sea is a vast sheet of metal plate.

Norman Shrapnel

Visit to Portmeirion
May 28 1954

The visit to Portmeirion last night gave some idea of what television can do by way of showing places which are on a small enough scale for the cameras to range about and see a good deal in one eyeful. It was never possible, in the views we saw, to get quite the perspective that would show this pretty Italianate village complete in its wooded setting, nor, of course, to see the colour which is half its charm. On the other hand, there were, piece by piece, glimpses of the sea, the hills, the roofs, and the campanile, and then the different buildings in closeup.

As the broadcast continued it gave a much more unified impression of the village as a whole, and the interview with Mr Clough Williams-Ellis, one of the rare people who appear natural and at ease before the camera, was interesting and amusing. Mr Hywel Davies, guide and interviewer, gave an air of leisure to this visit. Some commentators seem to seize a broadcast and subordinate it to their plan. Mr Davies went along easily and put the place and the people (who included Richard Hughes, the novelist) before himself: this is good television manners.

The visiting card
July 1 1954

I had some hundreds of yards of net drifting with the tide, and I sat by it in my small, light, rowboat in the summer darkness. This manner of catching salmon and sea trout is a usual pursuit of mine in the six-month season beginning in spring and ending by autumn, so the circumstances were not unusual. All was quiet, except that now and again a black shadow went overhead and I heard the harsh honk of the heron which had been the shadow. But I had a sense that there were salmon around, as well as other sea life, and the latter I took to be grey seals which often plague me by plundering from my nets. Apart from that knowledge – based on experience – I had a niggling suspicion that there was something else around; some creature that watched me.

I waited in the dark silence, eyes peering and my ears hearing and interpreting the sea noises. Far off in the night the sound of gulls gorging themselves on fry; a distant light splash that told me a fish had jumped out and hit the water as it fell in again; then I heard the blubber-bumping-thunder-splash that told me a seal had dived deep and steeply from the surface after salmon. I was relieved that it was some distance away from my nets.

Then all the sounds were gone, and on the flat, calm sea there was not even a rippling of water against the sides of the boat. My oars were in my hands, ready to row quickly if I heard a fish strike the net. There is no mistaking it, for it sounds like an express train swishing through a tunnel; it is made by the agitation of the float corks, shaken and pulled by the net as the fish struggles to get out. It is this sound that makes an excitement in the night.

Out of the now profound silence, when the world seems to have died, I heard that noise some fifty yards from me in the net. My oars hit the water with a smack, my back straightened to give rowing all my weight. The light boat jumped forward as I rushed it on to catch the fish before it broke out or escaped. It is always a race against time. I saw a shadow on the starboard side as I raced for the net; it passed me, going like a speedboat. There were now two competitors for one fish, myself in a boat and this other creature. It looked odd to be a seal, and small for one from all I saw of it as it passed me by. In great anxiety I rushed on towards the sound of splashing; when I neared it ceased. I looked down and all I saw was the swirl in the dark water and again unbroken silence, profound as it had been. It was evident that my competitor had caught the fish in the net, plucked it out, and dived away in the seconds between us.

Careful of making any undue noises (for fish have an acute sense of sounds as vibrations) I rowed slowly back along my net and waited, wondering if again I would have to compete with this voracious creature robbing me of earnings that are meagre enough. A Manx shearwater screeched in that spine-chilling fashion peculiar to it, the bird banshee of the darkness. It started me and cooled my skin – it always does; the ghostly noise in an echo of darkness was a taunt at timidity. A green crab started wandering around scraping at the boards inside the boat, but I could not find it to fling it into the sea from whence it had come.

As the light of morning moved overhead, starting the dawn from the brightness on the roof of sky that moved towards the east, I looked round with greater ease. I saw two lines of corks: the black one that I see at night, the light brown one that I see in day; in this odd light of morning I see them both – it is a strange phenomenon, – each a ghost of the other. I could see no seals then, but high overhead I saw the dark outlines of the seagulls on their way from their night's roosting places in the cliffs to their daytime feeding grounds. Now I knew as the day was breaking that the fish too would go out into the deep sea until night again. It had been an unsuccessful night, like so many others. All my chances of catching a fish were gone.

I went along my net searching just in case some silent fish had become caught in the darkness; it occasionally happens. Down deep in the water I saw a shining salmon. I pulled up the net to get the prize, dead, of course, for it was without movement. When I lifted it aboard I saw a clean round of flesh cut from its thick shoulder, and I knew my erstwhile competitor by that visiting card – it had been an otter. The fish as such was ruined for the market; I had been twice robbed in the night, so far as I know, by the creature watching me. However, the fish left over by the otter made a meal or two. I had learned the hard way that otters leave the rivers for the sea in search of food sometimes.

Thomas Skelton

Just like the railway posters – Margate in the sun
August 2 1955

There is only one advantage the Mediterranean resorts have over those of the English south coast – the weather; and this weekend they have lost that. Indeed it is more agreeable here than it is at Cannes or on the Lido, for a light breeze comes off the sea and makes it possible to play beach cricket and Jakarta, which is a one-man game of tennis played with a captive ball on an elastic string. There are, it is true, human salamanders who would prefer to be baking listless in the Italian sun, but they are provided for, too. For sixpence they can hire a canvas screen which acts as a windbreak but is officially called a suntrap. On the average August day the screen is a necessary protection against an east wind, which blows meanly between exposed shoulders, but this weekend it is a luxury demanded only by the most sybaritic.

The south-east coast looks for once as it does in the holiday posters the Southern Region puts up at Victoria. Sea and sky are blue, sand is golden, and the crowds on the beach, instead of looking from the distance like flies in their dark protective clothing, seem to be clusters of forget-me-nots. Even the grandmothers are in pastel colours and grandfathers are wearing teenage clothes, open-necked short-sleeved shirts and trousers daringly held up by belts.

Before the kiosks on the Promenade are queues for cups of rather thin tea and ice cream made by the great London distributing firms. The ice cream is all safe and hygienic and is liked by everybody who cannot remember the delicious combination of frozen custard and the vanilla-flavoured wafer which the Italians used to sell before ice cream became big business. And in those days, when the container of the ice cream was inevitably biscuit, all was consumed. No cartons or wrappings were left littering the beach.

For many of us, this weekend and the days which preceded it, have brought back memories of the long summers of childhood. They are evoked more easily because the seaside resort has changed remarkably little in 40 years. I have been staying on Marine Parade in an Edwardian boarding-house which would start Mr Ivor Brown and Mr John Betjeman into nostalgic rhyme – Victorian spaciousness without Victorian gloom. The bedroom has an immense bay window overlooking the sea. The curtains, suspended from a white pole, are of a pink that matches bedspread and curtains. The jug and bowl are missing, but the running water is hidden in a cupboard meant for clothes. The pictures on the walls are strictly of the period – an old peasant reading his Bible, a troupe of children playing on a baroque marble staircase. There is a mounting block to enter the bath, a cork seat across its top for those who fear to immerse themselves fully, a speaking tube so that one may communicate with the outside world in case of need.

Some change there is for the better. Under the pressure of competition from holiday camps and the liberal continental hotel the rules of the house have disappeared from the bedroom wall. 'But why,' asked a child, 'should we not take the towels down to the beach? Why must we not clean our shoes in the bedrooms? Why must we leave buckets and spades in the vestibule?' Useless to explain that these were rules impressed too deeply for us to forget, and though they no longer exist in statutory form they are part of the unwritten contract between the well-mannered guest and the landlady.

The food is much the same as it used to be, innocuous, innocent, flavoured with mint or sage, but never by garlic. The meals are rather exiguous, but include something you never get in the continental 'en pension,' there is afternoon tea for those who can haul themselves from the beach, with new bread and sometimes new cakes. With food prices mounting, with help more difficult to have than ever, with a season too short, the proprietor of the seven guineas a week boarding house still does well by her guests. And she provides something which one never finds in the grander continental hotels, a drawing room with comfortable cretonne-covered chairs that look into a lawn surrounded by antirrhinums and hollyhocks.

At night there is no casino. But the follies are there in the municipal pavilion. Their task is harder than ever now. The audience has seen everything that film and television has to offer and will not put up with simple sketches and excerpts from Max Miller. The pierrots I saw the other night had solved the problem by getting some of the nicer lyrics and sketches from revues which have played in the West End in recent years. Among them was an older work, a sketch in which Stanley Holloway used to play long years ago. He appeared as a henpecked Lancashire man, going on holiday with a wife and mother-in-law, who surprisingly orders himself a grapefruit. From this strange request wife and mother-in-law build up a suppositious picture of the paths of depravity he must have been treading to acquire such a strange taste.

In the years since the sketch was written grapefruit has become democratised and Stan Holloway's successor has to demand instead 'a dozen oysters.' It might be noted that some of the songs from the West End revues were put over better in this seaside pavilion than they were in the original productions, for the simple reason that in a seaside concert party an artist has to be able to sing.

Miscellany: Non-stop fishermen
March 20 1958

Posters are in the nature of things ephemeral works of art: seen today, overpasted tomorrow. A few of the better examples are revived at exhibitions. Certainly none has enjoyed the enduring fame of 'The Jolly Fisherman of Skegness.' Fifty years ago John Hassall sold an oil painting for £12 to the Great Northern Railways. It was used to advertise 'Non-Stop Corridor Excursions' on Sundays from King's Cross to Skegness: 3s return. It showed a plump, rather improbable fisherman skipping blithely along the beach. The caption read 'Skegness is So Bracing.' It is still the town's unofficial motto. By our standards, Hassall's colouring was a little thin for the hoardings. The artist himself admitted that he had done better, but 'this just happened to catch on.' The excursionists poured into the quiet Lincolnshire water place. After long and compelling service, the poster, or rather, the original, is now a museum piece. It is on permanent loan to Skegness council, who have hung it reverently in the town hall. The owners of the poster are the British Railways, and to mark its golden jubilee they have reissued it, altering only the wording – and the fare – to bring it up to date. The Jolly Fisherman has become a Skegness hero in his own right, and in the form of a silver statuette is presented to important visitors.

'Bucket and spade mob' move in
August 11 1958

Scarborough used to be 'posh', and it owed its prosperity to the ailment of a Mrs Farrow – some call her Farrer – who first had the idea in 1630 that the water springing from the cliffs in the South Bay might do her rheumatism some good. That was how the Spa was founded. Mrs Farrow's rheumatism was quickly forgotten, however, and the tonic waters became an excuse for fashion and high, if respectable, living. Nowadays a building sits solidly across the top of the well, the contents of which dribble wastefully down the seawall on to the sand below. The Spa is just another name, like the Olympia or the Palais – a place of entertainment without any special significance in its title.

But the great change has been a social one. No longer is this the home of high fashion, no longer can retired brigadiers suffer their gout quietly away from the miners and their families on the popular side. The corporation has taken over the Spa and, with commendable democracy and a practical show of economics, has removed the old toll gates and given over the buildings to what is fondly termed 'the bucket and spade mob.'

Scarborough corporation took over from the old Spa company last year, and it cost it £112,000 to do so; a further £20,000 was spent on improvements. But the corporation is sure that it has backed a winner. The return for the last financial year – the first under the corporation's management – shows a profit large enough to allow the inhabitants of Scarborough town hall an indulgent, perhaps self-satisfied, smile

It is hard to see exactly when the Spa began its decline. It became exceedingly popular in 1845, when the railways clattered into Scarborough. More than 20 years later the Prince of Wales became the first member of royalty to patronise the Spa, and thereafter it became 'fashionable' to visit the town. In 1880 much of the Spa was rebuilt after a fire had destroyed many of the original buildings, and Irving, Kemble, and George Alexander played to politely enthusiastic audiences at the newly open theatre. All this time the waters were sold for 2d a glass or 3d a bottle and the toll gates shut the Spa off from the other Scarborough, which was already beginning to push a rude forefinger in its direction.

Between the two world wars the Spa still remained aloof and it was not until 1945, a few years after the corporation had made an unsuccessful attempt to buy the property, that the company began to realise there were more people coming to the town who were not so poor. What it did not realise was that the barrier between 'posh' and popular still remained: the toll gates. The corporation tore them down and the results were astounding. On average nowadays 7,000 people dance at the Spa ballroom each week, conferences are held there well into the winter months, and the corporation can afford to spend £27,000 on dance bands, light orchestras, and artists without worrying too much about it.

The Spa is now returning to its golden days of prosperity; and if the pattern of entertainment is different, the old days are not entirely forgotten. For instance, the Spa waters, forgotten for twenty years or more, are to be marketed for the general public next year. And, although the corporation pulled down the gates with many a grand gesture and gave free admission to the Spa, it now costs you 6d to hire a deckchair. In the old days you might have paid your 6d at the gate, but at least you got a free seat.

A paddle-steamer Atlantis
September 20 1958

Lundy's Clear
Rains A'near.

So runs (or so I am rather unconvincingly assured) an Old Devonshire Proverb. Certainly there lingers around the island of Lundy, in the Bristol Channel, an agreeable aura of folksy romance, eminently conducive to fables and premonitions. There it stands on the holiday horizon, a paddle-steamer Atlantis, distant enough to be hazily compelling, near enough to be home again for supper (and if the worst comes to the worst, well, their yellow jumpers are nearly dry, aren't they, Muriel?). Lundy stands about halfway between Ilfracombe and Tenby, and the pleasure-steamers will whisk you there at the drop of a pale pink bathing cap.

It is an island of heathland mounted upon cliffs, three miles long, half a mile wide: high, austere, well-watered, and speckled with heather. Your ship drops anchor, with a flurry of back-paddling, in a small green conspiratorial inlet. A small but proper castle frowns down upon you from the headland. A white lighthouse gleams beside you. A string of motor launches, manned by seamen in blue jerseys, conveys you ashore in an atmosphere that might be, were it not for its toffee-apple overtones, distinctly cloak-and-dagger. Lundy lives up to its distant suggestive silhouette; and as you clamber up the hillside with your babies and your buckets you may close your eyes (if you are that way inclined), sniff the heather, rock slightly to the Atlantic breeze, and fancy yourself smuggling brandies or staggering ashore with the proceeds of piracy.

And in fact, when at last you reach the picnic plateau, the place turns out to be wonderfully rich in curiosities. If you stand on a high point in the centre of the island, surveying its broad fields from tip to tip, you may (for example) observe the following phenomena: the sad barbettes of the pre-dreadnought *Montagu*, ignominiously wrecked here in 1906; the fortress of the redoubtable De Marisco family, who struck up an alliance with Holdbodii the wicked Viking, and introduced the rabbit to England; a lighthouse abandoned because it was too tall and got mixed up with the fogs; some of Lundy's herds of 30 deer and 27 wild goat; the little fishing tender Lundy Gannet, which is the island's own link to the mainland; Mouse Island, Rat Island, Puffin Gully, Benjamin's Chair, Hangman's Hill, and the Ugly; and the big granite church built for the islanders by the Rev Hudson G. Heaven, whose tenures of office as lord of the manor, curate-in-charge, and vicar of Lundy gave rise to the witticism that unto him was the kingdom of heaven.

Bold, varied, and spectacular have been the owners, occupiers, or tenants of Lundy: the Vikings, Sir Richard Grenville, Lord Saye and Sele, Captain Nutt, the pirate, the knights templar, the father of Mr John Christie of Glyndebourne, the notorious trickster-parliamentarian Thomas Benson, and successive patriarchs of the Heaven family. It is still a private island. The last of the Heavens inherited it with a heavy mortgage, but unfortunately without any money whatsoever; for a year or two he tried to live off the island, with its berries and roots and lobsters, and then sold it with a sigh to less ascetic proprietors. The present owners are the three children of Mr MC Harman, who bought it in 1925 for £16,000, and who had so potent a sense of insular independence that he minted a coinage of his own, bearing a somewhat forbidding profile of himself on one side and a plump little puffin on the other (so upset were the authorities by this endearing stroke of bravura that the matter went to the House of Lords before it was decreed that puffins were, alas, not legal currency).

The heart of this entrancing island is the cluster of houses around the church, a little tattered at the edges, attended by grazing goats (who provide all the island's milk) and elevated by the presence of the Marisco Tavern, which suffers from no licensing restrictions and is both stone-flagged and cider-soaked. Twenty-two people now live on Lundy. It has always had a shifting population, and none of the present inhabitants was born on the island. The Harman children are all married (another son honoured Lundy's lusty traditions by winning a brilliant VC in Burma) and spend half their time on the mainland, half in the lovely old manor house that crouches twinkling in the gully beneath the church.

Mr Bendall is the farm bailiff and boatman; Mr Ogilvie the shepherd and goatherd; Mr Smith the tavernkeeper; Mr Cannon the gardener; and Mr John Spink is entitled a retired gentleman of leisure. Mr Dixon the priest, Dr Ruddock the doctor, Mr Ross the dentist, Mr Dyke the artist, and Mr Copp the builder are described as part-time islanders. The oldest inhabitant is Mr FW Gade, the agent, who has been on Lundy since 1926 and has written an admirable little book about it. It seems a gay, uninhibited, friendly community, at least on those days when, in a cloud of potato crisps and suntan lotion, the holiday crowds toil up the hill from the landing-beach, and the lord and ladies of the manor put on their aprons and help with the cottage teas.

Other kinds of fauna and flora are more abundant. If you peer over the southern cliff you may see the gloomy entrance to Seal's Hole, where the grey seals breed. Peregrine falcons have occupied one eyrie for centuries. The Lundy pony is a cross between the Welsh mountain pony and the New Forest species. The deer multiply so successfully that now and again a sharpshooter is imported to keep them down. Brassica Wrightil is, so Mr Gade's book says succinctly, 'an ancient member of the cabbage family which is found nowhere but on Lundy.' In 1850 they discovered on this surprising island the skeletons of two giants, a male of 8ft 6in, a female of 7ft 8in. There are no reptiles on Lundy, but there are pygmy shrews, puffins and crawfish, not to speak of the trippers.

Wherever you wander on Lundy, before the siren summons you helter-skelter back to the sea, you will observe the proud signs of its individualism. At the village store you may buy the Lundy postage stamps, aesthetically delightful but philatelically valueless: they are priced 'One Puffin', or 'Half Puffin,' according to Mr Harman's currency system, but at a pinch the shop will accept sterling (Lundy, in essence, is no more than an unproductive country estate, costs its owners a good deal of money, and even the 1s 6d landing fee charged to each seafarer does not cover its expenses). There are no rates to be paid on this Elysian resort, no taxes on income earned on the island, no licensing hours, no policemen. The Lundy islanders maintain a three-mile fishing limit, liable to be extended (one imagines) at any moment.

The island has never been really independent, though, perilously close though it must have been to the distinction in its brave piratical days. Indeed, at one time or another it has performed its services for the kingdom. It has been a lighthouse station and lookout post. Its granite helped to build the Charing Cross hotel. It put up a stiff fight, once or twice, when the French raided its cliffs, and it has sheltered many a royal ship, guided them up the channel to Bristol, offered them matins in its church and victuals in its inn, and sent them on their way rejoicing. Today it seems to be part of Devon in a hazy, lazy, private, roistering sort of way; and when the Queen Mother recently hove in sight in the royal yacht *Britannia* the islanders gave her a cup of tea and a sandwich and belaboured her with no nationalist petulances.

Another old proverb may come into your mind as the steamer churns its Edwardian passage back to Ilfracombe: 'He who tasteth Lundy's Air, Evermore Returneth There'. Nobody can complain of an island that matches its proverbs so genially and so curiously confirms its distant prospect: but – quick, Muriel, catch him, it's all down his front!

James Morris

A back way to Brightlingsea
December 7 1959

We left Whitstable in the family seven-tonner for the Essex shore, and as always on these occasions we had no set idea as to where our landfall would eventually be. It is a peculiarity of our family (or is it a peculiarly? I will take that up in a minute) that we have a preference for those places where we can berth alongside, or in some other way step straight ashore, rather than be obliged to moor or anchor; so Maldon, or Walton-on-the-Naze approached through the sheltering backwaters, were two obvious alternatives. But we should be lucky to reach either in a single day. We should be content to stay the night at Brightlingsea.

There seems good reason to doubt whether it is we, rather than the rest of the British sailing community, who are out of step in this preference of ours for tying up to the shore, alongside or end-on as the case may be. From Copenhagen to California tens of thousands of boat-owners are accustomed to securing their craft in well-protected marinas or yacht haves, and then stepping direct on to small piers leading to the shore. In home waters the considerable rise and fall of tide have something to do with it, but it must be pure masochism that makes so many Britons content with the mooring in mid-stream, the inevitable gyrations when wind is against tide, the dinghy that too frequently goes bump in the night, and all the minor inconveniences involved in a separation from the shore. All this is perhaps by the way, but it helps to explain why Maldon or Walton was our ultimate destination for a short stay.

Near low water that morning *Barcarole* had been beached for a scrub, and we did not leave Whitstable until noon. The wind along our coast was a moderate north-easterly, so we sailed close-hauled on the starboard tack. The direction of the wind and of the incoming tide jointly decreed that our course made good was something like NNW. It was past three o'clock when we reached southern end of the Swin, near the twin pairs of posts which mark the Admiralty's measured mile.

In contrast with the steamer lanes of the main estuary, the Swin seemed deserted. For the sailing barges it had once been the main highway to the east coast; there are only a dozen or so of these handsome craft still left and it would have been asking too much to expect to see one or more of them running up towards London river with a bone in her teeth; yet we were sorry to see that ahead of us there was no coaster or tug, nor even a small yacht.

For the bargeman or the yachtsman who is heading 'down Swin' for the Blackwater or the Colne there are normally two alternatives. There is the route through the Swin Spitway about five miles south of Clacton, and about 18 miles from where we found ourselves at that moment. Only two or three feet of water are to be found in this channel at low water springs. It shifts a good deal, and hundreds of craft must have run aground there. If we chose this passage we should have a long turn to windward and then (if all went well) we should be running up the Wallet against the ebb as darkness approached and the wind disappeared.

The other route is by way of the Crouch entrance and the Raysand channel. At high water and on a rising tide one can 'cut the corner' over Foulness sands, and the course from the measured mile is something like N N E. But high water was only half an hour away, the tide would soon be ebbing eastwards, and no risks could be taken with the sands. We should have to round the Whitaker beacon and then run towards the Crouch against the ebbing tide, past the W Buxey buoy, before turning north again.

'Work your tides' is the bargeman's maxim – plan to go with them and not against them, particularly at times when the wind may be falling light. There was only one way to do this. I eased my sheets a little and headed straight for the shore still hidden in faint mist, and with it the mouth of Havengore creek. Havengore was once a haven of some account; now it is no more than a short cut, when the tide is in, for yachtsmen on their way between the Crouch or Roach and the open estuary. Even at spring tides there is only a maximum of four or five feet of water over the bar – the ancient 'broomway' connecting Foulness with the mainland. With the wind on the beam, and our trust in *Barcarole*'s shallow draught (only three feet), we made rapidly towards the land.

The leadline was soon showing little more than a fathom of water and we took the precaution of reefing the mainsail to reduce speed. We aimed carefully for the centre of the two lines of posts that mark the twisting way across the bar. In the bows a conscientious daughter was calling out the depth: 'Five feet.' 'Four and a half feet.' Her brother stood by the mast in case the worst should happen, to let go the halliards with a run. But everything went according to plan and we finally found ourselves in the creek, with its full two fathoms of water.

A gaff-rigged boat had been about half a mile ahead of us, and the bridgekepper on the Foulness road had waited to deal with the two boats together before he started to wind up the lifting span by hand. This was a bit of luck; we went through the bridge without a check and were soon in Narrow Gut, where the creek is no wider than a country road. The marshland cows gazed at us contemplatively. In half an hour we were tacking down the river Roach, as the tide began its powerful sweep towards the open sea; in another half-hour we were in the Crouch and the tide was helping us even more. The wind was still against us, and dropping a little, but with the strong tide in our favour we hardly cared. We were in the Raysand (to be pronounced 'Rays'n,' we are told) channel before it was time for the ritual of hearing the evening shipping forecast. The leadline was in use again, and sometimes there was little more than a fathom under us as we picked our way between the Dengie flats and the Buxey sands; but as it was growing dusk we fetched the NW Knoll buoy and the Colne was before us.

We had almost certainly saved ourselves an hour or two by our back-door approach, for the wind was now very light indeed. As we entered the Colne the tide was at last unfriendly, but we did our best to cheat it by sailing in the shallow water near the mainland shore. We looked up the directions in our Pilot before following the leading lights that show the way into Brightlingsea's narrow creek. For the last quarter of a mile the auxiliary engine was turned on and we chugged to a berth at the harbour trots. The seabirds were calling to each other as we tied up and looked forward to a snug night.

Philip Hays

Poised for the Plunge:
1960-1979

Room to stretch
July 16 1960

Newcastle, with its skyline fretted out of black velvet, and the black Tyne, flowing viscid as fuel oil past the clangour of the riveting hammers, keeps more southerners out of Northumberland today than ever Berwick, with its strong flowing river and the Cumberland, Brass Mount, and Windmill bastions, reinforcing its walls, kept out Scots. Between them there runs, still virtually uncorrupted, a strip of coastline which those who have learned to love it, not merely over the years but over generations, would claim as the noblest in Britain.

From Alnmouth in the south to the northern sanctuary, Holy Island, the sands stretch for mile after firm mile, flanked on the west by fertile farm and wood land, on the east by a sea that is now jay blue, now hammered silver, now blocked in with solid ultramarine. Far out are the islands haunted by saints and seabirds; far inland, like a backdrop, the humped shapes of the Cheviots. Green and blue boats go bucking out of the little harbours to set crab and lobster pots; and the castles – Dunstanburgh, Bamburgh, and Holy Island – are so madly romantic that only their sheer mass saves them from being gimcrack.

Here, it seems, is a paradise ripe for the spoiler. But it can hope to remain relatively inviolate because this holiday land is self-selective. To begin with, as the guide book to Belford rural district says with engaging honesty, 'Weather in these parts is not predictable.' (It goes on to say, equally truthfully, that the annual rainfall – 24.5 inches – is only a fraction of an inch more than that of the driest part of the British Isles and that the figures for winter sunshine are high). In fact, you can predict fairly safely that you are never likely to be insufferably, or even blissfully, hot. A common sight along this coast is that of women holidaymakers, wearing plastic macs as windcheaters over hopeful cotton dresses, sitting in the lee of something solid, and knitting woollen garments which they might be happier wearing. All the same there are days when you can bask in the hollows of the sand hills. The bathing is excellent and safe almost everywhere (the danger spots are marked) but the temperature of the water by comparison with the Isle of Wight let alone the Mediterranean is character-building.

The area is pretty well supplied with hotels and boarding houses of various grades but the standard is average English – nobody would come here just for the fleshpots. This, like all generalisations, has to be qualified. There is at least one hotel, not externally the most impressive, where the food is outstandingly good, and there are surprises among the common run – superlative roasts where most of the vegetables come out of tins and excellent coffee where the custard is what the Americans call accurately 'corn starch.'

Best safeguard of all, there is 'nothing to do' – which means that for the walker, the birdwatcher, the botanist, the geologist, the archaeologist, the contemplative, there is everything to do, but that night life is represented by an occasional village hop, a small shy cinema here and there, and a coffee shop or two that stays open after tea. And there are no 'attractions' at all except for some ponies, mild and sleek as mice, at Alnmouth, swing boats for four children at Boulmer and ice cream nearly everywhere. So the wrong holidaymakers usually find out their mistake early on and light out for Whitley Bay if not Scarborough.

The right ones will be confirmed in their choice once they are fairly into Alnmouth, where the pink and crimson roses splashing the grey stone houses are a reassurance that Northumbria is not grim, and where a cliff path strikes north offering a panorama of the Farne Islands and dropping down into villages most of which can hardly be called resorts. Boulmer is no more than a huddle of houses, a few boats drawn up on the hard, and some discreet caravans. Craster is a colder Cornish fishing port – Mousehole or Polperro without the godwottery. Perhaps not so cold at that, since roses are rioting over the slopes that drop steeply into the tiny harbour, but certainly no godwottery. 'A Present from Craster' is likely to be a box of kippers claimed to be the finest in England (this keeps the Isle of Man out of the contest). Sometimes here you can watch the fishermen tying up the murderous claws of live lobsters before sending them to market. Today they are mending crab and lobster pots with swift movements of leathery hands and the blue flash of the knife blade. 'A laddie cut his hand this morning,' says one of them casually. 'Nipped two arteries. Doctor had to put in seven stitches.'

The tattered walls of Dunstanburgh stand sentinel on the cliffs between Craster and Beadnell. Beadnell is fashionable in a very small way. Fishing cobles work out of the harbour – the great arches flanking it are the remains not of another castle but of an eighteenth-century lime kiln – but there is sailing within the sheltering arms of the bay and a certain number of new-looking 'desirable residences.' Here too, there is a caravan site but of the better sort.

Seahouses, by contrast, is a working port and, at first glance, a Continental one, with the brilliant light of the north-east sharp as a razor on the painted boats and the fishermen in overalls faded from russet to shrimp pink. There is boat building here as well as inshore fishing and crab and lobster potting and a motorboat service to the Farnes, which offer St Cuthbert's chapel as well as Grace Darling's lighthouse, a bird sanctuary in which eider duck are found along with the more usual seabirds, and a nursery of the grey seals.

From Seahouses the sands go in a majestic three mile sweep to Bamburgh. The castle growing out of the rocks like Edinburgh is traditionally Lancelot's Joyous Garden. If so it was a long way from Camelot. The village would not shame the Cotswolds with its wide main street bordered by lawns rising to a tree-planted green. Bamburgh is high drama. Beyond it the coast levels out to the broad spread of Budle Bay with a caravan site (again discreet) on its shores and throngs of seabirds on its flats. Then comes the coda. Lindisfarne.

Holy Island, as it is more commonly known today, epitomises in its 1,350 acres the whole of this tract of Northumberland. There are vast sandy plains, there is a Gothic fantasy of a castle crowning a mound, there is land fertile enough to grow wheat, there is a harbour dotted with bright boats. Here in 634 St Aidan set up the monastery of mud and wattle from which he evangelised the whole of Northumbria. Here Cuthbert, the Lammermuir shepherd boy who became a hermit-bishop, was first buried. Here Eadfrith, one of his successors as Bishop of the Church of Lindisfarne, wrote the Lindisfarne Gospels, 'For God and St Cuthbert and for all the Saints in common that are in the island.'

The Gospels are now in the British Museum though not the cover which 'Billfrith the Anchorite, he wrought as a smith…. and adorned it with gold and with gems, also with silver overgilded, a treasure without deceit.' King Henry VIII melted that down. Here in the eleventh century the Benedictine monks of Durham built a priory of rosy sandstone whose ruins survive today.

Standing at the island end of the causeway which has taken most of the perils out of crossing from the mainland, you wonder what is the peculiar quality of this country. Behind you the coarse bents of the dunes are combing the wind. Before you are the Cheviots with above them a sky out of the border ballads, wild and torn and tangled. The air glitters; the black-headed gulls scream and scuffle with a twinkling of wings; the sea and the sand flats are illimitable.

And that is it – the sense of space. What this coast gives the holidaymaker is

'Room for soul to stretch and split,
Before the world closes in on it.'

Nesta Roberts

Sandflats and saltings
July 30 1960

There are no half measures about sandflats and saltings. Some people go melancholy mad after 48 hours among them. Others, at first sight of the endless levels and the huge skies overhead, know that this is a landscape they will love until they die. Since the northern coast of Norfolk, from Blakeney east to Scolt Head Island in the west, consists almost wholly of sandflats and saltings it is well to be certain which group you belong to before deciding on a quiet holiday in this area. It is well to remember also that a quiet holiday here is very quiet indeed; that, except for seals, it is not often the place for basking (though fuschia here and there survives the north-easters), and that even in summer there are a good many days when the North Sea is the colour of porridge, or, alternatively, of a pensioned-off battleship.

To go so prepared is to be surprised by joy. Come in from the south-west and you pass first through lavender farms and then through rolling harvest fields, rustling barley, dancing oats, the heavy swing of ripe wheat. The steep-pitched roofs are of pantiles that glow orange-red as though lit from within; the gardens are full of roses and clematis, honeysuckle and frilled hollyhocks. To the north the marshes stretch for mile after mile, showered with lark song, the green washed with purple where the sea lavender is in bloom. Farther out are the lion-coloured sands; beyond, infinitely distant, a line of indigo with a narrow flounce of foam to mark the sea's edge.

Bed and breakfast accommodation is less common than, say, in the Lakes or the West Country, but almost every village has caravanners or campers. Hotels and guest houses, from the small to the fairly large, are numerous. Quality does not depend on size. A rather pretentious three-star hotel may offer the usual lamentable selection of puddings (which means that, in the proper sense, none of them *are* puddings), synthetic cream, and a tatty cheese board. A one-star restaurant not far away has an enterprising menu including a generous platter of fresh vegetables (deep-freeze means that today's luxuries are properly cooked cabbage and carrots, straight from the garden). To confuse the issue, your dinner will cost much the same at both.

If you are the right man – or woman – for this coast, what to do is no problem. There is fair, though bracing, bathing right along it, if you pick your spot carefully and take notice of local warnings. The commercial fishing is mostly for mussels and whelks, but holidaymakers can hope to take skate, mackerel, and sea trout as well as whiting and flounders. On shore there is dab-pricking in the shallows with a four-pronged fork, raking for cockles, shrimping in the primeval ooze of the creeks, and gathering samphire (it is said to make 1s 6d a pound in Norwich market – retail, of course).

It is not essential to sail in order to enjoy a holiday here, but it seems a sad waste of opportunity not to. Most of the creeks provide stretches of sheltered water where you are unlikely either to drown yourself or smash up your boat while you get your experience.

And if you have not a boat of your own and do not manage to get taken on as somebody's crew, the village shop windows (between announcements of the church fete and such heart cries as: 'Wanted daily cook for August. Four grandchildren coming to stay!') often contain notices like: 'For hire. 10 foot lug-sail centre-board dinghy.' Similarly, you need not be a naturalist to come to the Norfolk coast, but if you leave its shifting dunes and banks of shingle and its wealth of sea and shore birds without a quickened interest in natural history your responses must be a bit sluggish.

Nature reserves mark off the area at either end. Scolt Head Island in the west, Blakeney Point in the east. Overy Staithe, near Scolt Head, is small and tranquil and blissfully unfashionable sailing – not that it is tiresomely smart anywhere round here. Near it are seven villages called Burnham in the space of four square miles. Burnham Thorpe, Nelson's birthplace, would be worth visiting for the beauty of its high, white church even without the relics it possesses. Wells-next-the-Sea is the nearest thing to a conventional resort in the area. There are beach huts on the shore and a large caravan site behind it. Nothing can make a large caravan site attractive, but at least this one is screened from the beach by dunes and pine trees and is next to invisible from the village. The harbour is well away from the beach. Fifty years ago Baddeley found it 'most depressing' at low tide. Today, with the waterfront crowded with sailing craft and the little main street prettied up with pink and blue paint, it is perpetually animated. Inland is a green, shaded with beech and lime trees, where the house fronts round the square suggest a cathedral close rather than a seaside village.

Morston is another Overy. Blakeney, with its clean-faced flint and pebble houses, and its great church which, from off-shore, looks like a yawl (the small turret stepped abaft the east end was built as a beacon for shipping) would be attractive even without its waterfront. As things are it is entrancing, whether the sails are crowding home in the evening, with the creek pale as glass and the marsh dimming from green to sage grey, or whether the bare poles are tiled over the low-tide mud, iridescent in the sun.

Motorboats go daily from the quay to the bird sanctuary on Blakeney Point. Here, on the seaward side of the shingle, is solitude. Oyster-catchers pipe; the terns, which look like ballerinas and sound like fishwives, plop into the water; groups of black-backed gulls stand hunched, facing the wind. The small bird that dodges across your sight is a snipe. The ringed plover running away with a trailing wing and plaintive cries as a brood near by which, with patience, you may find. Perhaps – it is about a 5,000-to-one chance – you will have the sensational experience of seeing a cockle leap, jet propelled, out of the wet sand.

The day is rich in possibilities. Meantime you are content to walk barefoot along the shore, now stepping into the water because it is cold, now back on to the sand because it is by contrast warm. In your right hand you carry a white pebble because it is smooth and round, in your left a whelk shell because it is grooved and pointed. This is the absolute of quiet holidays.

Nesta Roberts

Dover
September 16 1961

With the exception of London itself, no place in the British Isles perpetuates our self-indulgent image as unflinchingly as Dover. Nature has been on her side in this matter. See how she stands at the beginning and the end of England, the very nearest outpost of Empire. 'Europe' is only 19 miles away here but to the English, who will not have it that they are as European as the Portuguese, it is a separate continent and a world apart.

Then consider the emotional appeal of her surroundings, the billowing chalk cliffs with their promise of solidity and independence.

Men have been known to weep with relief at the sight of them; others are said to have shaken their fists in frustration at their symbolism – a fossilised assurance that Britons never shall be slaves.

You should bring with you to Dover a healthy respect for the whims of Nature, which in these parts are not to be trusted. A few miles outside the harbour are the Goodwins, that wickedly playful bank of sand which will swallow three ships in a day at one moment and at the next allow cyclists to race upon it – as they did in August 1877. But it is the sea's toying with the land which is at least as treacherous and more awfully fascinating. There is a place in East Anglia, Dunwich, which has been bodily removed by the sea. Hereabouts the waters are more calculating in their transformations, slowly withdrawing or altering course, and leaving proud ports to waste and die.

Around the coast, beneath the snout of North Foreland, Richborough moulders glumly in the estuary of the Stour. It was once the chief port in Britain, and the Romans built a pharos on the heights of Dubris to guide their galleys safely home. Yet the saddest decline of all, if you have any feeling for the past, is that which has overtaken the Cinque Ports. Hastings, Sandwich, Hythe, Romney, Winchelsea, and Rye – for these, too, the tides have slowly changed, leaving them high and dry in pensive recollection.

Only Dover remains a port to reckon with, and her preoccupations now are with the workings of entrepot, whereas once they were with the fitting out of men-of-war. For 200 years after the Conquest the Cinque Ports provided the Crown with its navy in exchange for their jealously held privileges of soc or sac, tol and team, blodwit and fledwit, pillory and tumbrel and the rest. Dover, in those days, was able to arm twenty vessels, each with 21 able-bodied men, and to keep them at sea for fifteen days. Whatever they may tell you in the wardrooms of Portsmouth it was around here that the Royal Navy had its foundations.

And though Dover shared the fate of her fellows as a place of seapower, she held tenaciously to her position as the gateway to England. There have been some notable comings and goings. Richard I and his warriors assembled here before setting out on the third crusade; Anne of Bohemia landed here in 1382 to become the bride of Richard II; in 1520 Henry VIII and his court embarked from Dover for the Cloth of Gold; and on May 25 1660, Charles II came from over the water to retrieve his father's crown.

In the calendar of almost every town you care to think of such events would each be the occasion of a cherished anniversary; in Dover they are almost a commonplace. She puts up her monuments to the birds of passage, to be sure, but they are to the likes of Captain Matthew Webb, who started the fashion in Channel swimming with his crossing to Calais in 1875, and to the Honourable CS Rolls, who in 1910 was the first man to fly to France and back. No doubt she clings affectionately to those gaudier memories as well, but you can see why new ways of making the crossing move her more to commemoration than royal progresses, however grand. Transition is Dover's stock in trade.

You can take in a sweeping bird's eye view of this shifting panorama if you mount the battlements of Dover Castle, balanced unnervingly above the town. Here, said old Matthew Parris, was 'the key and draw bars of the whole realm,' a daunting fortification which Harold started in 1064, commanding the valley of the Dour and threatening the narrow Channel passage – as the Spaniards found when their wind-blown Armada came in confusion from the West. From these breezy turrets Dover, indeed, appears to lie in ambush for her enemies, huddled confidingly along the sides of the slender river valley, peering cautiously around the corners of her cliffs, which are, in truth, not as fond legend would have them, but rather the colour of dirty whitewash except when the sun is at its hottest height.

They have been riddled and runnelled with passageways for ages past. Out of them once came the smugglers and their pack horses, bearing brandy for the parson and baccy for the clerk in the conspiring parishes of East Kent. Now they contain heaven knows what military devices. There are enough antique barrack buildings in the scrub above the foreshore to remind you that this has long been a garrison no less than a port; but Dover's latent belligerence goes deeper than that. Nor is it held in check only against the Queen's enemies. The shores hereabouts are groined and fortified against the manoeuvrings of the sea; the dredgers trudge up and down the harbour, buckets clanking, holding their own and only just. Dover remembers Richborough and keeps watch.

The sea has none of the majesty of the western approaches, with that sweeping, battering surge which must be met by granite if there is to be resistance at all. It is, after all, a sea and not an ocean; it has its own vitality, which is a hard chop chop, persistent, and knowing that chalk will eventually yield if it keeps it up long enough. And across the narrow, baleful bit of water, a faint thickening line behind the sea fret, there is France, a little remote today but sometimes, as they will tell you in Dover, seeming so close that you'd think you were over there. It has frequently been too close for comfort. On the Marine Parade they have a monument to its proximity, a piece of armour-plating from one of the German long-range guns which was mounted near Calais and which helped to pitch 2,226 shells on to the town between 1940 and 1944.

After this sort of bombardment you might reasonably expect nothing of pre-war Dover to have survived. Astonishingly, it is still preponderantly Victorian in character. True, an enormous and angular block of flats occupies one half of the sea front, a phoenix from the flames; but the curve is completed by a seemingly undamaged stretch of Regency terracing. The market place is evidently a reconstruction; but as you contemplate the grey nineteenth-century homes streaming away up the valley, you begin to wonder where all those shells landed.

It is down there, however, at sea level, that you can really feel Dover's pulse. There is a length of Snargate Street which might have been plucked from any old maritime context. It is replete with chandlers, where professionals can fossick among the transome gudgeons and the fixed rudder pintles for a spare riding light; and across the road are their tarry yawls and opulent yachts, a-flutter with bunting and bright with spit and polish, taking their ease from the up-Channel haul.

But to catch the very essence of Dover you must involve yourself in the bustle around the sea front and on the moles. Anticipation is in the air as the motor coaches come rolling into town from Lincolnshire and London, from Birmingham and Leeds, bearing hefty old women and nervous-looking young men to their first tentative taste of that worrying world across the water (Six Countries in Eight Days – £50 All-in). They may have their counterparts in France and Holland and Belgium, but if such people exist they must make their entry at Folkestone or Newhaven.

For the ones who arrive in Dover seem to be all jaunty and practiced, and mobile to a degree scarcely ever achieved by the English. They disembark late at night, perhaps, and in your early morning stroll along the beach you have to pick your way around sleeping bundles, swaddled in quilt and unconscious of the train which is trundling gently down the road at their side, preceded by a man with a red flag. Then it is *en avant à Londres* with the hope of a lift along the Dover Road, perhaps from a compatriot who is still gingerly testing the left-hand rule in bottom gear.

It is as busy as Waterloo station down here at the height of the tourist season as the ferry boats shuffle past the breakwater, sixty times in a day and a night, all round the clock. There is nothing particularly elegant about these ships – the *Prince Phillipe* and *The Lord Warden*, the *Artevelde* and the *Twickenham Ferry*. To the purist's searching eye they are perhaps too squat or too gaunt or even, it may be, a trifle homely. Most of them have the grace of a bus, which is not altogether out of place, for they inhabit the same workaday world. They rate only an occasional glance from the anglers on the Prince of Wales pier and are barely noticed by the hearties at the

Royal Cinque Ports Yacht Club. But for getting huge numbers of people across the Channel you can't beat them. They will land you in Calais in eighty minutes or at Ostend in a little more. And they make a mockery of our inhibitions and our ancient insularity.

This brisk traffic across the Channel is heartening if you have dwelt too long on the symbolism of Dover's cliffs and on some of the assumptions that lurk behind them. And if it strikes you uncomfortably that Dover has for centuries been too readily primed for attack and defence, a mile or so to the west you will find one more hopeful portent for the future. There, at the foot of Shakespeare Cliff, is a tunnel which they dug in 1881, which stretches 2,000 yards under the sea, and which would have gone on to Gris Nez if the chauvinists had not had their way. If ever we are to have a Channel tunnel this could well be the English end of it. The Gateway to Europe would sit splendidly among those cliffs.

Geoffrey Moorhouse

Holidays of old
July 18 1962

My great-grandmother disapproved of holidays. She despised the idea and thought they were rather vulgar. So she remained at home. But her four lovely daughters, my great-aunts, frequently 'paid visits' and enjoyed them enormously. Great-grandpapa brought 'the girls' to London. They stayed in rooms which were the mode (only the rich or the overflow of the naughty regency age stayed in hotels) and they crammed everything into those few days.

On one occasion, great-aunt Mary writes that 'she woke fresh as a daisy, went to the Royal Opera to see *The Huguenots*, then off to Drury Lane to see *The Somnambula*, and to the Olympic, because there was a special benefit night for Pillycodie Robson who was playing *The Yellow Dwarf*. Then off to the Cremorne, to dance, to listen to music, and to coquette!' That was the way to enjoy yourself on the extensive scale, and my great-aunt Mary must have been very young, and very energetic. The Cremorne Gardens must not be confused with the modern Festival ones for they had rose bowers where one sat 'with gentlemen,' and partook of a posset!

My grandmothers travelled, staying always in the best places, for the best places were tremendously important to Victorian ladies. And always with papa. It was dangerous to travel alone. Brighton was popular and gay. Bath was delightful, and Tunbridge Wells quite ravishing, and oh, so select! Harrogate was becoming popular, and Scotland of course 'the thing,' for did not the dear Queen always go to Balmoral? Some aristocrats went abroad, generally to the Riviera, though Rome was possible. Paris was not on the list as being a suitable resort, the idea being that only naughty gentlemen went to Paris, and it was not at all the correct atmosphere for ladies.

At the beginning of the century my family took a holiday about once in five years, that being the best we could afford. We went to the seaside. Rooms were booked ahead, and if they were advertised in the *Church Times* they were sure to be good. Landladies greeted us on arrival, wearing small lace caps which smelt of stale hair oil, beaded bodies, and always about them there was the remote suggestion of gin.

A double room for parents and two small ones for the children were our lot, and the use of the front sitting room, which was usually quite frightful. There was never a bathroom but that was not a worry. After all, what was the sea for? The wardrobe smelt of other children's decaying crustacea brought home in buckets in triumph, but immediately dying. Mother did the shopping, and old Mrs Somebody-or-other cooked and served it, thereby splashing her jet-trimmed bodice a good deal more.

We sat on the beach. We bathed from appalling bathing machines wearing extensive costumes 'in case anybody saw something they shouldn't,' and we dug on the beaches, while mother did crochet, and father read the *Church Times*. When we wished to have a fling, we hired a landau and drove up and down the front. All the horses wore hats and we were always given a linen dust sheet to put over our knees. We attended pierrot shows, and went to the weekly change of programme at the theatre. When we came home we brought with us a long piece of seaweed, which was said to have the ability to predict a change in the weather. Everybody of 'our class' took the same holiday, and behaved in exactly the same way, but we all came home bursting with enthusiasm for the marvellous time we had had.

Today on my sideboard is the souvenir of all those holidays when I was a fat little girl who wore pinafores. It is a magnificent cut-glass decanter which was given me by a certain Mrs Buncroft, on the eve of my departure from Great Yarmouth one summer.

Mrs Buncroft was not by any means a teetotaller, and I only hope that she did not regret later her noble generosity, for I should have thought that a decanter was something that she could not spare. I had been ill, and when the parents went out to evening shows she came and talked to me. She adored talking, and I have always been a delighted listener. Apparently I charmed her, for on the last night she appeared with the decanter. She said that I was such a little duck, she was sure that I would marry (God bless the lucky gentleman, etc.), and she wished to bestow upon me my first wedding present. She kissed me with deep affection, nearly asphyxiating me with the stench of gin. She was, of course, very drunk, though I was far too young and innocent to know it.

The decanter stands there today for all to see, a reminder of whatever it was about the old-time holiday we do not get today.

Ursula Bloom

Power point
February 19 1963

They are building an atomic power station at the point at Dungeness. The local hermits shuddered some years back when the cross-Channel air ferries opened their airfield at Lydd; but until this last year the marsh had retained much of its loneliness. The small chubby aircraft buzzed noisily down to scatter the flocks of tern and plover, but the disturbance was no greater than local hazards of wildfowlers and an occasional pack of beagles. The rolling mounds of shingle begged for gravel workings until these slowly filled with water, splashing grounds for the hosts of golden-eye and scota that settled down there off the sea.

Then came a further irritation: a miniature railway, of all things, rattled its way out of Hythe right down to the water's edge, and brought with it the inevitable trippers:

'Oh, look mom, sheep!'

'Oh, look mom, look't all them birds, bet they got cold feet in all them puggles.'

But this was only a summer hazard. In the autumn and winter when the east wind over the flats shivered the woolly sheep right down to the mutton, then Dungeness was left in peace. You could stand at the lip of the surging waves, snuggle down into three coats and four pairs of socks, and watch the Vs of duck quickly winging overhead into the shallows back on the marsh. And then the wind sang down over the breakers, cresting each wave with a silver spangle of driving foam, and the rain clouds massed like the canvas of billowing spinnakers running free down to Beachy Head or on to the Lizard.

It was such a fresh and cutting easterly that sent me to shelter under the hull of a squat round-sided little rowboat, high up on the beach like an empty conch shell, to watch the real ships pass by: a tanker with BP on the funnel, steaming out of London and going to warmer seas; dirty little coasters puckering the swell with anxious shudders of their grimy sides; and, farther out, the stately whiteness of a large liner waiting the tide or the pilot boat out of Dover.

The sea here is always humdrum with activity and every tide brings its treasure of oddments up on the pebbles. Ships of every nation pass this point, so close that the eye can read the registration on their sterns: *Keynes*, a Tynesider that one; or the *Ely Jensen*, with the gold, black, and red of the Dutch flag at her masthead. And on the beach, the only upright figures other than myself and my shelter, were the lifeboat station and on the other side, the sleek symmetry of the lighthouse, buttressed against the easterlies by all the beauty of her shapely concrete shell.

But this is Dungeness, a sparse salty coast riven by its memories of ships and gales; home for the duck and waders, stopping ground for the geese as they fly south at winter, and home too for the fishermen in their scattered huts and shanties among the pebbles. These fisher people are a race who live with their boats; every tide takes them out, their bright little craft scooping up the trawls of plaice and sole. Their pots, with bobbing corks and rough cordage placed at the exact spot at the exact tide, never fail to bring up a fair catch of crab and lobsters for the Folkestone market or down the coast at Hastings.

On my day at Dungeness the men were out with the boats. An old woman with a basket of shrimps pointed back to her cottage: 'Over there at the window if you want some, luv.' The window had a notice 'Shrimps 2s' in large lettering above it, and a young girl handed me out a bag: 'Just cooked, they are,' she said, and the shrimps were as salty as the grandmother.

Today, walking down to Dungeness across the marsh is like approaching a lunar city. The scale of the marsh had been set by the massy, squat Martello towers, monolithic hunks looming like the stumps of primeval tree trunks over the misty flat dikes. The station stands out above the Martellos like an illustration for

Kafka's Castle; a vast edifice of differing planes, squares, rectangles, cylinders towering oppressively against the skyline, the Manhattan of the marshes. The birds are leaving the reserve; but the fishermen like it. It brings the workmen, and still more trippers, and then the shrimps are three and four bob a bag.

Allan Chidgey

A Country Diary
October 24 1964

MACHYNLLETH: A man I used to know had a passion for curlews. His house overlooked the estuary of the Dovey river so closely that the tide washed against his garden wall and curlews were his constant neighbours. He saw other creatures too. Sometimes with the tide came grebes, divers, mergansers, or big leaping fish with porpoises or grey seals after them. And when the tide ebbed off the mudflats he would watch the wader flocks gather for the worm harvest. Sometimes he slept badly and would lie awake listening to the estuary: the gentle lap-lapping of a neap-tide under his wall; or the urgent hissing and gurgling of the great springs. But on some nights even the estuary would be quite without sound, the whole vast expanse of mud and water lying in absolute silence through the sleepless hours.

But sooner or later, lying there he would be sure to hear the deep wailings and liquid bubblings of the curlews and this gave him intense delight. When he died he left behind him several scrapbooks in which he had collected a mass of curlew lore; poems and bits of prose clipped out from innumerable books and magazines, every one of them about curlews. Clearly he was not the world's only curlew-devotee. And now I live by the estuary at times I wake in the night and hear the curlews crying in the darkness. Then I remember my old friend.

William Condry

Our coastline
June 28 1965

A few weeks ago we went down to Cornwall. It was in the nature of a sentimental return, since we had not been to Cornwall for more than ten years. For me, Cornish holidays go back to childhood. My home was in Somerset, so Cornwall was easily accessible; but even when we children had grown up and left the West Country we used to return each summer. My own children's first seaside holidays were in Cornwall, beginning soon after the war, when barbed wire and tank traps were still not cleared from the beaches. Our last Cornish family holiday was in 1954 and we wondered how much we should find altered on this return visit.

Whereas we always used to go in September, this time it was late spring, and the flowers astonished us. The deep ferny lanes were brilliant with bluebells and campion, foxgloves, bugle, and star of Bethlehem. The stone walls near the coast were covered with sea pinks and bouncing Bess, and the fine close turf of the cliffs were embroidered with bird's-foot trefoil. Gorse blazed. Little paths leading down the cliffs were unbelievably bordered with the kind of flowers you connect with inland places – moon daises, cowslips, garlic, foxgloves, ragged robin, and bluebells – flowering all the more magnificently, it seemed, for being exposed to the salt winds and spray.

We found remembered tracks to deserted coves – still deserted; and on the beach we used to go for shells we found cowries on exactly the same stretch as we used to find them. Nothing was altered, either, on the beach where we used to take out a little dinghy. We walked by the farmhouse where, as a family of six, we stayed four Septembers in succession. It lies in a fold of its fields, above and between two blameless beaches. Not another house in view, just sea and headlands and farmland. Nothing was changed except that the farmhouse looked in better repair with a new front door and the garden was decidedly better tended. It was bought four years ago for the National Trust, with 134 acres and one of the beaches. Its remoteness can never now be encroached upon. And many other parts of the coast we revisited are in the same way safe from new building, because the National Trust owns or protects a great deal of Cornish property.

But we were appalled by what is happening in some of the unprotected places, in particular near the splendid surfing beaches on the north coast. Sand dunes behind the beaches and valleys leading down to the bays littered with promiscuous building, with bungalows, beach huts, chalets, caravan sites, souvenir shacks, and tea rooms. It is estimated that the natural beauty of the coastline of England, Wales, and Northern Ireland is being lost in one way or another at the rate of five miles a year – it's as bad as that. Just before our visit to Cornwall the National Trust launched Enterprise Neptune, an endeavour to raise £2 million within two years for the protection, acquisition, and endowment for the nation of some 900 miles of the best remaining stretches.

When I first heard of Enterprise Neptune it struck me that it would have been a wonderful purpose for the Winston Churchill memorial fund. And now, after seeing for myself the contrast between the protected stretches of the coast and the unprotected, I feel this even more strongly. What could be more appropriate as a memorial to the man who defended our beaches from foreign invaders than an endowment towards saving it from the despoilers within our shores…?

'That England, that was wont to conquer others,

Hath made a shameful conquest of itself.'

Launched on St George's Day with bonfires on every historic beacon, Enterprise Neptune has a Churchillian ring to it and would surely have appealed to the late Lord Warden of the Cinque Ports. I am convinced that many more people would have subscribed to the fund if some at least of it were destined for such a grand, imaginative, Churchillian cause as defending our coastline from commercial despoilers.

However, there is nothing to prevent these people subscribing instead to Enterprise Neptune – and every reason to entreat them to do so. The address is the National Trust, 44 Queen Anne's Gate, London SW 1. This is something that is desperately urgent. What's done in the name of 'development' can never be undone. And every motorway opened, every new car on the road, makes it easier for people to get to some unspoiled piece of coastline. If its beauty is not protected now, there will soon be little left to protect.

Alison Adburgham

A Country Diary
December 4 1965

SHETLAND ISLES: As in all maritime communities, beachcombing is a favourite Shetland pursuit. At 60deg. N a gale from any quarter can bring to these shores the debris of the Atlantic or the North Sea, and a rising wind sees a trickle of men heading for exposed beaches and headlands. In part, beachcombing is a necessary activity. The islands, almost treeless as a result of constant winds and nibbling sheep, lack an indigenous source of timber. Consequently, we depend for firewood on what the tide brings in. Its most frequent gift is the fishbox, washed overboard from either the local seine net fleet or from passing trawlers going up to the fishing grounds round Faroe. Most Shetland fires are kindled with chopped fishbox, but there are many other interesting items for anyone prepared to watch the beach for long enough.

Almost every winter sees deck cargo washed off freighters in northern latitudes. Last winter dozens of pit props off a vessel bound from Norway to South Shields came up on our eastern shores. The Russian fishing fleet, which spends each winter on the Shetland grounds, is a regular source of long barrels, of a variety of uses on the croft. Some weeks ago the *Birgitte Frellsen*, a heavily listing Danish freighter, was national news as she was towed to Lerwick through heavy seas by a Russian tug. Local concern for her safety was complemented by an active interest in the whereabouts of the deck cargo of timber jettisoned fifteen miles to the east. The wind held, the *Birgitte Frellsen* arrived with a sensational list, and local rumour has it that some byres and steadings in Yell and Fetlar are being extended with salvaged baulks of timber.

CRPL

Pulpits in the sand
August 10 1966

I liked the summers at Seaview; the pier, croquet in the garden, ponies on the beach, and what seemed to be, at 10, the quite enormous sum of 5s every week to spend on Isle of Wight ice cream. But Seaview was not Seaview, not the quintessential Seaview, until the August camp strike of the CSSM. The Children's Special Service Mission – college men in blazers, teachers-in-training in floral skirts and anoraks, a multitude of smiling patient friends to little children – built pulpits in the sand and shouted out God's word. The love of God extended to prize fights, sausage sizzles, scavenger hunts, and occasional fizzy feasts. The love of God was very clearly indispensable. At 10 I believed, and I had a super time.

The first healthy tang of a seaside evangelism overtook Llandudno in 1867. Josiah Spiers, a Christian on holiday, spelled out 'God is Love' in pebbles on the sand. Children gathered round, singing hymns. Over the century that first Llandudno text has been taken south to Perranporth and north to Portmakomack, adorned the summer beaches at Colwyn Bay and Bude, encouraged infant converts on Isle of Arran shores. This year there are 76 children's missions, some seaside, some inland, with a thousand unpaid workers. Forty-seven, off and on, muster children at Frinton, following – headquarters states – the footsteps of Our Lord, 'who was perhaps the real pioneer of seaside and inland missions.' Workers waylay children and parents in the streets, give them mission programmes, hope to meet them by the banner which somehow stands firm against the Frinton gales, proclaiming the work of the CSSM.

The mission lasts all day. At 7.45am Gold Diggers meet 'to dig for gold in the Bible.' More than 12 hours later the CSSM epilogue finishes the vigorous schedule of activities. No wonder that parents, entertainment problems solved, entrust their children willingly to the mission,

'Wide, wide as the ocean
High as the heavens above
Deep, deep as the deepest sea
Is my Saviour's love.'

A hundred and fifty children on the sand bellow the chorus, eyes on great black word sheet, gestures following the big keen chorus leader. Young men bound up to the pulpit – 'Hello, children, aren't we all having a marvellous holiday? There were 75 of you at Gold Diggers this morning. That's very good, but let's make it more tomorrow. Close you eyes and now we'll pray.'

Quick lunch, mission strong men re-erect the banners. The banner on the greensward summons Tiddlywinks, the smallest, to an afternoon of nice and cheerful games for under-eights. Pygmies, eight to 10, get 'a run in the sun,' a scavenger hunt for teeth and pins and Frinton oddments. Commando, 11 to 13, have a swim or 'a walk and a natter' if the Essex seas are cold. The holiday club, for more sophisticated teenagers, lays on 'battle of the beach huts 1066.'

They are eager at Frinton, and at CSSM headquarters, to tell you that the missions are far from what they were. Modern missions are closer to heaven in democracy: men workers no longer wear white flannels on the beach. The Oxford and Cambridge dominated house party, normal a decade ago, is thoroughly diluted; the development of missions inland, on city commons, is reaching the less prosperous child on holiday at home. Besides, the teenage clubs, run by expert social workers (eg the Rev Ronald Preece, BD: 'Rev. Ron to you'), have increased the CSSM programme so wildly that the movement needs all its robustness to cope.

The scope of the CSSM may have changed, but centralised and streamlined, classless and matured, it keeps the basic methods of a century ago: hearty personal contact, rambles, sports and claps on backs, evangelistic street talks, God's name for ever dropped. Round CSSM coffee bars, through teenage doubts and sorrows, 'someone,' they assure you, 'is always there to point out that the only final and satisfying meaning is to be found in Jesus Christ.'

From saints and sinners coffee bars to pygmies on the beach the CSSM principle is friendship for God's sake. This is obvious at Frinton where every mission worker takes on six children and invites their beck and call. This was, for me, the great Seaview amazement: that these large and glorious people would devote themselves to me. I remember Mr Edmonds, resplendent in white knee socks, reading me the Bible: graven close; ideal. I liked the Seaview summers with ponies, creaky saddled, the yachts in the Solent, the shrimps in my net, and my heart leaping softly in a yellow summer shirt for the love Mr Edmonds mixed up with the love of God.

Fiona MacCarthy

Where the tide makes Canutes in reverse
August 12 1967

Nobody could call Weston-super-Mare cosmopolitan. Few of its visitors would want to. But multiregional it undoubtedly is. Children scream in many dialects, with running commentaries from their parents in various shades of Midland, West Country, and Welsh.

It's the position that does it, the luck of the geographical draw. If you could possibly talk of a central seaside resort, Weston would be it. The town is easily approached from most of the big population centres, London included. There's a saying that it's not far to Weston wherever you start from, but it's a long way to the sea once you get there.

Super or no super, arrive at low tide and you see what they mean. In fact you could almost say that when the tide is out there is only local tradition, supported by the name of the place and other corroborations of folk memory, to persuade you that Weston is on the sea at all. This is the town's great worry, amounting to a positive anxiety-neurosis with some citizens. Shading their eyes and watching how far the tide goes they fear the day may come when it will walk out on them altogether and never return.

It has made them Canutes in reverse, eager to find ways of turning the tide forward instead of turning it back. A vast sea wall linking the outer points of the bay would no doubt hold enough of the commuting water to solve the problem. But sea walls come expensive, particularly at a time when Weston is treating itself to a central development scheme of a kind that nearly all the resorts feel they have to indulge in, rather in the way that a competitive household has to have a new car.

Weston's development plan is in a strange state of evolution just now, oddly dramatic for a town that doesn't go in much for drama. A pedestrian way is in the making. White concrete pillars like the columns of temples, supporting nothing yet, march down to the sea. A flight of dazzling white steps, leading nowhere yet, contribute to the uncanny air of ruins out of the future. The traffic-free Dolphin Square is finished, boutiques and cobbled geranium-beds and all; but Weston doesn't take easily to patios. It rapidly anglicises them. You would know at a glance that those old dears on the benches enjoying themselves so quietly and so uncomplainingly were no tourists in Italy. You half expect to see garden gnomes.

It is the large gesture, whether of nature or of man, that the British are so determined to cut down to size. Weston is a standing monument to our national disinclination for grandeur. Its site is incomparable, its homeliness indomitable. Poised on its many-coloured, widely sweeping bay, fringed by wooded hills, the place has an Adriatic splendour of situation. It is a positive feast for the eyes, and they insist on serving it with chips and vinegar. Even the resulting contrasts, which could be piquant, are somehow dissolved.

The Grand Pier with its mighty green-and-white Kremlin at the end – that, as you would expect, is a just a spectacular money-extracting machine. There is also the charming Old Pier at the end of the town, its timbers creaking under your feet, which generates such an air of adventure that you might be setting sail round the world instead of across the estuary to Wales. The last place to play pop music is at the end of this pier. Naturally, they play it.

Cheek by jowl with the flashy new boutiques are traditional old-lady-and-eat general stores, where behind the same window can be seen buckets and spades, Weston rock, pork sausages, cheeky postcards and – strangest offering of all – bags of pebbles for 1s 3d. Undeterred by the smart traffic, a window-cleaner on a bicycle tows his ladder-cart behind him. On the enormous beach a helicopter buzzes the donkey-riding children. There is hardly a mini-skirt in sight, but a whole procession of topless buses along the front. Real barbed wire guards the make-believe castle guarding the model village, a piece of ye oldery that really brings them in. There are warnings about broken glass but not about unexploded mines, the subject of a scare the other day that emptied sands and sea.

'Why did they chop his head off, daddy?' demands a child as he frolics out of the chamber of horrors. 'Cause he was naughty,' comes the answer a Birmingham Professor Higgins would locate around Acocks Green. 'What did the naughty man do?'... But this conversation will obviously have no end. There has been an animal welfare service attended among others by dogs, cats, ponies, tortoises and a pair of budgerigars which travelled by bus. At the same time a church for people has just been offered for sale, reserve price only £500.

'Deck Chairs Here Today' says a mysterious sign. Will they be gone tomorrow? Perhaps, at ninepence a sit, the simpler customers may run away with the idea that they have bought the things. But most baffling of all is the all-night gambling club where you can stake up to £15 a go at roulette, or play dice with 5s minimum and £25 maximum bets. None of these holidaymakers look like candidates for such goings-on. Can there be another holiday population that only comes out at night?

Night or day, blackjack and dice or bingo and chips, there are complaints from some traders that takings are down. In so sunny a season, this brings the resorts face to face with a new spectre. Much is nominally in their favour this year: the weather, the foreign travel restriction. And yet the quiet revellers at Weston are certainly flinging their coin around with something less than abandon. They sit, they talk, they read, they sunbathe and – tide willing – they even swim in the sea. If the resorts are going to have to watch their customers getting into the way of being satisfied with such novelties as these, pirate pleasures which remain untrappably free, the holiday industry will be compelled to do some fairly profound rethinking. Weston would be a good sort of place to start.

Norman Shrapnel

The Naples of the North
January 30 1971

When I was a little boy, my way to school took me by the railway station. One day I saw there the most beautiful picture in the world. It was called 'Llandudno, the Naples of the North. Go by LMS.' I had been there twice and by LMS, but it had not looked like that. There was a great sweep of shore, dividing esplanade and sea; blue, gold, and white. At each end a headland, green and grey with rocky outcrop. There was a pier reaching into the sea and a white steamer trailing its curving wake to balance the arc of the shore. Over the left side was the red-roofed town and sunlight was everywhere. There seemed to be a 'lift' in the picture that made you think, 'Ah, I could be happy there.'

I knew Llandudno, as I said. I had plenty of experience of cold sea water, flinty pebbles, cabbage, stewed plums, my sister getting lost, and endless bickering with the man who took the collection at the Pierrots. To think that the Great Orme could look like that! I just never knew! When the poster was replaced by an instruction to proceed to Skegness (It's So Bracing), I felt much as the abbot must have done after Henry VIII had called.

We were off to Llandudno that summer but, owing to a financial sanction, my mother was to take my siblings on the train while my father and I went by bicycle, about 60 miles, we believed. It should not have been a long ride, but we were not used to such exercise, nor had we reckoned with the Welsh hills. They were backbreaking and we seemed to walk beside the machines more than ride them until at last we came to Rhos-on-Sea. When I saw the ascent then before us, I wanted to cry. It was late afternoon. We were tired, dry, hungry, not speaking to each other as we plodded up, up, up, my father first and me with my head drooping over the handlebars, staring at his rear-lamp. I was counting my steps, '1,541, 1,542...' when he suddenly said, 'Stop.' I stopped. And there at my feet was my picture.

Our road turned right and then fell sheer away so that the foreshore seemed to spring out from under our feet, miles below. Then the great curve of yellow sand led our tired eyes on and on to the Great Orme, green and grey and sleepy. Just as I had seen it, the long pier stretched out to the sun over the Irish Sea. All was bathed in light.

But this was a living picture. In the clear air, no detail was missing. There was St Tudno's church, a white dot on the headland miles away. Farther still the West Shore, the Conway river, a glimpse of the castle, the town, and then, the eye drawn still farther to the blue-grey mass of Snowdonia and 'darkly Penmaenmawr.'

In Llandudno the gulls were wheeling, flashing into the sun to match the white esplanade and bathing machines. The little beetle-boats were coming in to the jetties with their hungry trippers and the last crowd of the day was gathered round Punch and Judy. All my personal treasures were there – the Grand hotel (more like a palace, where Charlie Chaplin had once stayed), Arcadia, Happy Valley, the railway station, and Vaughn Street, where our lodgings were and where my mother was waiting.

I think that, for the first time in my life, I was filled with beauty. Many a time since I have returned, pausing where the road forks right and swoops down to surprise the eye and catch the breath, and I hear again my father say, 'I will lift my eyes unto the hills.'

There have been other scenes since, awful, awesome, awe-inspiring: the icy majesty of the Alps, the mountains of festering dead at Dachau, the misty islands of the west, the New York skyline, a sinking ship, Mardi Gras, but sharper in my memory than any is my first gaze at the golden crescent of Llandudno shore, caught in the evening sun, 'A sight to dream of, not to tell.'

When I had recovered my speech and we were free-wheeling like birds into town, I asked my father (I was only 10, remember), 'Do you think they ever call Naples the Llandudno of Italy?'

WA Tait

Golden mileage
September 8 1973

A flick of the ceremonial switch and once again Blackpool is into its Indian Summer. For 52 days longer than any other British resort the till owners of Blackpool will be hard at it. The next seven weekends will be even busier than the last seven. The illuminations themselves are denser and more spectacular than ever before. Everything seems fine; business as usual. But, of course, it's not. Quite perceptibly over the last 10 years Blackpool's role, its social and economic fabric, and inevitably its appearance, have changed. Consortia of one kind or another have snapped up family or locally owned businesses; the car and the day tripper now predominate over the railway and the one or two-week 'long stay' holidaymaker; the developer and the tarter-up are at work. The Golden Mile itself is being ripped to pieces. While the Grand Theatre, with its fashionable Victorian interior was being saved at the eleventh hour, much else that was unique about Blackpool, and no less valuable for being untidy and vulgar, had already been destroyed.

Blackpool was founded on noisy and glorious vulgarity and it has known no other way of life. Nothing so far has ever been spoilt by commercialism in Blackpool. There never was anything to spoil. Its whole raison d'etre was the spending and the making of money in the righteous pursuit of happiness.

In the late 18th and early 19th centuries Blackpool had its little pretensions to gentility. There was a time when a bell would ring when the ladies were to bathe and the gentlemen were to leave the beach (the penalty for peeping was a bottle of wine) but all that was forgotten when the railways made working-class holidays a reality and the rush began. There were never any rock pools at Blackpool; no cliffs or hills or scenery. The beach was good but the water was always muddy brown. Commercial attractions were the only way in which the resort could have been developed.

Blackpool became a classic case of the boisterous, self-indulgent, and good natured seaside rip-off. And in response to its own success, Blackpool developed an appetite for publicity, repeatedly upstaging its competitors. Hence in 1879 the Blackpool Improvement Act which first allowed public money to be spent on advertising a resort; hence in 1894 the astonishing gimmickry of the Blackpool Tower and in 1912 the first string of bulbs across the prom. Last night Gordon Banks switched on a quarter of a million pounds worth of light.

Further illumination is available in the Tower building. If the spirit of traditional Blackpool lives on anywhere, it is in the Tower Ballroom. Reginald Dixon no longer presides; his successor is Earnest Broadbent. The blinds are drawn for an afternoon session to make it seem like evening, but the dancers are in their plimsolls and their day-time frocks. They drift around the edge of the floor to Ernest's Dixonesque medleys, and although the tunes were from *Cabaret* and the Beatles, the rhythms were the same and the valeta and the barn dance were being assiduously danced.

The old Blackpool was definitely in the air until the very moment when Ernest and the Wurlitzer graciously descended and the blinds opened. Elsewhere in the building, the excellent aquarium, the tiny zoo, and the circus, were going on much as before. But the building is already heavily scarred by insensitive designers. The ascent of the Tower is now smothered with the bland and belittling imagery of the space age. 'Blast off' and 'Splash down' for up and down. You have your cup of tea after the trip to the Countdown cafeteria.

The view from the tower tells much of the rest of the story. Immediately to the south is the enormous triangle of what used to be the railway terminus, with the old Central station (now with almost traditional irony a bingo hall) at its apex. The station was at the heart of Blackpool's prosperity and it is much mourned by the old-timers. An eloquent pre-war regular observed that his favourite Blackpool pastime was 'to stand on the top of the tower on a bank holiday morning, and see far below the trains arriving like little clockwork toys; to watch tiny train after tiny train burst, as it were, into a moving mass, dark, close, packed as swarming bees; to see this swarm disperse and melt away in different directions, and another swarm arrive, and another, and another.' The triangle is immediately behind the Golden Mile and is now the scene of massive redevelopment.

It is probably the economics of property ownership in the 70s rather than the urge to tidy things up that has destroyed the Golden Mile, but the effect is the same. A few fortune tellers' huts and seafood stalls, a few hotdog kiosks, and the odd roundabout hang grimly on in the rubble, but the brave new pattern is clearly set. Your vision of the future is the Golden Mile centre, a sort of entertainment precinct. Flashy new slot machines and electronic games are rooted in grubby carpet and upstairs (up the escalator, that is) are your roundabouts. An upstairs roundabout set in carpeting can be a depressing spectacle.

Where once there were inventive barkers inviting you to believe what they said and waste your money, hypnotic tape recordings now aim for your subliminal blind spots. The fat ladies, the almost naked ladies, the freak shows have gone; their neat and polished American successor is Ripley's *Believe It or Not* Odditorium. Waxworks of actual men with four eyes and tales of men who wore the same collar stud for 48 years are bound to stir the imagination to some extent, but when all's said and done they could be anywhere. And indeed, according to the robot barking machine outside, who seems to have missed the point completely, so they are: in Miami, Chicago, and Las Vegas, for example.

It may be some time before Blackpool is completely anodysed. There is still much to enjoy and much for Blackpool to be proud of, but the achievements of the precinct makers give the old Blackpool, the Gypsy Lees, the deck chairs, the bizarre chaos of signs and advertisements, something of an air of old world charm or of trendy kitsch. That was never its purpose.

Blackpool, like many another town, has lost the purpose for which it was built and is struggling to adjust to the loss. The pattern of holiday making has altered and left the town stranded. But seaside holidays are really the only thing Blackpool knows much about. It worked best when nobody really thought about it, when it grew up unplanned out of raw needs, with the air of a railhead or frontier town. The move to the precinct culture is evidently not something it can take easily in its stride. The new commercialism really isn't fun.

Barry Coleman

Piers de resistance
February 28 1975

Britannia up to her knees in water! There can hardly be a better example of English compromise than our piers. Where else can you be all at sea yet high and dry and safely linked to land? There's nothing quite as British as the sense of self righteousness that follows a stroll along the pier. Yet we have allowed them to go to seed. In the past five years several have faced financial and structural crises. Many are a hundred years old and in a very sorry state indeed.

Brighton's west pier was built in 1889 to supersede the original chain pier. The architecture of this popular pleasure palace is symbolic of the moral and immoral delights of the traditional seaside holiday. Just before Christmas came the announcement that the pier was to be demolished without any testing of public opinion in Brighton, Hove, or elsewhere. John Lloyd, in the throes of running his Brighton art gallery over the holiday period, launched a 'We want the west pier' campaign and collected 4,000 signatures. A protest group marched to Brighton town hall and caused the decision to be postponed.

Mr Lloyd said: 'In 1851, the Royal Pavilion was derelict. There was a proposal to pull it down and redevelop the site. Fortunately, the council of the day found the £50,000 necessary to buy it and now it is a lucrative asset. In a time of crisis we should remember the more enduring qualities of a civilisation.'

Southend's pier has been more fortunate. The resort's policy and resources committee is recommending that the council spends £1.5 million of ratepayers' money over the next 10 years on repairs and maintenance rather than demolish the mile-and-a-third long pier. Gavin Henderson is adamant that, whatever the likely fate of the majority of the our remaining 40 piers, we should make every effort to preserve at least three: Brighton's two piers as well as the one at Clevedon in Somerset. This is a special example with its set of

Brunel-designed railway lines.

'One might have to accept the fate of a pier as rather like a ship with a limited life,' he said. 'But we should feel impoverished without, say, the *Cutty Sark* or the *Victory*. Piers are as totally British.'

Mr Henderson has a lifelong interest in piers. He started his working life as the manager of the rifle range at Worthing pier and it was there that he had his first engagement as a professional musician. Now, as director of York festival society, he travels throughout the country, making a point of taking a stroll along any available pier. This interest, backed by lengthy research, will be the subject of a book on piers to be published next year.

The doyen of pier engineers was Eugenius Birch of Westminster. His first was the Margate jetty, completed in 1855, a new departure in marine construction. Piers from his designs were erected in resorts around the country. Birch was also the first to construct large sea-water aquariums like those at Brighton and Scarborough. His last design represented a huge ship arranged and fitted up as a first-class hotel to be erected at the end of Brighton's chain pier. He died before this could be carried out.

Gradually piers became seaside amenities in their own right. 'It was a fashionable place to be seen,' said Mr Henderson. 'People dressed in their elegant best to take a stroll along the pier.'

In the late 1850s they began selling prints, early forms of seaside postcards, and souvenirs, now eagerly sought by the Victoria and Albert Museum. The camera obscura was introduced, amusements were all very genteel. The advent of the railways introduced the day tripper but piers did not go through an overnight knees-up metamorphosis. Brass bands, maybe, but also some of the finest orchestras in England played at the end of the pier. It was possible to see Elgar and Sir Henry Wood. Concert parties offered good clean humour, although the pierrot show was considered not respectable. That was kept in its place, on the beach. End-of-the-pier humour with its slot machines of the what the butler saw variety came much later.

A piece of Victorian sentiment or a commercial proposition? How should we look at the question of their preservation? The cost of maintenance is high – can they be made to pay? Mr Henderson said: 'The sentiment industry is growing; piers are a unique part of our heritage and their tourist value cannot be assessed merely by the number of people who go through the turnstiles. The British holiday is booming with an accent on cities with an historical interest. In York, the Arts Council has given grants for a medieval centre where one can learn about the medieval way of life. This could be done with a pier: a living museum of a past way of life which would appeal to a large cross section of people.'

Because of the recent controversy, Brighton's west pier has come under the spotlight. Suggestions have been made which, if imaginatively directed, could prove profitable. While the basic Victorian layout would not be changed, it is obvious that the pier must cater for the tastes of the 70s and 80s. 'You cannot expect people to be satisfied with the fish and chips, jam sponge image,' said Mr Henderson. 'The quality of food will have to be better – perhaps there could be a fish restaurant overlooking the sea. What could be a nicer place to have a meal? I am not advocating a rich man's playground but the idea of a casino could have potential profit. There might be a theatre on a flexible basis, perhaps a children's theatre or a crèche with a children's entertainer. Many of our piers will have to go but some, as a unique facet of British holiday life, must be retained. If they are demolished it will be a national crime.'

Jennifer Pilling

A Country Diary
September 18 1975

SOUTH DEVON: Crabs are still caught by Beesands fishermen but for local consumption only. The big markets are now supplied by the motor vessels operating from Brixham. The coastline here, between Beesands and Strete, is unique in Devon, having two long sand and shingle barriers which separate the sea from two freshwater leys similar to Dorset's Chesil beach. The coastal path passes along both shingle ridges and between them it climbs and descends a hill where it meanders through thickets where rose hips, bryony berries and bitter sloes remind one of the approach of autumn. From a vantage point swans and their cygnets could be seen on the unruffled waters of the ley and flocks of house martins circulated overhead. Slapton Ley, larger than Beesands Ley, is also the largest stretch of natural freshwater in Devon and one of the largest, situated so close to the sea, in the British Isles as a whole. It has abundant aquatic flora including extensive reed beds and water lilies, and it is famous as a reserve. A field studies council centre, through whose natural history courses thousands of students have passed, is situated conveniently close to it. The ley is a habitat of regional importance for both the sedge and reed warbler. Kingfishers, whitethroats, blackcaps and the migrant, fresh-water black tern were being reported as we passed by. Late on we saw sandwich terns on the mud banks of the river Dart. Along the beaches adjacent to the leys sunbathing Britons in their hundreds were looking browner than for some years.

Brian Chugg

Old salt seller
August 1 1977

Skegness celebrates this month the centenary of its third foundation. The first Skegness, founded by Skeggi the Viking, was engulfed by the sea in 1526, and now lies three miles off the coast. And the second, a fishing village of 349 people, was engulfed by the ninth Earl of Scarborough in the 1870s with his grand plan for a purpose-built resort that now lies along five miles of the Lincolnshire coast.

Everybody knows this third Skegness, if only from John Hassall's famous 1908 poster of the jolly fisherman prancing along the beach with the slogan 'Skegness is so bracing.' Though the *Guinness Book of Records* is silent on the point, this must be the oldest advertisement still on continuous display.

But does the poster still tell the truth? There are no jolly fishermen prancing anywhere in Skegness today. Nor perhaps, were there any in John Hassall's day. And that 'bracing' air does not brace everywhere in Skegness. If you stand on the Grand Parade, it drifts into the nostrils, tainted with fried onion, whiffs of hamburger, and the tang of vinegared chip. The same air is also loud with the litany of the bingo caller, chanting over the bowed heads of the devout: 'On the yellow, all the twos, twenty-two ...'

John Hassall did not visit Skegness until nearly 30 years after the publication of his poster, which probably explains his curious choice of a fisherman. But what else can one say about Skegness on an Easter Monday but 'bracing'? It is a description that Skegness, wisely, has stuck to through the years. Sometimes in unlikely context. In 1926 the council ordered its assistant clerk to take two weeks' leave because he had not had a holiday for 25 years. 'The bracing air of Skegness,' he announced, 'was sufficient for all my physical needs.'

After the last war, new promenades were built and called the Bracings. Mr Stanley Webster, the foreshore manager, who knows a good slogan when he sees one, has a set speech about bracing Skegness. It has, he says, 'a tonic effect on the jaded and restores the invalid. Chronic bronchitis sufferers can without doubt gain much relief and have the fullest possible chance of recovery from the disease.'

Skegness was also the birthplace of the holiday camp. Mr Billy Butlin, who started as a hoop-la stall owner, was watching despondent Skegness holidaymakers sheltering from the rain when he hit upon the idea of a holiday camp where he could move the entertainment indoors when it rained. He opened his first camp, a mile or two up the coast from Skegness, in 1936. It housed 1,000 campers. The idea could probably never have been conceived anywhere else but Skegness. The resort has much of the jolly brashness of a Butlin camp. There is nothing like a week in Skegness, or a week in a Butlin's camp, or domicile in Australia, for exploding the notion that the English are a stuffy and reserved race.

I first knew Butlin's at Skegness when it became HMS Royal Arthur, a Royal Navy shore establishment, during the war. Lord Haw-Haw, broadcasting propaganda from Germany, claimed three times that the Germans had sunk it. Would that they could, and would that they had. Unheated chalets in winter and inoculation fever made life a misery for young sailors. So did a petty officer who behaved like a madman and claimed that he was the only man in the navy who could prove his sanity. He said he had a discharge certificate from a mental hospital declaring him sane.

Butlin's revisited showed that many of the prewar chalets were still in use, looking seedy and in need of repair. Billy Butlin created an ethos, and it survives intact. It should be inscribed above the entrance gate: 'A good time will be had by all.' And nobody more personifies the Butlin spirit than Professor Splash, alias Mr Harry Wilcockson, a miner from Mansfield Woodhouse, Notts. He has been a paying guest (they no longer call them campers) at all eight Butlin camps in the United Kingdom since 1947. He devotes most of his holiday to entertaining children by dressing up in outrageous clown costumes. We saw him in his queen's guard outfit of bearskin, tail coat, kilt, jubilee knickers, and skiboots with bells on. This splendid man, who has raised over £20,000 for charities, gives his services free. He once worked so hard on a holiday at the Filey camp, giving three shows a day for children, that he collapsed from exhaustion when he returned home. A few Redcoats have resented his success. After all this time, the very least that Butlin's could do would be to offer him free or cut-price holidays.

Sir Billy Butlin, now 77, and living in retirement in Jersey, will return to Skegness next Monday to switch on the centenary illuminations. He will find Skegness greatly changed since his early days there. It still has one of the finest beaches in the country, and the fourth longest pier, and bracing air away from the chip-fryers. But the Tower cinema now has special adult late night shows – Sextet, plus Clockwork Nympho. Mrs Whitehouse would probably want to bring a private prosecution over some of the comic postcards on show on the front.

Sir Billy will have arrived too late for two all in wrestling bouts, one featuring Giant Haystack, monsterman, 6ft 11in, 31-stone mountain, versus Big Daddy, 300lb blockbuster (ring specially strengthened), and the other featuring the Fabulous Royal Brothers versus The Skinheads of Liverpool, mean, moody backstreet brawlers.

If he strolls through the town, Sir Billy will see what else Skegness has to offer its visitors. A coach firm advertises excursions to Grimsby, and suggests that visitors might care to visit the docks. The Embassy theatre offers old time music hall on posters which protest, surely not seriously, 'Ignored by the Arts Council.' The shops sell pension-book cases, 'My lucky bingo board,' and plates with couplets like

'True friends are like diamonds, precious but rare.
False friends are like autumn leaves, found everywhere.'

Skegness has always had a streak of vulgarity. In 1937 the wretched Harold Davidson, unfrocked rector of Stiffkey, was mauled by a lion at Skegness and died two days later. Davidson was unfrocked for immoral conduct. In a campaign to proclaim his innocence, he made a spectacle of himself at seaside resorts by fasting in a barrel or going into a lion's cage. When the lion struck him down, the tamer, a girl of 16, pulled Davidson out and was given a gold watch for her courage. The owners of the lions promptly doubled the charge to see them perform and were packed out every day.

In its centenary year Skegness is thinking of twinning with Bad Gandershelm, a resort in the Hartz Mountains of Germany. The Germans would probably enjoy the beach and its donkeys, the pier, the gardens, boating lake, bowling greens, swimming pool and pleasant tree-lined streets behind the front. Much of the rest, alas, would be pure culture shock.

Michael Parkin

Going out in style
April 11 1978

Sir Clough Williams-Ellis, the architect who spent his life designing buildings to give pleasure, decided he wanted his ashes sent up in a firework rocket. Now, after his death last Saturday at the age of 94, Sir Clough's family are working out how best they can carry out his wishes.

Mrs Kate Williams, promotions officer for Portmeirion, the village Sir Clough created on the north Wales coast, said he made clear in a letter nearly five years ago that he wanted no funeral service. His body should be 'just sent off to the handiest crematorium in a truck or Portmeirion van.' Most of his ashes were to be used 'to fertilise the crematorium's garden.' But some could be retained 'in a tobacco tin and incorporated in the next big rocket to be let off in a Portmeirion fiesta.' Mrs Williams said firework displays were a feature of annual balls held at Portmeirion.

Ancient solace in the Cinque Ports
June 15 1978

The Cinque Ports, once England's frontier towns facing France across the narrow seas, yesterday got down to the serious business of celebrating seven centuries of their unbroken confederacy – 700 years of history, including at least 800 years of make-believe. And to mark them, a blush of crimsoned mayors and a huff of macebearers.

And the Queen Mother, too. In the face of such sustained if stubborn vigilance by the five ports, two ancient towns and seven limbs, it seems churlish to let on that the sea long ago left Rye, Sandwich, and Romney high and dry. However, the proceedings to mark the anniversary were held in Hastings which still has a watery doorstep.

The choice of meeting place was the only concession to reality. The rest was sustained British dottiness, with tradition and precedent giving it impeccable pedigree. How else can you explain away an assembly calling itself the Courts of Brotherhood and Guestling, summoning the mayors and officials of 14 towns to pat itself on the back for having existed for so long and latterly to such little purpose.

Brotherhood and Guestling sound like two classes of membership of the confederacy: one category, a medieval fraternity perhaps, the other for extremely small people. Not so. A helpful man from Hastings council produces a rare work of scholarship, researched ages ago by a Manchester academic. This indicates that the two words are place names. Such arcane considerations, of course, are quite irrelevant. For there in the municipal pomp of the white mock pavilion, the rules of an antique game were read out by the Official Solicitor. They come from the Black Book 'compiled in the 36th year of the reign of Elizabeth I.' Namely, that any deputies who speak more than once, or who interrupt another while speaking, shall be fined three shillings four pence.

So the speaker, the mayor of Rye, Mrs Joan Gwendolen Yates, declares freedom of the debate. And never has there been such an orderly gaggle of councillors and clerks. The heart of the matter is a resolution to commemorate the granting of King Edward's charter in 1278 – thanks to a saving clause (sub section three of section 271 of the Local Government Act, 1972, actually) which allows the courts to continue in being.

The proceedings were wrapped up in 30 minutes, but the central historical figure was missing. The office of Lord Warden and Admiral of the Cinque Ports has been vacant since the death earlier this year of Sir Robert Menzies. The office is in the gift of the Crown and within the next few months the name of the 160th incumbent of the oldest military role in Britain will be issued from Buckingham Palace. Sir Robert, who succeeded Churchill, will be missed, for he took his duties seriously and spent a month each year in a little apartment that had been fixed up for his family in Walmer Castle.

No longer does the lord warden hold the narrow seas, as he used to in the time of Edward the Confessor; nor does he fight all England's sea battles – as he used to until Sir Francis Drake bowled along. But he does, in theory at least, have jurisdiction over the sea from Essex to Sussex. A lord warden needs to have a sense of history and a sense of fun. How else can he hold, straight-faced, an office which, on one hand entitles him to a 19-gun salute when he is passed at sea and on the other allows him the perk of picking flotsam and jetsam. In what other make believe situation would a beachcomber be allowed to dress in a cocked hat, heavy gold epaulettes and gold striped pants? Sir Robert had the measure of it all right. He used to pick up flotsam and as for the uniform, he once told the Melbourne Age: 'I shall take it back home ultimately and present it to the nation. People may as well get some fun out of it when I am dead.'

Back at the Courts of Brotherhood and Guestling, the mood was certainly not funereal. After the Queen Mum, who brings a sense of continuity to these things, had departed, the town crier told the company 'to hie yourselves' to the Queen's hotel for lunch. And so the mayors of the Cinque Ports, the ancient towns and the limbs, having proclaimed the said anniversary, trooped off for cucumber soup, poached salmon and strawberries – 'such repast and refreshment,' as the Oyez man put it winningly: 'as may be provided and ordained for your comfort and solace.'

John Cunningham

The Pleasures of Ports and Piers: 1980-1989

Edging slowly round towards the end
May 16 1981

The Tamar marks an old frontier into Cornwall, and crossing it now, one enters a place which still feels remote. The light is brighter, even on a cloudy day. The smell of the ocean is in the air. Villages with their flowers and white cottages look scrubbed clean.

During the effort to stamp out smuggling in the 18th century, a path was made which allowed excisemen and coastguards to patrol, on horseback and on foot, the entire coastline of Cornwall. Though little known, this coastal footpath – clearly marked and in good condition for most of its length – is now Cornwall's greatest asset. It slips away inconspicuously from the caravans and car parks, and within minutes there is nothing around but the grassy clifftops and the sky, and the sounds of the wind, the birds, and the waves.

On one side, great cliffs descend into clear, clean water which has a Mediterranean blueness not normally seen in Britain. On the other, heathland and meadows with thousands of tiny wildflowers. Stone stiles are set into slate walls between fields. The walls themselves are covered with green plants and look like rock gardens. Few people walk far along the path and it is easy to find oneself completely alone. Along the south coast there are rocky coves, tiny, sandy bays, and little fishing harbours. The cliffs of the Lizard and Lands End peninsulas have among the finest walks in Cornwall, with glorious views over Mounts Bay.

There are three or four guides to the coast path and the best of them, Letts', tells you how easy or how tough the going is, and gives titbits of the history of each stretch, and the names of bed and breakfast places and pubs along the way. (*The South-west Peninsula Coastal Path*. Parts I and II. Letts Guides, £1.25 each.) The path is ideal for any type of walking, from a short stroll to a long hard hike, and with the help of the guide, it is possible to find what suits you, drive out to the area and start from there. Without a car, you have to take the path as it comes.

Andrew Sanger

Anglers squirm at worm rule
February 4 1983

Anyone digging for lugworms on Cleethorpes beach without a licence will find the borough council coming down on them like a ton of sand. Nearly 20 lugworm poachers have been taken to court and fined. Sea anglers visiting Cleethorpes, who want lugworms for bait, are objecting to what they call KGB tactics.

The council has relied in its campaigns against lugworm diggers on more recent legislation, in the Cleethorpes Improvement Act of 1902, and the Humberside Act of 1982. The latter states that no person can dig on or take from the foreshore sand, shingle, rock, or other material, Lugworm or any other bait without written consent. In this context, 'written consent' means a licence costing £1 a year and available only to residents of Cleethorpes and Grimsby.

Mr John Timmins, a sea angler and secretary of the regional federation for sport and recreation, said yesterday that the Humberside act made an offender of a child digging for a sandcastle, or a visitor picking up and taking home a pretty shell or stone from the beach. Magna Carta, he said, gave the public the right to fish off all shores and in all tidal waters, except where the right had been lost before 1215. 'If you have the right to fish, you must have the right to get bait to catch the fish.'

Mr Richard Wilson, senior assistant solicitor with the council, said that the Cleethorpes Improvement Act did not cover removal of lugworms. Prosecutions were brought for removing sand. Sand had to be removed when digging for lugworms and the lugworms themselves were largely full of sand. Mr Wilson admitted that, technically, the wording of the 1982 Act would cover a child digging for a sandcastle or someone taking home a shell. But any suggestion that the council would prosecute for these offences was ridiculous. Holidaymakers were on the beach at the council's invitation.

Michael Parkin

Going down to the sea in slips
August 13 1983

The seashore of Aphrodite, William Golding, and Benjamin Britten is a mythic place, a place of inspiration, of regeneration and even of death. Death in Bridlington, then. That is where I went for the purgatoria of the annual holiday. Of course, if you set off in that frame of mind, then you do not deserve to enjoy yourself. But I was more amenable, more open to persuasion, at least to begin with: at least until the rapturous gulls screeched holes in my cerebellum at half-past four on the first morning.

I knew from that moment that it was a horrible mistake. But holidays also partake of the quality of myth and it was no more use wishing that I had not come than it would have been for Tamino to tell the Queen of the Night to blow her own flute or for Siegfried to object that his journey up the Rhine was a waste of effort. After the third cup of black coffee I even began to chide myself for having been churlish about seabirds at the seaside; it is, when all is said and done, neat and proper for them to squawk at 4.30 in the morning. I decided that what was needed was a dissociation of sensibility, a radical readjustment of my consciousness so as to make it appropriate to the mythic ambience of the holiday.

Though not everyone was on holiday. The men who clean the streets of all that was left of last night's far from mythical glee, vomit, and procreation were already thundering along the gutters in their noisy and noisome chariot that beats hell out of your eardrums as it sweeps as it cleans. I went out into the disinfected streets and was immediately propositioned by two men. 'Fishing today, sir?' He grinned at his mate in the purple sweater and the leather boots and I suspected for a moment that fishing was only a euphemism. He had the hair of a Gorgon and sepulchral teeth. He reminded me of Tony Hancock's Captain Ahab act.

I declined as politely as I could, and as I turned away I concluded they had only asked me for a joke. My library pallor betokens no mariner. Embarrassed, I ducked into the only place open at that hour, a snack bar. (Not Allen's Nosh Bar – I tasted Allen's nosh later in the week and it was much superior to that first breakfast, bacon and tomato, like cold blood, hot oil and old rubber.) However early in the day, there is always someone about at the seaside. There was a man in a checked cap standing by the hot hand rails talking to the waiter. It was like something by Harold Pinter:

'There aren't many in.'

'There were one or two in earlier.'

'I expect there'll be a few more in later.' (Lights another cigarette.) 'Later. Later on, that's when they'll all come in.' (Pours mug of tea.) 'They're waiting till it gets a bit later.' 'There's always a lot in teatimes Fridays.'

'Teatimes Fridays, eh? You wonder why that is.' 'They're wanting their tea I expect.'

'I expect that's it.'

After breakfast I returned to the flat. The rest of the family were up. 'Couldn't sleep for the gulls, and something rolling through the street like a tank. I was dreaming it was the French Revolution.' I had gone off the idea of myth by now. Given the gulls and the tumbril and the practical absurdists in the snack bar, given at that moment my eldest son staring at the test card for Channel Four on the landlady's decrepit television set, everything seemed more like a glum plot by Sam Beckett.

As we set out for the beach, a brown mist descended over the town like a tarpaulin. However, this was soon dispersed by a ferocious southwest wind (no heatwave for our holiday, of course.) We used a leftover sandcastle for the stumps. The first ball hurtled past me and through a greatcoated family huddled over their chilly picnic. It was blown along until forced to stop by the breakwater where the ebb tide seethed among the greasy flotsam of last night's fish and chips. There were plenty of people on the beach and most of them looked as if they were waiting to be taken off by landing craft. Most, but not all, for there were a few puritans determined to remain constant in their pursuit of enjoyment come wind or weather.

We took refuge from the squally shower in Madame Tussaud's where, among waxworks which could have taken for holidaymakers marooned last year, there was an account of the woman with the biggest bust in the world. It was written: 'Her breasts measure seventy-two inches and weigh nine and a half stones.' There were women who looked like that on the seaside postcards.

On the whole, these were disappointing. I think I remember that they used to be funny, but not any longer; no clean meaning, only single entendres of such lurid explicitness that they made Arthur Askey's old seaside landlady, bending in search of her little pussy seem positively innocent.

In the middle of all this salaciousness was the Catholic Repository like an oasis of sanctity in a naughty world. The shop window was full of pasty statues looking as if they would pock mark if you poked them. There were cut price figurines of the Pope rather irreverently marked 'To clear.' My cast of mind had been perverted by the postcards and that word repository aroused a smirk. Repository, an unscheduled double entendre reminding me of the worthy missions to seamen who call their evangelising newspaper Hello Sailor! Back to Sea I would say; definitely Round the Horne. Repository gave me the nasty suspicion that, if they could not shove religion down your throat, then some other means of entry would be found.

If you have been to the seaside with your wife and kids, you will know how difficult it is to find a pub that will let you in for a drink even in the daytime. One saloon bar window displayed the notice: 'No dogs, No children, No customers' own food, No parking.' We eventually found a place near the harbour. The children had to be left in a sort of sanforised cellar that smelt of paint and was austerely lit by loudly humming fluorescent, striplights. You had to go upstairs to the bar and fetch the drinks down again on a tray. That children's room was like the third level of Dante's *Inferno*. The prince of this world, the jukebox, was turned up so loud that conversation demanded the art of the lip reader. Babies, toddlers, and young children who were as yet unschooled in this skill were obliged to bide their time until the heavy metal subsided, when they could all bawl at once for more crisps and shandies.

Occasionally one of the braver kids would make a break for it and run out into the busy street. They were always retrieved by their dads, who could then be seen but not heard upbraiding them:

by gesticulations and mouthed threats. Periodically, one of the bar staff would come in, stare at us all as if on the lookout for any sign of incipient ingratitude, wipe the plastic tables, and rush off upstairs again with a tray full of empties. If you happened to catch the eye of a fellow holiday maker, you always got a desperate smile. We knew we were supposed to be enjoying ourselves.

The town centre seemed quiet after the pub. And between ten and twelve minutes past two, the sun slid out briefly from the clouds like a gold coin among grey rags. The kids wanted to play the amusements. This proved expensive since all the penny slot machines now took 10p – all, that is, except for an avenue of what the butler saw machines where you could still wind your own handle and glimpse a bit of chintz naughtiness, which seemed almost virtuous beside what they were showing at the Odeon. The older kids playing the machines looked bored stiff, apathetic, as if, like their fathers sitting in that children's room, their hearts were not in it. As if they were acting the part of being teenagers, or worse, living out some horrible predestination. Perhaps it is just the style, like the solipsistic rockers with their personalised stereo headphones that have replaced the trannies.

In the afternoon we walked along the front again past the crazy golf and the pleasure park, past the architectural modernism of the hotels, one of which looked exactly like our 1940s utility wireless set. There was still plenty of that cream and mushroom paint about that went along with A-line dresses – they are back, too – and stockings with seams down the back.

More than anywhere else, I think, the seaside still bears witness to fashions that were all the rage in the early part of this century and to a way of life long since past: a milieu defined by the wash stand and the chamber pot once found in your digs but now immortalised only on those rude postcards. There is something of art nouveau about it all. The absurdly ornate and vaguely oriental design of the Spa Theatre. The roof of the ladies and gentlemen in the seaside baroque of curved stone. Just past the lavatories there is a row of seafront cubicles, obviously built on the style of the old bathing cabins. From these at half-past three rushed middle aged ladies with middle aged spread going, as it were, down to the sea in their slips. Further along towards Sewerby, it is all modernism again in the form of the hotel expanse where I longed to turn that letter 'a' into an 'e'. Then it is back to the old style again with the pavilion and the iron railings of the park, testimony to the expansiveness and flamboyance of the last decade of the nineteenth century. In this part you could think you were any minute about to see your ladies with long dresses and parasols picnicking opulently beside the cliff top oval while their fiances with whiskers and queer shaped crickets bats bat out the lazy summer afternoon.

Seasides need no museums. They are themselves museums with a strange and haunting capability of making the past live alongside the present. To the north stand the real and savage cliffs of Flamborough, protruding green and white like a rotting jaw. The weather was not bad all week and we ended up enjoying it all in a masochistic sort of way. In spite of the kitsch of the Repository and the silly gift shops, there is a quality about Bridlington which even the gaudiness and the commercialisation cannot erode. I think it is the sea itself, and the harbour, the real fishermen and their boats, the old lighthouse just up the coast standing severe as a Victorian parent over the plastic, the cheap trinkets, the Muzak, and the electronic follies of the arcades.

But what there is left that is genuine will have to be preserved. Entrepreneurs beware. Folks will put up with a certain amount of nonsense if they can still feel that the real seaside remains underneath it all. It is that reality as a remembrance of things almost past which still attracts the crowds. It is the myth of the sea and the shore as a magical place, a place that belongs essentially to childhood.

Peter Mullen

From suicide notes to sunshine and serendipity
March 24 1984

I began the path from the Cardigan end, on the last evening of August. The sky was clear, the air warm and the grass high after one of the finest summers for years. Ahead of me lay the Pembrokeshire coastal national park and 180 miles of footpath. I walked three of them and camped out in some sand dunes. At first light my tent collapsed around me; blown out of the ground by a force nine gale. I crawled out to find summer had disappeared for good, kicked in the teeth with a boot that had flattened everything from insects to trees. In minutes I was drenched and there was nothing I could do but start walking.

I kept going all day; so did the storm. That afternoon, totally despondent, I trudged into Newport and took shelter in a launderette. I sat there in socks and shorts and tried to re-examine my motives. Before I'd set out, I'd accepted that walking a long distance footpath wouldn't be a normal holiday. I mean I wasn't doing it for the girls, the glamour and the night life. In fact I'd convinced myself a journey like this would awaken senses in me that years of travelling by motorcar had blunted. I had a lightweight tent and sleeping bag, a little stove and some waterproofs, and I was set for a week or two of getting back to basics. It was only after I'd completed the path ten days later, that I came to realise how, on a walk of any distance, the bad times are as frequent as the good, and the sense of achievement at the journey's end is, more often than not, the result of some hard work.

Certainly, the postcards I sent from that north coast all read like suicide notes – 'I can't take it any more, I've had enough . . . etc.' – and all I gained from those first few days was a strange discoloration of the toes, which I could only diagnose as trenchfoot, and the knowledge that there's no truth in the term 'waterproof.' My big mistake was to walk the path from north to south right into the teeth of the gale. Nights I spent clinging to the tent poles and days, plodding along the monstrous cliff-tops, where waves hit the rocks below with such force I was sprayed with foam a hundred feet up.

The wind was ridiculous; it blew a gap between me and my rucksack and forced me to walk at an angle of 45 degrees, just to keep upright. Meanwhile, walkers heading in the other direction sailed past with a shout and a wave unable to keep up with themselves. I remember passing a bizarre cricket match, where the outfield was strewn with leaves and broken branches, and the fielders wore overcoats as, from one end, a fast bowler had difficulty making the ball travel 22 yards, while from the other crease, a spinner took wicket after wicket with meteoric deliveries the batsman never saw.

Finally, just before St David's Head, a gust of wind blew me uncomfortably close to the edge and like the many exhausted sea birds I'd seen along the way, I too, decided to turn inland. They took refuge in the woods and rocks on the headland; I opted for the back room at Mrs Thomas's, The Gables, St Davids. B & B £6.50. Bath 50p extra. Toast cooked on one side only. St Davids is supposed to be the smallest city in Britain; indeed, it's no bigger than a village and was a pleasant place to rest up and weather out the remainder of the storm.

Next day I strolled around the streets hearing snippets of Welsh conversation in the shops and wondering if all cities were once as pretty as this, until in the afternoon the sun finally made an appearance and I headed back towards the coast, feeling a lot happier. After the table-top bleakness and struggle of the north, the west coast had a serendipitous quality that was wonderfully refreshing. I began to round headlands and find off-shore islands, basking; and breathtaking beaches, such as Marloes Sands, curving away into the distance.

Villages, like Little Haven and St Brides Haven, would appear tucked into the hillsides, and I'd come across tidal inlets, where all I could do was sit on a rock and wait till it was possible to wade across. For three days the walking was a joy, as I strode around St Brides bay and the Sale peninsula. The nights, too, were peaceful and I found some really wild places to camp. Then early one morning I rounded St Ann's Head and came into Milford Haven; as I did so the sun went in. Nelson once called this harbour the finest he'd ever seen. Twenty-five years ago, the major oil companies came to the same conclusion and built the second largest oil refinery in Europe on its shores. Jetties and pipelines snake far out into the deep water channel, collections of oil tanks sit on the hillsides like caravan sites, and the horizon is broken with the dark silhouettes of refineries and power stations.

It's a sort of industrial Disneyland, and I walked through it for a while, awestruck. But after a mile or two it seemed a bit daft, and in the end I caught a bus. Not until the path turned south again, past West Angle Bay, did it recapture its craggy beauty, but soon after that the restricted MoD area around Castlemartin caused a lengthy diversion inland, and it was St Govan's Head before I was able to rejoin the coast. By then the rain had returned and I saw little of the last stretch as I walked head down, until I bumped into Tenby. There, children in school uniform queued at bus stops with holidaymakers – the surest sign that summer is over. I had a cup of tea in a beach cafe and pressed on to the walk's end at Amroth. It had taken me 11 days to travel 180 miles; five hours later I was back in London.

Mark Wallington

From Land's End to John o'Groats by public transport
August 4 1984

'John O'Groats 874 miles,' says the signpost on the cliff edge. The sea below is the colour of washed-out poster paint, and so still that there is not the narrowest frill of foam round the rocks. But nearer is a crammed car park, a hotel, and an area where, by paying £1.80 for children and for geriatrics one can see exhibitions about rescue and heritage and Wurzel Gummidge. There is a case for going somewhere fast, and, even if 874 miles is a fair step, the alternative, New York, is 3,147.

The local-looking bus just ready for off, whose driver says Land's End is a lot better than it used to be, they've tidied it up, seems hardly to be clear of the first and last everything before it dives down the dramatic incline to Sennen Cove. The inshore water is green blue and translucent and the height above is peopled by motorists gazing down at it, some of them not merely beside but actually still in their cars. After that the landscape of small stone-walled fields and roadsides flushed with campion and foxgloves is that of any western peninsula from Brittany to Galloway until we run down a leafy tunnel into Newlyn, with its fresh, fishy smells. There is time to eat one of the most delectable cream ices in Cornwall – though you think that wherever you eat them in the West Country – and idle round the harbour before walking on to Penzance, partly beside the regency and Victorian houses of the promenade, which is one of the sea fronts where I should rather like to live, partly barefoot along the tide line, splashing in and out of the shallows.

The Plymouth bus veers away from the sea after the turning for Marazion, with St. Michael's Mount floating on the water rather than rising out of it, picks it up again briefly at Hayle, where there is a glimpse of bright sand dunes behind the soggy mud of the estuary, then keeps inland through country that gets softer and greener and more flowery as we move further from the craggy extremity of Cornwall. Hedge roses and rhododendrons and hawthorn and escallonia and veronica and elder now, as well as the foxgloves and campion, and I see my first Devon red. One of the debits of modern farming is that you can no longer tell where you are to a county or so by the breed of cattle that are grazing over the hedge.

These days you see everything everywhere, and half of them fill-bucket Ayrshires. My neighbour is a Cornishman who has lived in Plymouth these thirty years, so it is hard to say whether he is at the moment leaving home or going back to it. He remembers driving along this road in his father's trap, but nothing is the same today. We've lost the old traditions. Look at Arthur Scargill and that McEnroe – Drake and the Pilgrim Fathers wouldn't think much of him. Most of the politicians have lost the old traditions, too, and it's never been the same since the Great Western went. We agree that what we want is a country run by the Queen and Willie Whitelaw, in double harness; they are about my favourite public people, the matter of whom one votes for having nothing to do with the case.

Then I sink into a contented trance, to be jerked out of it when a narrow shape flashes down the sky ahead and, for one idiotic instant, I think: 'A peregrine!' before marking it down as merely a jet fighter. But earlier today, I did see a buzzard loafing overhead, and at least the jet has shaken me properly alert to details like the splendid classical Wesleyan chapel at Camborne and the even bigger one at Redruth. We stop in Truro's marketplace for long enough to make one wonder why, in some quarters, it is fashionable to deprecate the cathedral. Probably simply because it is Early English of 1910. The point is that this Early English comes off.

Then we are into industrial Cornwall, with the evening light glancing off the distant alps of the china-clay spoil heaps north of St Austell, and the chimneys of the disused tin mines raising warning fingers. Liskeard has a granite church so enormous that it is hard to believe it is only the second largest in Cornwall, and many of the wayside cottages and small town terraces we have passed have been granite also, and blessedly unpicturesque. Can one build really badly in stone?

With Saltash we are in frontier territory. The Tamar estuary marks the boundary between Cornwall and Devon; the new – well, 1961 – road bridge by which we cross into Plymouth gives a chance to admire the railway bridge, Isambard Brunel's masterpiece of 1859, 100ft above high-water level. It was too early to eat seriously at Penzance before leaving, and now it is too late to eat in Plymouth, unless I settle for battered frogs' legs or a 16oz point steak (I am allergic to fish and chips), so I go fasting up to the Hoe to look for the old traditions. Drake is secure on his plinth, surveying the Sound from the headland that is the quarterdeck of the city. On the green behind him a group of shirt-sleeved gentlemen of a certain age are finishing a game of bowls in the last of the light. The broad stretch of grass before him is spattered with the detritus of the ambulant eating which is one of the three curses of our age, the other two being Muzak and the cult of the anti-hero, but the outward prospect makes up for it.

The bay is brimming and lustrous with the sleek heads of the late swimmers bobbing up like curious seals. The sky promises another flawless day tomorrow. Getting away from Land's End was one thing, but why go farther than this? Then an American voice near at hand says: 'We're going all round the world. Polperro and Mousehole tomorrow, and Gretna Green and Edinburgh. It's a tease of a tour really – they just give you a taste of everything. The guide made us go through St Paul's [she throws the accent on the Saint] in 15 minutes, so there wasn't time to see the crypt or the whispering gallery Oh, and we're going to York.' Who am I to feel that John o' Groats is excessively far?

Nesta Roberts

A day out at Frinton and Clacton-on-Sea
August 16 1985

Why, I was asked, do you want to go to Frinton-on-Sea? Because it is there, I replied, and waving two fingers at the weather seized my bucket and spade and headed for Liverpool Street station, which surely deserves some kind of award for being so outstandingly unpleasant, untidy and ill-designed. Thence by a tremendously bumpy train (doubtless designed by Rowland Emmett) to Thorpe-le-Soken (where do they find these names?) where I took another train which was littered with discarded copies of the *Financial Times* and smelt of cat's pee.

I had been told that Frinton is elegantly refined, populated by retired gentlefolk, old buffers with white moustaches and little old ladies who can make a cup of coffee last all morning. This turned out to be absolutely true. The average age appears to be about three score years and ten. Most inhabitants carry a walking-stick, if not two. It's a town that is making valiant attempts to behave as though Queen Victoria was still on the throne. The shops in the broad treelined main street don't just sell you things. They purvey them, and as often as not they are bespoke. Frinton is so genteel that it actually boasts about what it hasn't got. A promotional leaflet proudly announces that there are no whelk or candyfloss stalls, and no funfairs. I'm told that it has never had a cinema or even a pub. Certainly I failed to find one of either.

There are plenty of churches though. A tiny Norman one (disused) in stone. A huge inter-denominational one in red brick. A Roman Catholic one in timber and stucco. A Methodist one that looks like a school. And probably many others I didn't see. Frinton may not have a pub, but it has lots of religion. Frinton is full of lovely gardens, public and private, and the beaches are splendid. Needless to say the weather was wretched. The grey sea merged imperceptibly into the grey sky. Still, there were children flying kites and playing cricket on the Greensward. That's the kind of place Frinton is. A place that has a Greensward and an Esplanade.

On the beach a father and son were building a sandcastle. The child, aged about six, was showing not the slightest interest in this activity. By contrast the father, bald, pipe-smoking, fiftyish, was completely engrossed and looked as happy as (what can I say?) as happy as a sandboy. When the heavens opened I decided to take the bus to Clacton-on-Sea. In distance it's only eight miles from Frinton, but in every other way (years, class, culture) it's very much further. While the Frinton theatre was showing Alan Ayckbourn's *How the Other Half Loves*, the posters outside Clacton Town Hall advertised Val Doonican and Frankie Vaughan.

Other forthcoming attractions were wrestling between Rollerball Rocco and Chic Cullen, the sensational lady wrestler Naughty Nicky v. Big Momma and the Fabulous Blonde Bombshell Miss Mitzi Mueller v. 46in Busty Keegan. If Frinton is herbaceous borders, panama hats and lapsang souchong tea, Clacton is bingo, fish and chips, ice cream, burgers, cockles, whelks, jellied eels, more fish and chips, ice cream, eel pies, and Fresh Bait for Sale, maggots white and coloured, lug, rag, peelers. And deafening amusement arcades.

In Frinton the little old ladies are so respectable, meek and mild that any one of them could easily be the murderer in an Agatha Christie novel. Clacton is not so subtle. If Frinton is the regimental tie and the woolly cardigan, Clacton is the broken nose, the cauliflower ear and the tattoos on the arms. When thunder and lightning broke out I decided against an eel pie and chips and took refuge in an expensive-looking hotel where I thought I would not be hurried over the meal and could spend an hour or so reading Raymond Chandler without being disturbed. I soon became aware that the people at neighbouring tables were mostly villains. One of them wore dark glasses and looked like the late Aristotle Onassis. When he spoke everyone else listened, and agreed. One exchange I overheard went as follows. 'Where did you get it?' The rather indignant reply was 'I nicked it.' Another occurred when some latecomers arrived and introductions were made. Man with scar on face: 'This is my wife.' Onassis: 'I thought you were a bachelor.' Wife: 'You're thinking of his father.'

Clacton really is different from Frinton.

Richard Boston

Bottom lines
August 23 1985

There was a certain desolate sound about *Kisses on the Bottom* (BBC2) like a lost donkey with its foot in a bucket and the tide coming in. You could try suing the BBC under the Trades Description Act for calling it a saucy comedy. It was an animated Donald McGill postcard: Mam and Dad, Buxom and Lecherous the honeymoon couple, a vicar and a Scotsman. The absence of the milkman can only be explained by an urgent prior appointment with a lady in a nightie. 'Milkman, do you have the time?' 'Yes, madam, but 'oo will look after my 'orse?'

There was a time before the war when the entire surface of Lancashire was in motion like the sea. Each cotton town moved as one to the seaside and back again at the end of the wakes week. It is something of a mystery whom they sent saucy postcards to as everyone they knew was there already. 'Do you keep stationery?' 'Sometimes I wriggle about a bit.'

Kisses on the Bottom by Stephen Lowe recreated their primitive charm quite cleverly, the bright red noses, the bright blue jokes, the bloomers huge and clean as cumulus. Judy Cornwall, lollipop sweet as Mam, was such a generous helping that even her feet seemed to overflow her Minnie Mouse shoes. If Peter Benson seemed a touch on the tall side for Dad it was because men don't grow as small as

McGill drew them.   'It'll be all right later. It always shrinks after it's been in the water.'

Kisses on the Bottom was a little lament for lost innocence or lost faith or just lost knickers. Mam and Dad are pensioned off and the honeymoon couple promoted as the new, nude model. Or perhaps it was about the way one generation meets another on the way down, a phenomenon commonly experienced when you look in the mirror and see not yourself but your mother with no clothes on.

Nancy Banks-Smith

Butlin's goes Somerwest
July 19 1986

Fresh from chalet No ZE 7 at Somerwest World in Minehead, here is an esoteric piece of good news on the employment front. The number of Redcoats at the Butlin's centre, the biggest of the half-dozen still run by the famous old firm, has been doubled this season. Anyone not familiar with Sir Billy's great creation may imagine that the whole concept is just a piece of nostalgia, on a par with conscription and sweet rationing.   Seaside barracks, with tea for 2,000 at one sitting, seem to belong to another world, before the arrival of the good fairy Marbella. But it isn't so. As many people as ever are taking the traditional week by the sea, four-fifths of them parents besieged by young children. As soon as Minehead opened in May it began to approach its 10,100 capacity – well above the population of the pretty Somerset nest where this tremendous cuckoo was hatched in 1962.

In some fundamental ways, though, Butlin's really has disappeared from the Somerset coast. The name itself has gone – to the distraction of directory inquiries which now has to look under 'S' for Somerwest World rather than 'B' for Butlin's.   And if knobbly knees are your greatest asset, then Minehead is no longer for you. The traditional contest was abolished this year as out of keeping with the shiny new Somerwest image. After a serious dip in trade in the 70s, money has been poured into improvements at all six Butlin's camps. The work takes time; £1m alone has to be earmarked just for new plugs in every chalet bath and basin.

At Minehead the first of the flashier results can now be seen – notably the £5m Sunsplash swimming pool. Although shacky-looking buildings with corrugated iron roofs and witch's hat chimneys are still around, Sunsplash points to the future envisaged by Butlin's owners Top Rank – a sort of Alton Towers with board and lodging. Three giddy waterslides spiral into a series of pools, dotted with palm trees, rapids and water-sprays. You can sloosh, mind-numbed, through the complete darkness of the Black Hole slide before sitting at the waterside under a banana tree, licking ice cream.

Another £5m has gone on improving the chalets and disguising, with the help of rose pergolas and redundant red phone kiosks, Sir Billy's original grid. The old impression of seaside back-to-backs has given way to something more like a succession of private estates – 'Georgian' fanlight doors, bow windows complete with bottle glass and the harsh old nameplates – A, B, C and so on – replaced by Ash Grove, Beech Lane, and Cedar Close. According to the centre's director Paul Rumke, whose 18 years with Butlins began with the job of operating the nightly tropical storm in the Beachcomber bar, the pressure is mostly at the top end of the market. Tenants can almost always be found for the half-board County Suites (up to £133 a head per week in high season) and the De Luxe self-catering flats (a maximum of £295 a week for between four and seven people).

But although claret is served and Rumke tells of customers bringing their own nannies and au pairs, Somerwest World is not on its way to becoming a playground for the SDP. The improvements are more of a reflection of the rising demands of Butlin's traditional market than an attempt to match the delights of the Dordogne. Mass middle-range custom remains essential for the business to succeed and accounts for a great deal of the 'old' Butlin's staying in place. Miss Lovely Legs and Glamorous Gran are in no danger of going the way of Knobbly Knees and the robotic twirling of sequence dancing fills a large room every night.

The main attractions, as a result, tend to be crowded, and Sunsplash is frequently rationed into sessions with a maximum number – though a very generous one – of swimmers and sliders allowed in. Scanning the massed bodies for a glimpse of water, you can see why the mere prospect of sharing 165 acres with 10,099 other holidaymakers makes Butlin's anathema for many.   The hardest sceptic might be rewarded, though, by buying a £5 day ticket just to have a look. (The price – £4 for children – covers unlimited entry to Sunsplash and endless free rides on the Monorail, fairground, and other attractions.) And Butlin's traditional skill at entertaining children would be worth any parents examining at greater length, with abseiling, archery, and home computer courses among the diversions now on offer.

Butlin's as a base for a day or two? Even a week, so that you can potter on Exmoor or dally in Dunster Castle without small voices saying 'I'm bored,' and demanding ice cream? It is a thought. But don't go to Somerwest World if tales of the 'chalet patrol' have conjured up an image of wild 18-30 Club nights of lust. The centres are family places, cheerful but well disciplined, and Miss Lovely Legs is likely to have her parents near by – and probably her glamorous gran as well. 'Just curl up and wait for a Redcoat to come to you,' said a loudspeaker suggestively during my visit. But it was only advising tiny jockeys what to do if they tumbled from their mounts in the Donkey Derby.

Martin Wainwright

Postcard blues
December 17 1986

Margaret Kenny, aged 21, a High Wycombe, Buckinghamshire, part-time postwoman who refused to deliver saucy seaside postcards claiming that they were pornographic was gaoled for seven days at High Wycombe yesterday after admitting not delivering the cards and opening 10 packages. She pleaded pre-menstrual tension in mitigation.

Islands apart
November 7 1987

Shetland certainly put on a show. After dinner, the sky was full of the green arcs, streamers, and curtains of the aurora borealis, more splendid than I had ever seen, even in the Arctic. But then Shetland is northerly, further north than Stockholm, on the same latitude as Helsinki. Shetlanders, many of them, would like to fly a flag which is closer to the Danish than the British, a white cross on a blue ground. Lord Lyon, King of Arms, is obstructive.

This is perhaps still a politically sensitive matter. Until 1472, which is very recent in the history of these northern parts, the islands were Danish. Only then were they handed over to Scotland as dowry when a Danish princess married a Scots king. More recently, in the 1970s, Shetland wanted nothing to do with Scottish devolution, against which the people voted overwhelmingly, considering themselves no part of Scotland. There is substance to this opinion. If you come to Shetland from London, Glasgow is little more than half way there. Shetland is so far north that there is generally no room for it on the maps of Great Britain. It is a deeply felt grievance of Shetlanders that their islands are often put in a box somewhere to the east of

Aberdeen, miles off course, and often not to scale. They get their own back by referring to England, Scotland, Wales, and Ireland as 'the adjacent island group.'

'No trees?' said Miss Andrea Manson, at dinner. Well, no, she said, there weren't: when her cousin first went to the mainland, at the age of 19, he sat open mouthed in the train. It was all the trees passing by. He wanted to know if there were names for all those trees. And his own greatest surprise, said Maurice Mullay, when he first went south, was a squirrel in Hyde Park. He had seen pictures, of course, but thought they were a good size, nearer that of a small bear.

Shetland animals do have difficulties of scale. The cattle, the ponies, and the sheep are smaller (and some of the sheep are spotted like dalmatians too), but Shetland mice are bigger. The winds are bigger too. I had landed in what was called a breeze but seemed to me half a gale. Miss Manson said the strongest recorded gust was 126mph, at which Mr Mullay said there had immediately afterwards been a stronger one, because it blew the anemometer right over a cliff. There is in fact one planted clump of trees in all the isles, and everyone stops to wonder at it. If trees were native, there would be a hundred names for their different parts, because Shetland is rich in words. There are words for every particularity of snow. A mourie caavie is snow so thick you can't see in it. Faans is a snowdrift. And what, Miss Manson asked herself, was the word for a huge flake? There was a word: it would come to her mind in February when she next saw one. What Shetland has are wild flowers with so strong a fragrance that fishermen, far out, can fix their position by the scent on the wind; and birds such as puffin, great skua, whimbrel, plover, and guillemot; and one neck of land so narrow that you can throw a stone the hundred yards from the North Sea to the Atlantic; and, besides, there is a road sign saying, 'Caution, Otters Crossing.' It is all very Norse.

It is even said there today that the Vikings did not deserve their bloodthirsty reputation: in a bloodthirsty world they were just better at the job than most. Next morning I learned the word for a huge snowflake. James Nicholson told me, at Scalloway. 'Skalva,' he said immediately, and then told me other things. Aali meant to entice with food or kindness. To stylk was to injure with a stalk of corn. This is all an extra vocabulary. The language of Shetland is enriched English. There is no Gaelic. Indeed there are so many Chinese restaurants that the second language may be Cantonese. I saw fried rice and chips offered for £1.75.

At Scalloway the Klondikers lay anchored in the bay. These are factory ships from eastern Europe which pay Shetland fisherman £110 a ton for their catch, and then gut, marinate, and barrel it. The crews come freely ashore without passports. Then of course there is oil. BP has recently handed the islands council a cheque for £5 million as land rent for the oil terminal at Sullom Voe. This is regarded as an insult. The council thinks it should be £100m a year. BP are called pirates and 'billionaire squatters.'

Never mind, there are consolations. More salmon are being caught in the clear, fresh waters, which can hardly, therefore, be at all polluted by oil. And Shetland is a place where the Post Office still works. Post a letter before 10 am in Lerwick, the capital, and it is often delivered on the islands that same afternoon.

One of the last things I heard before I left Shetland, and the first I heard when I arrived in Orkney, was that a Shetlander is a fisherman with a croft, and that an Orcadian is a farmer with a fishing boat. You can see the truth of this at a glance. Shetland is rugged, and all fjords: Orkney is softer, flatter, greener – desolate only when the sun goes in. And it does feel much farther south than Shetland. The southern point of Orkney is only seven miles north of John O'Groats. But where is it historically? One of the splendours of Orkney is the cathedral of St Magnus at Kirkwall, which this year celebrates its 850th anniversary. The diocese of Orkney was first subordinate to the archdiocese of Hamburg, in 1154 was transferred to the Norse see of Trondheim, and only in 1472 (after the same dynastic marriage that made Shetland Scottish) did it come under the jurisdiction of St Andrews. But Orkney is not so adamantly un-Scottish as Shetland, though, on first hearing, the lilting Orkney voice sounds Welsh.

That isn't true of Alistair Scholes's voice. He is the councillor who runs tourism. He has lived there for years but is still regarded as a ferrylouper – someone who loped off the ferry. This may have something to do with his Glasgow accent, which is the thickest I ever heard. He is an accountant, he runs a BMW and a Mercedes, and at dinner he made it clear that he wanted no two-postcard tourists, only big spenders. Well, Orkney is not poor. The council gets £1m a year in barrelage from the oil companies. The fishermen of Westray can earn £19,000 a year, though in a four-day voyage they may get only four hours' sleep. As for tourists, they tend to be rather of the Adventurous Club of Denmark kind, who do crazy things like running husky races to the Pole, and last year turned up trying to buy Orkney back for 60,000 old Danish florins.

Still, it's not all mad, big-spending Danes. The story I liked best when I was there was that of Mr George Sinclair, shopkeeper, who said that customers had been apprehensive he would change things when he took over from David Foubister, but he didn't like fancy displays and had seen no reason for change. It then emerged that Mr Sinclair, who was now retiring at the age of 80, had taken over from Mr Foubister no less than 40 years ago.

What Orkney mostly has, apart from the northmost whisky distillery, is archeology, and an unmatched history of maritime wreckage. There are stone circles like Stonehenge, and neolithic villages like Skara Brae, which was inundated with sand just as Pompeii was with lava, and was in the same way preserved. There is a chambered tomb, built about 2700BC and later looted by Vikings, one of whom scratched the following runic inscription: 'Ingebor is the loveliest woman.'

And then the wrecks. Here, in Scapa Flow, 74 interned ships of the German high seas fleet scuttled themselves on June 21 1919. It is not a story that redounds to the credit of the victorious allies, who showed a shameful lack of magnanimity to a defeated enemy, and a miraculous incompetence in providing that enemy with an anchorage deep enough to suggest and encourage scuttling. Unless, of course, that was a not unwelcome result: rather no ships left than have to share them out among the allied navies? Most were raised for salvage, but *SMS König, Markgraf,* and *Kronprinz Wilhelm*, together with other smaller vessels, still lie at the bottom.

There too is the wreck of *HMS Royal Oak*, torpedoed by a U-boat in 1939. Every year the Royal Navy sends down divers to lay a new ensign over her, and has just had to deny that this custom would cease. It's just that a smaller flag will be used from now on. The charm of these northern islands is distance, but their trouble is distance too. Most people manage. Some never leave the islands at all. Some leave and return. I spent an afternoon with a young woman who had lived ten years in Paris, of all places, and had happily returned. But distance is expensive. British Airways' ordinary one way fare Shetland-London is £144. Shetland-Glasgow is £113, one way. You can roam around for a lot less, getting a Highland Rover airpass which gives you eight flights, all between different destinations, for £157.

I am an enthusiast for aeroplanes. My father was an engineer, and some things stay in the blood. On these Highlands and Islands routes British Airways fly 748s, twin-engined jet props of the same sort the Queen's Flight uses. I came back from Orkney to Aberdeen on the flight deck of a plane called Glen Fiddich. The first officer flew it. The captain, who had come back to what he called real flying after 10 years of long hauls on Boeing 747s, pointed out first the oil terminal in Scapa, and then the contours of the Scottish mainland. 'Cross wind from the left,' he said, as we came into Aberdeen. 'Crabbing in a bit.' 'Thanks for the comfort, sir,' said his young first officer. Having returned from far northern parts, we touched down gently on the tarmac of what those fierce northerners would call the adjacent island group.

Terry Coleman

Bathing machine trundles back into fashion
January 5 1988

The tide is turning, at last, for the horse-drawn bathing machine. Its
return to the British beach seems likely at the resort where George
III, stark naked, first took the plunge 199 years ago. Weymouth,
in Dorset, is considering a plan to bring back the sort of bathing
carriage last seen more than half a century ago. The new machine,
which may make an appearance this summer, will be larger but, in
other respects, more modest than the wagon which bore the bare
monarch into the briny. King George's personal bathing carriage
was embellished with the royal coat of arms and a lion's head door
knocker. He was escorted into the sea by maids, with their flannel
skirts tucked up, and fully-dressed bandsmen who stood knee-deep in
the waves playing God Save Great King George. Victorian bathers
at Weymouth 75 years later had to be a little more circumspect. By
then the bathing machine operators were required to provide carpets,
a looking glass and, for male bathers, pairs of drawers. A bylaw was
introduced in 1864, laying down that any bathing machine must
remain separated by at least 50 yards from another used by members
of the opposite sex, on pain of a one Pounds fine. A man bathing
without drawers after 8am was liable to be charged with indecency.
The return of the bathing machine, hauled into the sea by a shire
horse, is being put to Weymouth and Portland borough council as
part of a package of proposals designed to enhance the Georgian
seafront. Other elements of the scheme include the creation of a
beach bar and barbecue on the sands and a 'continental' sunbathing
area with ranks of sunbeds and parasols. Mr Harvey Bailey, the
borough's leisure and entertainments general manager, said the
idea was to add to the resort's character. King George's carriage
remains preserved in Weymouth museum. He first descended on
the town in 1789, the year of his recovery from derangement. His

condition had given rise to concern when he approached a young tree, shook it warmly by the branch and struck up a conversation with it. Weymouth's health-giving properties were later celebrated by the clown Joseph Grimaldi in a verse: There are bathing machines in a row/That you ride in to pickle your skin/ Kept by Scriven, Ford, Saxon and Co./ They will cleanse you of all but your sin.

Andrew Moncur

A degree up the Celsius scale – fourth division England
March 9 1988

Well, you can't be too unkind about Devon, can you? Not when you've been to some of the places I've been to lately. It does look splendid. And the average temperature is a good degree and a quarter Celsius above London's. Never has so much been made out of one and a quarter measly degrees. In 1847 *Murray's Handbook* assured its readers that Torquay's climate would cure 'lassitude and depression.' In 1857 C. Radclyffe Hall, 'physician to the Institution for Reduced Gentlewomen Affected with Diseases of the Chest', helped popularise the place by recommending it to sufferers from chronic bronchitis, asthma, chronic affections of the mucous membrane, neuralgia, pure rheumatism &c &c. In those days, when it was the height of fashion to be swooningly delicate or at the very least have something chronic in your mucous membrane, that must have constituted extremely sophisticated municipal marketing. Torquay is still at it today; it's just the approach that has changed. This year Torbay borough council is running an advertising campaign using the time-honoured slogan 'The English Riviera', making comparisons with Cannes, Miami and Deauville, and showing pictorial combinations of palm trees, birds in wet swimsuits, melting lollipops and skies the colour of a Greek August. 'Come off it,' I said to Tim Whitehead, the borough tourism officer, 'it's never that blue.' 'It is,' he said defensively,

looking out of the window into the February twilight. 'Sometimes.'
And even in February, it is true, the breeze felt surprisingly kind and
unrheumaticky, and the town was surprisingly lively.

Arriving in February at an English seaside resort, especially one
with a fourth division football team, you expect howling winds,
creaking shutters and streets deserted but for the odd stray cat. In
fact by the harbourside even some of the souvenir shops were open,
selling clotted cream toffees and porcelain pixies; one of them sold
a bucket and spade the other week. Madam Rosina the palmist was
closed. But generally trade, if not roaring, at least proceeded at an
acceptable winter whimper. However, something else surprised me.
Having been in Burnley and Hartlepool, I came to Torquay seeking
contrast. In fact, the three towns have more in common than Torquay
will ever admit. The characteristic of fourth division England seems
to be dependence on one inexorably declining industry. In this case
it happens not to be coal or cotton or ships but another product of
the same era: the English seaside family holiday.

Just after I arrived, I sat down for a cuppa in the Tudor Rose
tea rooms. A pair of elderly ladies were at the next table. 'We were
madly, passionately in love at the time,' one of them was saying
between mouthfuls of toasted tea cake, 'but now he gets on my
wick.' At the time I just counted this as a splendid eavesdrop. But
I came to realise that this was the essence of the town's problem.
Couples don't often choose Torquay these days when they are
madly, passionately in love; it is a place for people who have started
to get on each other's wick. Hence Mr Whitehead and his posters.
'Repositioning the resort's image,' is the official phrase.

What it means is that if you want to arrive from Swinton in
August with your knotted handkerchief you are still welcome.
As long as you pay your money you can take your choice. But
Torquay would rather you brought your executive sales team or
your 12-metre yacht. In the past 10 years the number of overnight
stays in Torbay (including the adjoining resorts of Paignton and

Brixham) has dropped by 22 per cent. There is still plenty of money sloshing about, heaven knows – property prices may be higher than anywhere else outside the south-east – but there are plenty of losers too. Winter unemployment is 18 per cent, the highest in Devon; and it falls only to about 15 per cent in high season when there are more jobs, sure, but many more people after them. Much of the work is breadline stuff anyway: kitchen portering and the like. 'Put a £100 a week job up here,' says the Job Centre manager Dan Cowan, 'and it's gone like a shot.'

The two Torquays sit uneasily and uncomprehendingly together. I presumed I wouldn't get past the door of the Royal Torbay Yacht Club so I went instead to Factory Row, the inappropriately named setting for the unemployment centre. This turned out to be even more depressing than I imagined. Factory Row has two main rooms, one a sort of day centre which was full of people playing chess and darts and listening to Radio 1. The other is an engineering workshop where a genial Yorkshireman called Ted Whitaker is willing to teach his skills to all comers. Mr Whitaker was sitting alone reading a fat novel; he has been sitting alone for much of the past 18 months. 'They're not interested,' he said sadly. 'The young lasses, they'll start a project and work right and see it through. But the young lads.' He shrugged. 'They have a look of despondency about them. I'm a little bit discouraged. In 18 months I can honestly say I can count on the fingers of two hands the people who've really got some benefit out of the place.'

So much for Torquay curing lassitude and depression. Bed-and-breakfast places have to decide which market they are chasing: the tourists or the homeless and jobless. Many of the adverts for accommodation in the evening papar have phrases like 'No DHSS,' modern Torquay's equivalent of 'No coloureds.' Torquay does have a working working class. Plainmoor, home of the football club, is a suburb well away from the sea which was built originally for the footmen and coachmen of Torquay's fashionable 19th century invalids. But most of the men there work for the gas or the electricity of the buses or something. The enthusiastic way the council officials list the town's industries is the giveaway that they don't really have that many to list.

'They're unbelievably dictatorial,' says David Smith, the Alliance leader. 'The mayor is always Tory, standing orders are manipulated to the Tories' advantage and we don't even get a say in which of our councillors goes on what committee. If they want to get a good speaker off a certain committee they just do it. They don't ask us anything. Torbay is actually run by a very small clique. Most of the Tories just put their hands up to agree.'

Similar comments were made to me several times by different people and Tony Key, the council leader, was not in the least surprised when I mentioned them. 'I presume,' he said finally, 'the same allegations are made against Liverpool. We most emphatically do take note of the opposition's ideas but some of the things they put up are crazy. And our party certainly doesn't agree on everything. We meet as a group in private on the Thursday before council and have our arguments there. There's nothing unusual about it.'

Some critics will name the handful of lawyers and businessmen who they reckon really run the town. But Torquay's future will actually be decided by the outsiders who vote with their feet on Mr Whitehead's repositioning of the image: on the new conference centre (set to lose £2m in its first year), theme parks, shopping centres and marinas; on the attempts to build up holidays based on nature rambles or sporting activities or the area's historical connections. Now this is the big year for Torbay history: 300 years ago William of Orange landed in Brixham Harbour to take the British throne and there is going to be a bit of a fuss about it come summertime. But the glorious revolution and all that does not rank high in our political culture these days, never mind popular culture – unless Torbay is chasing the Northern Ireland market. And other than that, it is a bit of a struggle to find Torbay's history.

Brunel almost lived here, according to the local historian John Pike; Bulwer Lytton caught pneumonia here; Agatha Christie got her expertise in poison by working in the hospital during the first war; and the sewing-machine Singer family lived at Paignton in a totally over-the-top mansion which now houses the borough environmental health officer. There was also Napoleon, who was in Torquay in July and August 1815. Well, not exactly in Torquay, you understand, but in the bay – aboard the *Bellerephon*, a prisoner of the British awaiting his departure to St Helena. About 1,000 pleasure boats a day were rented out to trippers who would occasionally be rewarded by the sight of the conquered titan and an exchange of pleasantries: '*Enfin, voila un beau pays*,' Boney would say.

Present-day visitors, of course, arrive from Paddington rather than Waterloo. The French connection is now kept going by the signs saying Town Centre (Centre Ville), a smattering of language schools and all this Cannes and Deauville guff. Mr Whitehead can take the place upmarket if he wants but I can't quite buy this jetset playground idea. Torquay is a place for love to flicker unsteadily and then be dissected over the toasted tea-cakes. It is extremely and exquisitely English – almost our secret, like the rest of Devon. I drove back east with a heavy heart and sure enough, just past Newton Abbot, it felt a good degree and a quarter colder.

Matthew Engel

Peninsular pleasures
April 9 1988

Beyond the collieries, steelworks and rugby-redolent names like Neath, Bridgend and Swansea, and close by the heron-priested shores of Dylan Thomas, lies a tongue of arable land whose elders are reported to remember a time when no Welshman lived among them. Gower – it is never prefixed with 'the' – is Gower because of an invasion which succeeded and one that never happened. Hastening from Hastings, the Normans – wily assessors – split the peninsula geologically. They kept the rich land of the south and east for themselves and drove the indigenous Welsh into a bleaker environment and a life of animal grazing – later coal-mining – rather than crop growing. A string of castles and fortified manors formed a stone manacle around their possession. This manacle is inset with a cluster of coastal villages: Llangennith, Rhosili, Port Eynon, Horton, Oxwich.

This last is probably the jewel: a tiny, white-scrubbed settlement looking out across its bay and a flat reedy nature reserve. It is watched from above by its castle – not at present open to the public – and from a distance by the faded grandeur of Penrice Castle. Penrice had its days of glory at the turn of the century; apparently Edward VII, when Prince of Wales, would stay here. Now sheep graze on its diminished estate. The other villages are similar to Oxwich. They are coastal dead-ends reached, Purbeck-like, by narrow lanes. Anyone wishing to drive from one to the other must always do three sides of a rectangle. Bumpy fields act as a carpark-cum-camp site, and now the tiny post offices have a trendy young cousin, a 'surf shop'. Some flat-roof blight – the sites of fixed caravans – can dull the picturesque limestone and whitewashed cottages.

And there other shades of Dorset's Purbeck coastline show: the same mix of walkers, wind-surfers, and jolly family outings. 'Emphatically a district for the pedestrian,' wrote Baedeker. Parents stroll and children scramble to explore caverns, pools, and limestone quarries. One can add pony-trekking and boardsailing which, as Baedeker might have put it, is prosecuted here with great success. Go though, early in the season when the landlords still have time to chat and the broad beaches belong to you. At Llangennith I stayed at Mrs Kneath's bed-and-breakfast. She's an epitome of Gower. 'I've only ever lived in two houses, you see: the one I was born in and this one.' Her birthplace stands 30 yards away. Yet she is no product of simple isolation. Her accent is Gower's unique, lightly intoned blend of Welsh and West Country. Her grandfather was a Norwegian sailor by the name of Knutsen who was shipwrecked off Gower. He stayed, married, and died in his accidentally adopted home. It would be easy to become a lotus-eater here. (Most settle for a holiday home.) Now Mrs Kneath accommodates Belgians, Dutch, and Germans: no shipwrecked sailors but boardsailers all.

It's typical of Gower. The people have been traders, seafarers and smugglers, and have remained detached from their mainland links, rather as Cornwall has done. Staring out of her living-room window across her back-garden potato patch and towards the weird tufted dunes which form a sandy fence between her and Rhosili Bay, Mrs Kneath recalls how Gower's rape was averted: 'The big house, well we always called it the big house, was owned by the old colonel. He loved Gower, you see, but he was an odd man. We had to be very careful when we walked to the beach. You couldn't stray off the path, you know.

'But when they wanted to build a road to Rhosili, if you please, well he wouldn't have it. They were going to have hotels all the way round, if you please. And then, you know, the war came and that was that. And there you are, you see.'

Soon after the war local farmers resisted the blandishments of Billy Butlin, and Gower soon became one of the first parts of Britain to be designated an area of outstanding natural beauty. We remain indebted, in part at least, to the threatening noise of Adolf Hitler. I felt that gratitude on first coming through the malformed tussocky dunes on to the beach of Rhosili Bay. A vast cuticle of unsullied sand arcs for miles, coming to a distant point at Worms Head where, in fables, a crippled and illegitimate boy was rescued from the sea by a flock of seagulls. When a young man he travelled to the other end of the bay, Burry Holms, where he lived and prayed.

The legend of St Cenydd still imbues this coast with Celtic mysticism, although it helps to visit on a grey wintry afternoon when the sea and sky are cold and churning. Celtic mystery dissipates fast in sunshine, sandwiches, beer cans, and beach cricket. Only so many can fit on to the peninsula in the summer, but even they chase away the vulnerable ghosts of old Gower. And every year a few more of these ghosts fail to return in the winter.

Stuart Rock

Fighting for the beaches
April 13 1988

Britain's first good beach guide has been published by the Marine Conservation Society as part of a clean-up campaign. The guide, compiled by Dr Anne Scott, was based on surveys last summer by hundreds of volunteers. It lists the whole range of beach types and highlights those worth protecting.

Dr Scott had no qualms about excluding some of Britain's most popular beaches from her guide of 180, including Blackpool and Yarmouth and several others whose sewage-infected waters put them outside EEC standards for bathing beaches – the first criterion for inclusion. She left out others because they are overlooked by heavy industry or nuclear power stations, a fate which may get Druridge Bay in Northumberland dropped from future editions if the Central Electricity Generating Board goes ahead with its plans to build a power station there.

Distant bangs from the artillery range next door have not, however, disqualified Lulworth Cove, Dorset, one of Dr Scott's favourites. Brighton is in favour too. 'The exciting, exotic and rather naughty seaside poster image remains,' Dr Scott said. So too are Eastbourne, Newquay and Llandudno, which gets an extra accolade as another of her 23 personal recommendations. This is just as well for north westerners on the other side of Liverpool Bay because Mersey pollution ensures that only Freshfield at Formby, qualifies.

'We don't want people not to go to these beaches,' Dr Scott says. 'Blackpool can still be a fun day out. But if you slam the beaches, people may become aware that they have problems and press the authorities to do something about them. 'We aim to get people thinking about what a good beach is. Some beaches are threatened by over-use, erosion, litter and so on. If we highlight what makes a good beach, maybe that will make people use them more carefully.' She admits, however, that once water quality, litter, access and other features have been taken into account, there is inevitably an element of personal choice. For Dr Scott, the ideal beach is 'far away with miles of golden sand.' And where is it? Like a true enthusiast of the remote and unspoiled shore, she prefers to keep that to herself. 'There are some that are excluded for that very reason – ones that would suffer if they had a lot of people suddenly appearing on them,' she confesses.

John Ardill

Peeping Geoffrey
July 21 1988

It's a fun book that I've always wanted to write, *The Canderel Guide To Beachwatching* (Rambletree Publishing, £4.95): a field guide to manwatching (or rather people watching) on the beach, something I have always been very interested in. I wrote it as a psychologist specifically for the interested layman, the kind of person who has spent many hours on beaches watching the comings and goings, wondering what it all means, if anything.

'But surely,' the sceptical reader will say, 'all that is happening on the beach is that people are trying to relax after a hard year in the office or factory? Surely their behaviour – the reclining on the sand, the beach football, the charges into the sea, the play fighting, the posture, the improbable bodily configuration or two doesn't actually mean anything in particular? It's just people relaxing and not doing a lot, and psychologists as usual trying to read too much into it.'

Well perhaps, but as the American psychologists Watzlawick, Beavin and Jackson wrote some 20 years ago: 'No matter how one may try, one cannot not communicate. Activity or inactivity, words or silence, all have message value: they influence others and these others, in turn, cannot not respond to these communications and are thus themselves communicating. The man at the crowded lunch counter who looks straight ahead, or the aeroplane passenger who sits with his eyes closed, are both communicating that they do not want to speak to anybody or be spoken to, and their neighbours usually 'get the message' and respond appropriately by leaving them alone. This obviously is just as much an interchange of communication as an animated discussion.'

Beaches are in fact a particularly good location to study human behaviour for a number of quite different reasons (apart from the obvious, that you can acquire a tan whilst you are doing it).

First, beaches are public places and behaviour is highly visible on the beach. Back in the office, you may be able to conceal your posture – behind the furniture, for example.

Second, although people do talk on beaches, often in quite distinctive ways, nonverbal communication, or body language as it is popularly known, plays a much more important role here. This is partly because it is not concealed (either by clothes or furniture), and partly because you end up sitting close to total strangers, whom you might not know well enough to talk to, but with whom you still can't help communicating through all the other means available to human beings, such as bodily posture, eye contact, and spacing. But how good are human beings at communicating through these other more primitive channels of communication? What misunderstandings arise because of differences in cultural or social background?

Third, beaches pose quite specific problems for urban man (and woman). People almost invariably remove at least some proportion of their clothing on the beach, and as we all know urban man relies on his clothes for sending out important (and instantaneous) messages about him or herself – about status, group membership, position in society. How does urban man and woman compensate when some of these props are not available any longer? And what happens when none of them are available, as with the nude sunbather? Beaches can be very crowded places, so they present special difficulties for the regulation of human behaviour.

A good deal of research exists which demonstrates that crowding can be associated with all kinds of social problems, perhaps most notably with violence. But beaches aren't necessarily associated with any of these problems. Why is that? I have spent many happy hours beach watching and contemplating some of these issues in a variety of locations from Skegness to St Tropez, from Cleethorpes to California.

In my experience, you can't get research funds to study behaviour on beaches, unfortunately. Like many other people who are to be found on beaches I sometimes feel a little guilty about sitting there all day, doing nothing. They end up playing endless games of beach cricket. I end up carrying out endless studies of people. The result of all this guilt and all those long days in the sun is the present book: a field guide to the shedding of clothes, if not inhibitions, the play fighting on the sand and in the water involving apparently mature adults, the defences of group territory and the territorial displays that people engage in on the beach, the public and private talk that tell us all so much, the silent communication carried out by postural patterns and postural echo and the intricate patterns of eye gaze, all furtive glances and blatant stares, that regulate and govern so much of human social interaction. The stuff of everyday life, all right.

Needless to say, the media has had a field day. You might say that I was asking for it. I admit that it wasn't entirely unexpected; indeed, the fact that Canderel were prepared to put some money into the book, which meant that all the illustrations could be in glorious colour, reinforced my faith that the book wouldn't be entirely ignored. But the magnitude of the interest, the ferocity of the interest, did surprise me.

A leading marketing consultancy company had been hired to co-ordinate the media campaign. There was meant to be a press embargo in operation until July 11, the book's publication date, but on May 11, the *Daily Telegraph* ran a short piece in their Peterborough column. The flood gates opened. Editors of major Sunday newspapers rang me direct to beg for serialisation rights. The *News Of The World* phoned to ask for an exlusive on 'bottoms.' 'Has anyone else got the bottom angle yet? Bottoms are in this year, and we want them.' I said that there wasn't much about bottoms in the book. 'Come off it, there has to be. Just answer me this – why do people bare their bottoms on the beach?' I said that I had no idea. 'What's the use of a book on beachwatching, if you can't answer that then?' And they put the phone down.

An American radio station asked me if I just did woman watching on the beach. When I told them that of course I watched men as well, and that it was a book about people watching, they hung up on me. The *Sunday Mirror* had me as a 'top psychologist' and a 'prof' getting 'an academic eyeful'. *De Telegraaf,* the Amsterdam newspaper, sent a photographer, who took me to a builder's yard. 'Just climb into the sand there with those binoculars,' he said. I told him that it might give the wrong impression. So after a few dozen photographs, he started sneaking the binoculars into the picture. 'Can we just leave them balanced on your knee then?' he asked pleadingly.

I sat in a variety of radio stations, which all looked the same, with the same ashtray and the same half-smoked cigar from some previous occupant obviously trying to maintain his or her image. The interviewer from Radio Sheffield said that she really liked the book when we met, but as the interview started she accused me in no uncertain terms of being both sexist and chauvinistic, because of the nature of some of the captions to the photographs. I tried to explain. I hadn't actually written the captions; they had been written by the wife of the publisher. 'They were written by a woman?' she blurted out. She was gobsmacked. 'What are you responsible for, then?' 'Just the maintext', I replied. It was rather like being accused of writing the headings on articles in the *Guardian* or the captions for the photographs that accompany the articles.

It's been an interesting time. I've probably learned more about people in the past few weeks than I did during my holidays. And I haven't even started yet. The publicity starts in earnest in the next few weeks: the Spanish, German, and Australian media are just starting to get in on the act (and act surely is the operative word). And now I hear *Sunday Sport* want an interview. 'If you don't talk to them, they can get very difficult. Just talk to them as if you are talking to a psychologist,' came the helpful advice from the marketing company.

Dr Geoffrey Beattie

A jolly good job on offer
July 29 1988

One of Britain's oddest jobs – impersonating the Jolly Fisherman of Skegness – is on offer as a matter of some urgency. The task of stamping round the Lincolnshire resort in waders, sou'wester, pipe and optional rubber tummy-stuffing has fallen vacant just before a planned reunion of more than 100 previous holders of the post.

Based on John Hassall's 1908 railway poster, the real-life Jolly Fisherman has become an important part of the town's attempts to rival cheap holidays overseas. For the past five years, the job has been full-time from May to September, with its holder welcoming trains, posing with children and holding beach birthday parties. Mr Les Shepherd, the resort's entertainments officer, said: 'The Jolly Fisherman is to Skegness what Mickey Mouse is to Disneyland or the Tower to Blackpool.'

Hurried adverts for the post, £2.56-an-hour with overtime available on a basic 35-hour week, have gone out after this year's two successive Jolly Fishermen landed all-the-year-round jobs. One possible perk is the chance to earn the Jolly Fisherman statuette awarded to people who have given particular service to Skegness. Holders include Princess Margaret, the wrestler Big Daddy and Edward Heath.

Martin Wainwright

Swallows' voyage of rediscovery
May 18 1989

It was very much a boat on dry land, marooned on trestles in an Ipswich park. The three ex-crew members who boarded her again yesterday for the first time in 55 years were sisters in their 50s and 60s, past any halcyon years afloat. But it and they were the stuff of childhood fable, equally potent for reminiscent greyheads in the audience at the East Coast Boat Show and for the little girl who got her father up at 6am to drive her from Yorkshire to get their autographs.

The yacht was the *Nancy Blackett*, which belonged to the children's writer Arthur Ransome, 'the best little boat I ever owned.' She was discovered rotting two years ago by an enthusiast, Mike Rines, and restored to youth. The sisters – brought together for the first time in public – were three of the original Swallows and Amazons who sailed her as the children of an Anglo-Irish Armenian family, the Altounyans, who befriended Ransome in 1930. There was Able Seaman Nancy the tomboy (Mrs Taqui Stephens), practical Susan (Mrs Susan Villard) and baby Bridget (Mrs Brigit Sanders) who to her enduring resentment was mostly left behind on voyages.

'It hasn't been yuppiefied,' Mrs Stephens said with relief. 'It still holds ghosts of memory for me. I remember lying on that forecastle bunk there. I spent a lot of my early life trying to prove that *Swallows and Amazons* wasn't our only existence. Now, funnily enough, I feel much more like Nancy than I ever did then.' Mrs Villard said: 'The boat seems much smaller than I remembered.' Mrs Sanders said she was overjoyed to see it 'resurrected.'

Ransome bought the craft in 1935, five years after leaving the *Manchester Guardian*, for which he covered the Russian revolution. The then editor, Ted Scott, who was desperate to keep him, wrote to a colleague: 'He has some stupid notion of a personal career.' By 1935, Ransome's career as author of the 12-novel *Swallows and Amazons* was established. At a time when there were often only two other yachts on the river Orwell, the wooden, eight-ton *Nancy Blackett* was counted a relatively big, prestige vessel.

The original lads and lasses of Ransome's stories now have 56 grandchildren. Mrs Stephens worked for the information section of the 1940s Palestine mandate. She married Robert Stephens, the *Observer*'s ex-diplomatic correspondent. Mrs Villard went to France and married a BP executive. Mrs Sanders wed a diplomat whose last post was as British ambassador in Panama. The boat, restored with the help of sponsorship from Black and Decker, will now house a new generation of children on voyages for the Cerdan Trust, which specialises in the disadvantaged. Over a private lunch, the sisters talked of absent Swallows – of the indomitable humourist Roger, who has died, and of the idealistic Titty, now grieving after the death of a daughter.

John Ezard

Beach nudity row prompts trust vote
August 24 1989

Nude bodies on a Dorset beach have forced a vote of 1,780,672 National Trust members. Believing bequests to the trust are being used for what is termed 'trendy purposes', 10 members have asked it to ban nudity as 'contrary to the spirit of the trust'. But the trust has been advised that it cannot stop people taking off their clothes on its property. Instead, it has put up notices warning visitors that 'nudists may be seen beyond this point'.

Corfe Castle estate was bequeathed to the trust in 1985, along with three miles of beach at Studland Bay used by naturists. Under pressure from the anti-naturist lobby, the trust put up the warning notices. But a spokeswoman for its council, Miss Emma O'Reilly, said: 'We have more complaints about noisy radios and dogs.' Of 1,200 people interviewed on the beach, 11 per cent objected to litter, 13 per cent to dogs, and only 2 per cent to the nudes. Some 16 per cent said they had come specifically to take their clothes off. Miss O'Reilly said: 'We try to be fair. Simple nudity is not a problem if people take their clothes off in secluded bits of our properties where they can be private. In any event we have been told we cannot get a bylaw to stop it, so we tolerate it. We are not a moral arbiter.'

Mr Rowland Hitchcott, the proposer of the resolution, said: 'Nudist areas effectively restrict access to these areas for certain groups – such as families, youth groups and individuals – who would wish to avoid them. This is contrary to the spirit of the trust.' Mr Ernest Stanley, controller of the Naturist Foundation, said nude bathing was for families. 'It is only voyeurs, male exhibitionists and parties of homosexuals who make a thundering nuisance of themselves that give rise to misgivings in ordinary decent people.'

Mr Hitchcott's resolution before the November annual meeting is likely to get a large majority. He claims the wording would force a nudity ban. The trust disagrees, but recommends members vote for it. Thereafter, the council says, nudists can carry on as before.

Paul Brown

Messing About in Boats: 1990-1999

Sailing in the North Sea
April 25 1990

The North Sea can be many things to many people. A sea of shallows and treacherous banks to those yachtsmen and fishermen who frequent the coasts of Essex and Suffolk; further north, on the east coast of England, a cold unfriendly sea which is slow to warm with the year. Yet, especially in the landlocked southern parts, equally slow to lose its summer warmth as the seabirds head out of its coastal habitats for winter quarters. Where the great knuckle of Norfolk sticks out provocatively into any northern blast there is bleakness and the imperative necessity of the Cromer lifeboat.

Sheltered havens have been created at the entrances to the rivers but getting into them, when the gale-force winds gather, is often a difficult and dangerous business calling for the same high degree of seamanship from the weekend sailor that the North Sea fishermen have had to learn in order to survive. The east coast is not a forgiving coast. The coasts of Sussex and Kent may have equally few harbours making for long hauls between one haven and another but somehow the south coast feels friendlier.

Maybe it is because of the long, low stretches of shingle beach that typically embrace such names as Dunwich, Aldeburgh and Southwold, small East Anglian communities lost at the end of no through roads. North of the Wash the coast roads stand even further back from the sea than they do in East Anglia. Further north again, where the curious claws of the Holderness offer the north-going sailor a challenge to the rounding of Flamborough Head, coastal habitation is the exception rather than the rule before the resorts of Yorkshire are reached. Large numbers of cruising yachts ply these coasts. The North Sea is their pond and the creeks, harbours, estuaries and marinas are fine hopping-off points for the coasts of the Low Countries. That often means the convolutions of the Schelde Estuary. A favourite starting point being the yacht harbour at Breskens on the southern shore of the Westerschelde that offers a shake-down haven before slipping across to Vlissingen and so into the Walcheren canal.

But the whole of the Dutch coast is open to the east coast yachtsman and it is a simple matter to cruise up round the corner of the Waddenzee to that pearl necklace of islands, the East Friesians, which ends with Wangerooge. However, on this side of the water there is one bit of nastiness that the North Sea spawns that is haar, fog so thick that in its clammy embrace may well seem like being entangled in hair. It will be well-remembered by veterans of the US Eighth Air Force as sometimes a greater hazard than the flak and the fighters when worn out aircraft and crews returned to find that haar had swept in across their East Anglian airfields. Today, just as then, North Sea haars wing in on the back of north-east winds. Air that leaves Scandinavia quite dry gathers water vapour with every mile it travels over the sea. The journey is long enough for the air to become laden with moisture and great banks of disorientating sea fog are the result. Yet, in the southern

North Sea especially, the wind only needs to shift a couple of points east and the fog clears as if by magic.

Alan Watts

A Country Diary
May 2 1990

LINCS AND NORFOLK: I have just spent a few days visiting nature reserves and especially, bird observatories around the Wash. My first was Gibraltar Point, renowned as an arrival and departure point for passage migrants. But, no doubt owing to the adverse conditions for departure – a strong and coolish wind from off the North Sea – no migrants were spotted apart from a single ring ousel, and therefore I turned my attention to the flora, and here what engaged my attention was the prevalence of miniature forms of familiar species. Thus the early forget-me-not (Myositis ramosissima), instead of being a few inches high and across, was blooming immediately on the surface of a rosette of foliage which could have been hidden by a 10p piece. Even more striking were dwarf forms of lamb's lettuce (Valeriana locusta) on similarly sized rosettes which were entirely of a pale mauve, for the flowers concealed the foliage beneath. Everywhere beneath the scrub of hawthorn and sea buckthorn the bright green foliage of spring beauty (the alien Montia perfoliata) formed complete ground-cover, and when I came across dwarf specimens of this on dry open ground, the truth dawned upon me these miniatures were not, as I had half suspected, some local sub-species, but merely starved specimens.

As to birds, a visit to the RSPB reserve at Titchwell, on the Norfolk corner of the Wash, lived up to expectations. Apart from renewing acquaintance with no less than 12 species of waders on the shore, I spent a fascinating hour watching a magnificent male marsh harrier patrolling the reeds, and for good measure, the brief appearance of two females which rose to join him, whilst all the while, immediately below where I sat, three bearded tits allowed fleeting glimpses of their activities up and down the reed-stems. On calling at the reserve office to report the sighting of a spotted redshank, apart from the purring of a turtle-dove and the songs of willow warbler, chiffchaff, and lesser whitethroat, all in the bushes around, the farewell bonus came in the form of a cuckoo which flew between me and the door.

W D Campbell

Barbara Hepworth's studio and garden
May 12 1990

Artists came to Cornwall in the 20th century the way Irish saints came in the dark ages. Most of the artists settled on the Penwith peninsula and most of those in St Ives. When Ben Nicholson arrived with Christopher Wood, they found an old sailor turned rag and bone man painting pictures on scraps of cardboard. His name was Alfred Wallis and, through their influence on Nicholson, his pictures helped to funnel one of the channels in the delta of 20th century art. Wallis's paintings were as fresh as mackerel and clear as a map of the town. The bright red, yellow and blue fishing boats bobbing in the harbour, the little lighthouse at the end of Smeaton's pier, the granite church tower that acts like a lodestone for tourists became leitmotifs in the grumpy old fisherman's painting. The effect on Nicholson was equivalent to Picasso's discovery of African sculpture.

On a wet day in August 1939 Nicholson brought his wife to safety in Carbis Bay, she reluctant and dragging with her their triplets. He stayed until after the marriage broke up in 1951. She stayed until 1975, when she fell asleep with a cigarette between her fingers; Mrs Nicholson (aka Barbara Hepworth) died in the fire, but her studio and workshop survive as the Barbara Hepworth museum. It's run by the Tate Gallery and, by 1992, the Tate should have a second

St Ives exhibition space, exhibiting its collection of the other St Ives artists, like Roger Hilton, Peter Lanyon and Bryan Wynter. National Heritage and the European Community have chipped in though there is, in the best tradition of these things, some local opposition, summed up in a letter to the *Cornishman* by the proprietor of the aptly-named harbour-front amusement arcade, Cuckoo Land.

It will look out across the Atlantic over Porthmeor Beach, but it can never be as beguiling as Hepworth's studio and garden, with clematis and honeysuckle climbing the walls and, planted among the trees and shrubs and alongside the small pond, her sculpture, some round and perfect as Carbis Bay pebbles, some as finely balanced as the prehistoric Zennor Quoit, some as big as Cornish megaliths. Hepworth gave the parish church a *Madonna and Child* in memory of the son who died when the plane he was piloting crashed in Thailand, and a pair of burnished steel candlesticks. To the town she donated the bronze *Epidaurus* on the terrace high above the harbour called the Malakoff, and *Dual Form* outside the Guildhall. Her memorial in Longstone Cemetery where she is buried is *Ascending Form*. In return for these works, St Ives gave Hepworth its welcome and its light.

That's why, after the first rainy evening, Barbara Hepworth stayed. Cornwall was like her native West Riding, rugged, bleak, scarred by ancient mines and clayworkings, bearing the scratch marks of Celtic efforts to bend the stony landscape to food production. But it was bathed in a light that she had only found elsewhere in certain places on the Mediterranean. Her sculpture is sheer, abstract, remote as the Parthenon. In St Ives, it opened up, became more organic. In her garden the wind blows through the holes in her bronzes, the rain collects in little pools in the recesses. Her life was etched by the divorce from Nicholson and the death of the son of her first marriage, but her sculpture expresses this in classical cadences, not the darker expressiveness of her older colleague at Leeds municipal arts school, Henry Moore; and in St Ives it is at home.

Michael McNay

Joys of a watery curfew
December 31 1990

Jeanetta McLair sounded peeved on the phone across the Fairlie Roads from Great Cumbrae island. 'It isn't very good for me either, that you've missed the ferry,' she said. 'I'll not get anyone else at this time of the night.' Harmony, and the McLair finances, were restored next morning when the two ferries returned to their 15-minute chug between Cumbrae Slip and Largs. But the episode, two empty beds on an island during its tourist season, underlined a fundamental point about British islet life. Miss the final ferry (and it's 8.15pm sharp for Great Cumbrae's 2,000 inhabitants) and you're away from home for the night. Schools, supper parties, shopping for extras all are governed by the sea's wash. A sizeable island like Cumbrae, three miles long and one of the 23 major Scottish Western Isles, is affected as much as any privately owned snippet with a causeway to the mainland.

'We lose our link altogether from time to time,' says David MacGill, retired bank manager and treasurer of Great Cumbrae's tourist association. 'The ferries were out for nine days in March this year because of bad seas.' Each day, the orange lamps flashed on tall poles at Millport headland, by Cumbrae's neat little capital town, to give local secondary school children the good news: no ferries, Largs Academy unreachable. Cut off by this watery curfew every suppertime, and sometimes more often, the islanders of Cumbrae have developed a social life celebrated locally.

'You'll sense the happiness when we get there,' said Glasgow toy salesman Cyril Shane, easing his Ford Escort, bulging with beach-balls and Teenage Mutant Hero Turtle hoopla sets, onto the *MV Loch Linnhe*'s ramp. The island's busy social life is mirrored, historically, by a worker-bee determination to get things done, and the need to get them done without the mainland's resources. Local government is now concentrated, cosily, in the person of George T Beagrie, district officer for Strathclyde council, and his two assistants, Margaret Meechan and Elizabeth McConnochie.

But below them, in the island museum, records fondly recall the Millport town council, 1864-1975, and its feverish record of building reservoirs, roads, a hospital, houses and piers. The councillors' efforts were helped, cannily, by regular joint appeals to Cumbrae's two landowners, the Earls of Glasgow and the Marquesses of Bute, who then vied with one another to make donations. Despite the island's summer influx of tourists, there is still room for more permanent invaders. Susan Murden, who moved a year ago from Oxford, offers clients a sheaf of properties at Thompson's estate agency in Millport. Prices are initially stunning by English standards: £6,000 or offer for a two-room flat. 'By local standards, though, Cumbrae is expensive now,' she says. 'It's mostly a holiday home market, too – very small properties.'

Legal curiosities may also deter the sassenach. The entire island, except the grounds of its tiny cathedral, now belongs to the Marquess of Bute (the Glasgows having faded, financially, earlier this century). As 'feudal superior', the marquess is entitled to duty payments on property and also has a veto on planning applications. 'If you put red tiles on your roof and he's sailing past in his yacht and doesn't like them, they might have to come off,' says Mrs Meechan, in the Strathclyde office.

The regulations have more force than the Millport bylaw, yet to be repealed by Strathclyde council, which requires males to sea bathe at Farlane, Kames Bay and Battery Points, and females to go chastely round the corner, hidden by the Eileann, Speug and Loig rocks. Penalty for contravention: a 40 shilling fine.

Martin Wainwright

Bexhill revels in sound of silence
April 2 1991

It is the very picture of an English tea garden: the tables on brilliant green grass, the borders stuffed with primroses and tulips, and a notice on the blue gate promising 'cream teas. No dogs.' But there has been no tea in the Miramar garden, Bexhill-on-Sea, over Easter. Kenneth Simmons has lost a three-year battle against neighbours who complained to the council about the noise, the deafening clatter of spoon on china. He appealed, and lost despite some neighbours writing to say they liked his tea garden, and a 2,500-signature petition from customers.

'Blooming ridiculous,' said Mr Simmons. But the war isn't over. 'I've got 12 grandchildren,' Mr Simmons said gleefully, 'and nobody can stop me giving barbecues for them in the garden.'

Ask anyone over 50 on the immaculate sea front what they like about Bexhill, and they'll say the quiet. 'We like a quiet life,' said a lady heading home from lunch in the De La Warr Pavilion – £5.50 for three waitress-service courses 'and it is quiet, lovely and quiet.' The council has just banned ice-cream vans from the seafront after complaints about their noisy engines. Anyone under 20 calls it the town of the living dead. With an estimated 60 per cent of the population aged over 50, it is said to be the oldest in England. Ball games, bicycles, skates and skateboards are banned from the front.

'They ban anything with wheels but not wheelchairs,' said James Rogers, a disgruntled 13-year-old. His sister Shelley, aged 11, was even franker: 'It's all old biddies, and there's only about two shops.'

It wasn't always thus. Bexhill-on-Sea was the brash Victorian offspring down the hill from Bexhill Old Town, which is really quiet. Bexhill-on-Sea had bathing machines and bands and fireworks, and the guests in the grand Victorian hotels featured in the society pages. The eighth Earl de la Warr built the Kursaal, famous for concerts. His son, the socialist ninth earl, gave the town its Grade I-listed modernist masterpiece, the De La Warr Pavilion. A Southern Railways poster of the 1930s ('frequent electric and steam trains ... cheap fares') shows its white seaside terraces festooned with bright young things.

Many who came first in the 30s came back to retire, and things got quiet. Only a handful of hotels remain. Belinda Rogers and her husband bought the Park Lodge three years ago. 'For the first six weeks I didn't have a single inquiry, no phone calls, nobody knocked on the door.' There is no passing trade, and no commercial travellers. She survives by advertising heavily in magazines aimed at the elderly. Several of her guests expressed dismay when she added the cheerful blue window awnings: 'It looks like a commercial hotel,' one said. 'It's like going back 30 years in time, it's so quiet and safe,' Mrs Rogers said brightly. Her children scowled. She added, 'within six months of coming here I felt I'd aged 10 years.'

Maev Kennedy

Britten's borough
June 6 1992

Even on the map, you can see that Aldeburgh is at the back of beyond. From London it has always been a long drive, the end of the line, an isolated community trapped defensively between the North Sea and the Suffolk marshes. The local people have lived off the sea, yet feared its menace, ever since the Saxons landed with fire and slaughter and gave the town its name. The invaders also brought with them a word that has somehow stuck to the place: weird.

Coming across the rabbity heath from the Ipswich road, the first thing you see is a golf course and an Edwardian clubhouse, a scene from an Agatha Christie or a PG Wodehouse. Further on, there's a parish church flying the cross of St George. Down the hill, a broad high street stretches towards a forest of yachts. Sometimes it's so empty there could be an air raid going on. Eastwards, behind dwellings lifted from the pages of David Copperfield, is a shingle beach, some black huts and a dirty sea. As a casual tourist, you might take in the Lifeboat shop, the British Gas showroom and the provincial Barclays and think to yourself, a typical, English seaside town. But you would be wrong.

Aldeburgh is not what it seems. Like many an English haunt, the place has a double life and makes a fetish of normality to disguise a darker complexity. The town, for instance, presents a picture of picnic innocence, yet without the newly rebuilt sea defences it would be swamped by the encroaching tide. The houses facing the ocean on Crag Path are bought and sold for London prices, yet for much of the year they stand empty. A few hardy swimmers plunge into the waves all year round, yet even on blue days the water remains grey or brown, like a Magritte. There's a bird sanctuary with nesting avocet and curlew on the walk to neighbouring Thorpeness, but the birdspotters' horizon is dominated by the Sizewell nuclear power station.

One person, among thousands, who would probably agree that there is rather more to Aldeburgh than meets the eye is Oliver Knussen, one of our finest young composers and an internationally renowned conductor of contemporary music. He and the American soprano, Lucy Shelton, have chosen to stay here in a cramped flint cottage, a stone's throw from the Martello tower. Their presence offers a vital clue to that other dimension of Aldeburgh's double life, its peculiar place in the history of English music and English literature.

Visiting writers certainly gave the resort some mixed reviews. Thomas Hardy noted 'the sensation of having nothing but the sea between you and the North Pole'. For Virginia Woolf, perhaps recalling holidays in Cornwall, it was 'that miserable, dull sea village'. EM Forster, who is still remembered here, agreed – it was, he wrote, 'a bleak little place: not beautiful'. Speaking of George Crabbe, the borough's most famous son, Forster added that the poet 'escaped from

Aldeburgh as soon as he could'. He had begun his broadcast with the words, 'To talk about Crabbe is to talk about England . . .'

The story goes that the young Benjamin Britten, in self-imposed American exile, read Forster's article in the *Listener* and determined to come home to his roots. The Suffolk to which Britten returned was the Suffolk of George Ewart Evans' folklore classic, *Ask The Fellows Who Cut The Hay*. To put it another way, this is Akenfield country.

Lady Fidelity Cranbrook, who was part of Britten's circle, remembers pre-war Suffolk as a remote, primitive place. 'East Anglia didn't exist in the 30s. Even east and west Suffolk were divided. There was tremendous suspicion. Coming here was like going abroad. The agricultural poverty was appalling. People were drinking water out of ponds. No one ever moved. If they did, they tramped from village to village, looking for work. With the war, agriculture became important. The war changed everything.'

In Suffolk, Britten could feel doubly at home. The war had changed many things, but it had not changed attitudes to homosexuality. In law, Britten's relationship with Peter Pears was still a criminal offence. Distant Aldeburgh, with its tight-lipped, seafaring population was in many ways an ideal place for those who feared society's oppression. Out here on the margin there was, it seems, quite a community of what Ewart Evans (using a quaint Edwardian euphemism) used to call 'the dillyboys'. And as a Lowestoft lad, Britten could easily mix with the natives.

Billy Burrell comes from a long line of Aldeburgh fishermen. After more than 50 years at sea, he's now a fishery inspector. In his heyday he was landing a ton and a half of shellfish a week and the fishing provided jobs for perhaps 200. Now there are barely 15 fishermen and the trade 'is slowly being stifled. It's survival, but only survival.' He recalls the first time he met Britten. ' 'I'm Ben', he said. 'I'm Billy', I said. There were no airs and graces, not with him.'

Elsewhere in the borough, there was the familiar claustrophobia of class. Billy Burrell used to bring Britten fresh herring for breakfast.

He will tell you with pride that he had the run of the house on Crag Path. One morning, coming in with the day's catch, he found he had blundered into a posh looking committee meeting. Seated round the table were all the local nobs. Britten, quite unaffected, said, 'Do you know everyone here, Billy?' 'Oh yes,' says I. And I did. And do you know, before that day, it was always 'Hello, Burrell', just plain Burrell. But after that, it was always 'Hello, Billy. How are you today?' Class distinction, you see.'

Aldeburgh has not shaken off its reputation for observing such social niceties. Billy Burrell's friendship with Britten was based on fishing and birdwatching, not music. 'Oh,' he laughs, 'I didn't like his music at all. Ben knew I didn't. I came in once and he was playing a piece on the piano, and I said, 'To think people pay good money to listen to that rubbish.' So he says, 'I expect you'd prefer to have it like this.' And so he hammers away on the piano and I says, 'Yes, I like that.' And he says, 'It's the same piece.' Billy Burrell raises his eyebrows at the memory of this musical legerdemain.

These were miraculous years for Britten's art. Oliver Knussen speaks with awe of the composer's output. 'If you take *Peter Grimes*, the *Serenade for Horn and Strings*, the *Rape of Lucretia*, *Albert Herring*, the *Spring Symphony*, the *Little Sweep*, *Billy Budd*, not to mention the Second String Quartet, *Saint Nicholas* and many songs, basically Opus 31 to Opus 50, you will find that they were all done in a period of eight years. I mean, it's unbelievably ridiculous.'

On top of all this there was the festival. This was Peter Pears's idea. The English Opera Group was touring Europe, becoming weary of the road. It was Pears who asked the crucial question. 'Why not make our own festival? A modest festival with a few concerts given by friends? Why not have an Aldeburgh Festival?'

It was done in a very English way. Britten came back and put the idea to the vicar and the mayor. He was accompanied by Eric Crozier, his librettist. Crozier has never shaken off the spell of the place. His wife, the singer Nancy Evans, a veteran of many Britten premieres, still teaches at the Britten-Pears School for Advanced Musical Studies. Crozier laughs at the memory of those days. 'The idea of doing opera in Suffolk. It was unheard of!' The local people rose to the occasion. Friends came down from London. 'Ben and Peter were inspiring people to work with. They brought together a marvellous ensemble.' Crozier, who collaborated in the first two festivals, later found himself excluded from the inner circle. He acknowledges there was a darker side to Britten. 'He could not tolerate criticism from anyone ... Even sailing, he could be very strict. No one, so to speak, could sail like Ben, just as no one could drive like Ben, or even carve a joint like Ben. He was a perfectionist.'

There are many people in Aldeburgh who knew the composer, but a suffocating air of protectiveness still surrounds his memory. Few will speak as frankly as Crozier and none has gone as far in their analysis of Britten's character. At one low point of his estrangement, Crozier committed his recollections of working with Britten privately to paper. The document lay in a drawer, unseen, unread, until Crozier showed it to Britten's biographer, Humphrey Carpenter. In his forthcoming Life, Carpenter makes brilliant and persuasive use of Crozier's sensational claim that Britten once confessed to him that he had been 'raped' by a master at school.

Aldeburgh has kept such secrets to itself. Privately, some allude to the settling of old scores but it is hard, if not impossible, to disentangle fact and fantasy. In this respect, Dr Donald Mitchell, the chairman of the Britten estate and now the most prominent keeper of the flame, finds the town 'quite a rum place'. Mitchell has recently published a two volume selection from Britten's *Letters and Diaries*, exposing once and for all the passionate, physical nature of Britten and Pears's relationship. I wonder about local reaction to these revelations. 'There's been a fairly deathly silence,' he says. 'Certain prohibitions and taboos were broken by the letters.'

Elsewhere, the mask of normality remains firmly in place. The composer's former assistant, Rosamund Strode, is a model of reticence. 'People want to make him (Britten) extraordinary, but he was much more ordinary than people imagine ... That's why people liked him.' Speaking of Britten and Pears as she knew them, Nancy Evans remarks: 'They didn't embarass anyone. There was no kind of exhibitionism, not like now. They were well mannered and discreet. They enjoyed being part of the community.'

In the early days, Britten's house was in the heart of the community, overlooking the beach. The composer Michael Berkeley, who knew Britten from childhood, believes that Britten's fascination with the sea is crucial to an understanding of the man. 'He was fascinated by innocence and by its potential for corruption. The sea is like that. It can provide and sustain life, and it can take life away. The duplicity of the sea is the mirror of his own character.' Britten drew obsessively on his surroundings. The operas are scattered with Aldeburgh names like Budd, Gedge, Upfold and Woodger. Speaking of the sea in Britten's music, Nancy Evans remembers one 'uncanny evening' at Crag Path. 'A new recording of the *Four Sea Interludes* had arrived. Ben was eager to listen to it. So after dinner we sat in his house on Crag Path and listened to the recording. I could hear the sea outside and there was Ben listening intently to his own sea music. And I thought to myself, this is a unique experience.'

Britten touched the hearts and minds of many Aldeburgh people with that potent sense of living through interesting times. Some devoted their lives to him. Among the most notable is Keith Cable, the long-serving festival office manager. Cable, a gentle, soft spoken East Anglian, collects Britten and Aldeburgh memorabilia. 'Have you seen the Crown Derby set?' he asks, handing me a platter engraved with scenes from *The Turn of the Screw*. We pore over his postcard albums, a hundred years of seaside snapshots.

Cable, who was born in the cottage next door, has had many brushes with greatness. Britten hovers on the edge of the conversation, a fidgety ghost. Cable shares with Britten a passion for sea swimming. By trade, an electrician at Sizewell, he admits that when he first started working for the festival, 'I would walk up the street with the programme under my arm and the locals would take the mickey.'

Another postcard. 'That's my Aunty May. She was the first carnival queen.' Now Cable tells a story that perfectly represents the relationship between Britten and Pears on the one hand and the people of Aldeburgh on the other. Every August there was (and still is) a carnival. 'Ben loved the carnival procession.' He produces a photograph of Britten watching the parade, an indulgent spectator. 'Each year, at the end of the day, Ben and Peter used to go to the Wentworth Hotel in their open car, collect the carnival queen and then drive her down the High Street to the carnival fair at the other end. It became a kind of tradition.' It would be hard to think of a gesture more loaded with symbolism.

Over the hill, there were mutterings in the club house. Some of the golfing set disapproved of the goings on down in the Jubilee Hall. JC Whately Smith, Esq., a retired prep school headmaster, and for 11 years the popular club secretary, is a reliable witness. He is typical of a certain kind of Aldeburgh resident. His family have been coming here for 'four or five generations'. His father married a local girl and, he remembers, liked to say that the town was 'full of remittance men'. A self-confessed philistine, Whately Smith seems chiefly concerned that I should not quote his opinion of the club's fairways. He describes the club as 'slightly toffee nosed, but much better than it used to be.' Incredibly enough, it still has an 'artisan section' for the horny handed.

'When the festival started up,' he says, 'there were one or two members who complained like hell and took themselves away on holiday for three weeks.' What was the nature of their complaint? 'Oh, they just didn't like it.' He looks away. 'Yes. The first few years were ... a bit tricky. Things have settled down now.' (Later, both Britten and Pears were made honorary members.) Indeed, when Britten and Pears left Crag Path to escape the curiosity of passers by, they moved to the Red House, overlooking the 14th green.

Here, in Michael Berkeley's words, 'they became lord and lady of the manor.'

Berkeley remembers the Aldeburgh of the 50s and 60s as 'an exciting place to be. Ben was at the peak of his powers. What was exciting for me was going as a boy chorister and staying in the Red House. It was slightly daunting, but it was made enjoyable by the fact that Ben was so good with children.' Berkeley was not alone in finding the atmosphere 'daunting'. The Red House became a byword for sycophancy and secrecy. Britten and Pears, it was said, were operating a peculiarly cold and manipulative 'court'. There was talk of 'an Aldeburgh mafia'. According to Carpenter, Robert Tear, the tenor, describes 'the terrible atmosphere of Aldeburgh, an atmosphere laden with waspishness, bitterness, cold, hard eyes ...'

There is no denying a certain grandeur in Britten and Pears. Both intimates and acquaintances were made well aware of being 'in' or 'out'. Donald Mitchell believes that such stories are 'very much exaggerated. Of course there was an entourage, but do you know of any great man who did not surround himself with a protective barrier of sympathetic people? Ben believed strongly in treating his musical gifts with respect. He needed space in which to compose.' Mitchell adds that, 'Life at the Red House was much more normal than Aldeburgh people imagined,' and suggests that such gossip was inevitable in a small town.

Letty Gifford, another redoubtable survivor, saw Britten from both sides of the fence. Mrs Gifford is a spirited, articulate woman who has managed the Aldeburgh cinema since 1974. A diplomat's wife, she seems happy to speak her mind, and agrees that she is 'a slightly improbable person to tramp round Wardour Street.' Her art deco cinema is a one-woman show. 'I just do it for fun. I don't make any money. It's a mixture of middle of the road and art house stuff, on Sunday afternoons in the winter. I'm kept well posted by my grandchildren and I take *Variety*.' She points to a headline: Fests Fight

Flic Famine. 'I love that. I enjoy hiring the films. Aldeburgh being Aldeburgh, the midnight matinee starts at 10 o'clock.'

The cinema programme has always been part of the festival and she knew Britten well. 'I was there for the dress rehearsal and the first performance of *A Midsummer Night's Dream.* That was rather amazing.' What about Britten's court? Letty Gifford laughs. 'Well, I was part of that coterie, so I have to say it was fun. But yes, Ben could be an absolute monster. He was absolutely ruthless when it came to his music. We'd say, 'He's behaving abominably, but ...' He was a genius, wasn't he?'

She believes that the festival 'went into the doldrums towards the end of Ben's life. He was very ill. It was an unhappy situation. It's picked up again now.'

Letty Gifford is refreshingly open about the past. I ask her about the local attitude to the festival. 'Oh, they're rather proud of Aldeburgh being on the map. They think it's a good thing, on the whole, though they complain about the traffic. Occasionally you hear estate agents say they won't let their houses to these long-haired queers, but they don't mean it.'

It seems to me quite understandable that the residents should, from time to time, get fed up with living, willy nilly, in a company town. Buy a pot of Dulux or a fillet of plaice in the High Street and you cannot escape Britten's legacy. Robin and Margaret Browning run the DIY store. Peter Pears used to have his pictures framed by Robin and when Margaret was mayor in 1986-7 she attended his memorial service in Westminster Abbey. Then there's Rostropovich. 'Slava' treats the Brownings as friends, bear hugs and kisses all round. He once bought a hammer and a bag of nails. Margaret winces. 'I can't bear to think of him with that hammer. Those hands!' The Brownings came here 20 years ago. Her husband chips in, 'I say that when people move here they become Suffolkated!'

At the other end of the street, their friends the Cartwrights run the fishmonger's. Alan was born here. Karen was not. 'They say you've got to live in Aldeburgh for 40 years before you're local.' Alan trained as joiner and went into the fish business eight years ago. He believes the place is changing, 'more in the last 10 years than I can remember.' There's music talk here, too. Their daughter is learning the violin. 'Slava has heard her play. "Tell her to come to me when she is 21," said the great man.' Alan has also had a walk-on part in the town's musical life. As a joiner, he worked for Wm C Reade. It was Reade that built the concert hall at Snape.

There had been a maltings at Snape, up the river Alde, since the mid-19th century. Bob Ling, who started work on 'the day gang' in 1938, remembers a lost way of life. 'At full employment there were a hundred men. We were a happy family, really.' Snape was a company village. At the Plough and Sail the men could exchange brass tokens for pints. In 1965, without any warning, the works were closed. 'It was so sudden. We all wondered what the devil we would do.' His wife Doris, who might have stepped out of Akenfield, breaks in: 'We went freelance. We had this Commer van, some grass mats, a couple of broken shovels and a fork ... There isn't an easy grave to dig.' As a husband and wife team of gravediggers they became local celebrities.

Back at the Maltings, Reade's men were building a remarkable concert hall, Britten's own. It was opened in 1967 by the Queen, who was ushered to her seat by Keith Cable. It was, he says, 'the high point of my career.' The Queen Mother is still the festival's patron and, according to Donald Mitchell, was genuinely interested in Britten's work. Nonetheless, there must have been moments during these years when the festival must have seemed part of the season, a bizarre burst of modernism, sandwiched between Ascot and Wimbledon.

Two years later, the night before the festival, the Maltings was burnt down. Many in Aldeburgh still remember the fire. Some people muttered darkly about arson, but nothing was proved. When the Maltings reopened a year later, Bob and Doris Ling were invited to become caretakers. 'I was amazed they gave the job to a couple of country hicks,' says Doris. For Bob, it was like going home. 'The times I've stood on the stage at the Maltings and thought that the singing were never done here it were done in the Plough and Sail.' Doris remembers that Britten couldn't keep away from the place. 'There weren't hardly a day Ben didn't visit the Maltings. He would come in for a cup of tea and a chat. He'd say, 'I'm bored, I'll come and talk to Bob and Doris'.'

Bob adds: 'I remember one night, during an interval, Ben was in his dressing room and he says to me, "Come out and listen to this." And there was this bittern a-booming away, an uncanny sound. There was what we call a rising dag, that's a mist on the marshes, and this booming sound. I thought it would sound good with the ghostly music of *Owen Wingrave*.' Bob and Doris have retired to Aldeburgh now, but they often return to Snape. Doris says, 'I was there the other evening and I said to Bob, "How could heaven be nicer? It's just like heaven in advance".'

Their job went to Pam and Bud Woolsey. He was a landscape gardener, she a hairdresser. At her interview, Pam said, 'I don't like this sort of music.' Now they listen to Radio 3 all the time. Pam says: 'You discover that Oliver Knussen is not only possible to listen to, but you get to enjoy it more than you might expect.' Bud, looks at his wife: 'You can easily cope with Stravinsky and Schoenberg now.' He might be talking about a troublesome neighbour. Pam again: 'Some of it's a bit iffy – plinky plonky music, I call it.'

Bud recognises that the festival has changed. 'In the old days, the artists used to live in Aldeburgh and just walk up the High Street to perform in the Jubilee Hall. The locals would be on the fringe of this big house party. Ordinary people in Aldeburgh miss seeing the stars.' During the festival, Pam and Bud are on call 24 hours. Pam laughs. 'I've been known to iron Murray Perahia's shirt!'

Britten died in 1976. The composer had said, 'I want Bob and Doris to bury me, and I want to be buried in the reeds (of Snape).' It was not to be. The family preferred the consecrated ground of Aldeburgh parish church. But Bob and Doris had the last word. They lined the grave with reeds from the marshes, and that's what everyone remembers. 'We felt he'd be happy with his reeds,' says Doris.

Pears died in 1986. He and and his 'companion', to use the code of the time, lie side by side beneath austere black headstones. In their will they left money 'to support and encourage the civilised treatment of homosexuals'. Many predicted that the festival would not survive them, but it did, some say by the skin of its teeth. Michael Berkeley makes a judicious summary. 'After Ben died, there was a hiatus ... It's become much more exciting since Ollie (Knussen) and Colin (Matthews) have been involved. There's a new sense of purpose and identity. They are committed to new music and they are prepared to take risks. Finally, the justification of Aldeburgh is that it's a place where some of the century's most important music was composed and first performed.'

Today, under the vigorous and imaginative management of Sheila Colvin, Aldeburgh music is reaching audiences never dreamed of by the founders. The festival has become just one moment in an almost continuous musical merry-go-round, nearly 100 days of live performance from Easter to Christmas. The Borodin Quartet is in residence. Box office takings have risen steadily for three years and the reviews, rather sniffy during the doldrum years, have become generally good. The annual turnover, a mixture of Arts Council grant, local sponsorship led by British Telecom, and ticket sales, has increased to £1.4 million. The treasurer, John Jacob, observes: 'We are no longer just a festival, but what are we? We have a concert hall, a music school, a research centre (at the Red House), an education programme, and an administrative office. Perhaps we're a mini arts complex.'

Significantly, most of the people involved in this mini arts complex never knew Britten or Pears. Sarah Gibbon is a typical new face. Her job is to take orchestras and chamber groups into local schools.

Her work is sponsored by Kleenex. Encouraged by the Aldeburgh Foundation, Suffolk has become an exceptionally musical county. 'It's not uncommon to walk into a classroom and see 10 Yamaha keyboards on the desks in front of you.' She enjoys living in Aldeburgh, but agrees that 'in the past, newcomers were scared of the place.'

Oliver Knussen isn't scared of Aldeburgh, though he's well aware of its reputation. 'If you blow your nose at one end of the High Street there'll be people at the other end ordering an ambulance.' He sits in the sun at the back of his cottage, drinking Diet Coke and smoking a cigarette. As a boy, he knew Britten and remembers 'a person of colossal charm, a very businesslike charm.' As a young composer he found Britten helpful: 'I was taken back to the Red House after a rehearsal of *Curlew River*. I'd just won a prize and he asked me very seriously about what I was composing. It was half an hour I shall never forget.' He has found living in Aldeburgh very conducive to work. 'I've done more in three months than in the last three years.' Is he bothered to be following in Britten's footsteps? 'The only thing we have in common is that we are both composers and conductors. Otherwise, I don't think about it.'

Knussen has been an artistic director for 10 years and has a clear idea of what he wants. 'The festival should have multiple themes, with Britten's music always a central theme ... You can do something new and outrageous so long as it's in a context that means something.' While he agrees that things were 'bumpy when I first arrived,' he believes the festival had rediscovered its purpose sooner than many music journalists recognised. By 1988, most concerts were sold out, even for Schnittke and Birtwhistle. 'The audiences started to trust us.'

If there's any in-fighting left over from the Britten/Pears regime, he steers clear of it. 'In this job it's virtually impossible to say or do something that everyone is going to agree with.' He's 40 this year, on June 12, and the festival is giving him a birthday concert. They'll play his *Ophelia Dances*, a Dutilleux item, Colin Matthews's *Suns Dance*, a new Knussen piece, *Songs without Voices*, *Four Compositions* by Poul Ruders (a Danish composer Knussen is keen on), and the first British performance of a solo flute piece by Elliott Carter.

Lucy Shelton, who is listening to our conversation, leans across to me, and whispers, 'The mafia'. But her aside is only pantomime and her eyes are smiling.

Robert McCrum

Dorset Diary
August 20 1992

I go to Dorset when I have a novel to write, as I do now. Its groomed resorts and dramatic, crumpled coastline have always appealed to writers: Jane Austen, Mary Shelley, Thomas Hardy, Paul Verlaine, Robert Louis Stevenson, Aubrey Beardsley, John Fowles ... A good county for a novelist to be born in, though no one gave it a thought that All Soul's day in post-war Poole when my mother, eight months' pregnant, conceived a burning desire to buy a strip of orange carpet for the hall, traipsed the long road into the town centre, returned triumphant, made watercress sandwiches for tea, and without further ado dashed to hospital to give birth to me before supper.

Because we left when I was three, early memories of Poole are mostly fragmentary and surreal – a doctor features, bringing an enormous stethoscope to my bed at night, and as I stand staring at him in the yellow light through the bars of my cot, he is definitely wearing a top hat. Another memory remains obstinately, photographically real. We are on the beach at Shell Bay, a long, wide, silver expanse of sand to the west of Poole. My mother, brother, father and I, are running in the sunshine. I spot a piddock shell, which is matte white with small regular indentations just like the rubber strip round the edge of the plimsolls we wore: 'Look, Daddy, it's a tennis white,' I say. I think I am stating a fact, not inventing one, so I am surprised my parents are so pleased with me.

Thirty five years later, my husband Nick Rankin began writing a book about Robert Louis Stevenson and had to research the period his author spent in neighbouring Bournemouth. (In 1885 Stevenson bought an ivy-covered house there; his enterprising wife Fanny grew tomatoes for their salads at a time when most Victorians thought they were poisonous, and Stevenson dreamed the wonderfully unhealthy dream of Dr Jekyll and Mr Hyde.) I went along for the ride and wrote a novel, *Light Years*, set on the Dorset coast. Ever since, I've been a regular.

Shell Bay gets overpopulated in high season, but there are still no promenades, shops or cafes to disturb the long stretch of sand which curves round towards Studland Bay and, beyond it, the battered chalk columns of the Old Harry rocks. The sheen on the sand probably comes from the extraordinary number of shallow, coin-shaped pearl shells, mostly white or honey-coloured but every colour from silver through to petrol blue, which the sea brings in and shatters.

Nudists have appropriated one remote strand for their pink private parties, rapidly reddening in the sun. A man (naked) tells me (swimsuited): 'We call people with their clothes on textiles' – not quite crushing enough to make me strip off. Poole Harbour is one of the largest natural harbours in the world, and it's beautiful to look at, dotted with islands and the canted sails of hundreds of small boats which are beached, at low tide, on the wet sand, among drifts of seagulls. At present, only 60 of the harbour's 10,000 acres are used commercially, the rest being enjoyed by holiday-makers, conservationists, fishermen, sailors and the birds who winter here – black tailed godwits and grey plovers. East of the harbour is Sandbanks, one of the 17 British beaches to be awarded a 1992 European blue flag for cleanliness, to the west the Dorset coastal walk.

Here begin the spectacular nature reserves of the Purbeck peninsula; Kimmeridge Bay with its dramatic black shale beaches, the jutting crags of Gad Cliff where cormorants rear their young, ruined Tyneham village in the heart of the army firing ranges where neglected hedges have sprawled into small woods. The chalk grasslands, paradoxically protected by the army's war games from the general run of human feet, support a rich carpet of cowslips and harebells, vetches and trefoils in spring. But time may have caught up with Purbeck, now that BP has discovered an estimated 100 million barrels of oil lying beneath Poole Bay. Its plan to build an artificial island in the harbour for offshore drilling was suddenly dropped last December, after local protest, but even the onshore development of the oil-field will bring more industry and more people to a remarkably unspoilted coastline. And the Ports Bill, which became law last year, threatens privatisation of a harbour which for nearly 100 years has been excellently managed by a trust, the Harbour Commissioners.

The government could still make an exception for Poole. It might be wise: Dorset people seem united in their opposition to privatisation, and they have always been a spirited lot. On D-day in 1944, four years before my mother bought her strip of orange carpet, a flotilla of ships from Poole joined the great assault on France. Men from the 1st Dorsets were the first Brits up the Normandy beaches.

Maggie Gee

Maggie Gee's latest novel is *My Driver* (Telegram, £12.99)

The bone ranger – Mary Anning
November 19 1992

Perched on the seawall at Lyme Regis on the Dorset coast is a museum uniquely positioned in both space and time. No other museum in Britain commands such a grand prospect. And no other museum encompasses the history of a place so pivotal in our understanding of our own location in evolutionary time. For Lyme is rightly regarded as a leading contender for the epithet 'the cradle of palaeontology', the study of ancient forms of life known to us only by deciphering the traces accidentally left as fossils.

The crumbling cliffs that have made the town a mecca for geologists have also been its prison, says the novelist John Fowles, who lived for years in a farmhouse that hangs precariously on the Undercliff. With only 3,500 inhabitants, the town remains small, the size it has been for centuries. Yet it has a history befitting a metropolis. As a result, its museum houses local objects that are also significant on a national and sometimes even international scale. Lyme's museum has launched an appeal to raise £100,000 to repair its weather-beaten building of 1901, and to conserve and better display its rich collections.

Funds are also sought to build up some of its fossil collections – 'Lyme's sheer international celebrity has caused its fossil treasures to be made off with as if they were the Elgin marbles,' says Hugh Torrens, geologist and historian of science at Keele University. Most intriguing is the plan to create an exhibition that will illustrate the town's extraordinary place in the history of science.

As if in a novel Fowles might have written, the story revolves round a network of women. In the early decades of the 19th century, two working-class women – mother and daughter, both named Mary Anning – made a living by selling the fossils they found in the cliffs around Lyme. The local newspaper of 1812 devoted just a column inch to one discovery, of a 'crocodile' in the Dorset cliffs. To the journalist, it was a curiosity, nothing more. In fact, it was the first complete skeleton – or at least, the first to come to the attention of scientists – of a 17-foot-long ichthyosaur, a dolphin-like reptile that swam in the sea 180 million years ago.

Mary Anning the younger knew it was important. She 'had a nose for valuable specimens that amounted to genius,' writes Fowles in his history of Lyme. Anning was the first professional collector to recognise the scientific significance of her finds, says Torrens, who now has plans to complete his half-written biography. What's more, she was 'the Rembrandt of geology,' spending weeks carving these objects out of the cliffs and developing them. For a brief decade or two, while the novelty of her discoveries lasted, she made a good living.

A shrewd businesswoman, says Torrens, she used her knowledge to capitalise on the rarity and novelty of discoveries, asking, and receiving, up to £200 for the most unusual – some £40,000 at today's prices. But as 'saleswoman to a new science' she needed to find specialist buyers willing to pay a high price for something new – at the time, geology and palaeontology were popular with the wealthy upper classes. 'They were perceived as novel, manly sciences, not yet obscured by the technicalities later introduced by professional scientists,' Torrens says.

Anning found her buyers with the help of her friends. She met Charlotte Murchison, the wife of a London geologist, in 1825 and they were clearly drawn to one another, Torrens says. Murchison told the many collectors she met of Anning's fossils, helping her to build up a remarkable network of contacts. Among her regular customers were virtually all the men now hailed as the founding fathers of palaeontology. One was William Buckland, professor of geology at Oxford and later Dean of Westminster. Thanks to the 'specific and vital help of Mary Anning junior', says Torrens, Buckland has gone down in history as the first to recognise coprolites for what they are – fossilised dung. He was a humorous and eccentric fellow; in the Lyme museum, you can see the tabletop he made of them.

Anning also had local patrons in the three Philpot sisters, who moved to Lyme in about 1805 to live in what is now the Mariners Hotel in Silver Street. Two of the sisters were keen fossilists, and they bought many of Anning's finds and introduced her to geologists they knew. Over the years, the Philpot sisters assembled a famous collection of Lyme fossils that is now the pride of Oxford University's collection. Many of the fossils are type specimens – the specimen from which a new species was first described, and many were found by Anning.

In 1823, Anning discovered the first complete fossil of the marine reptile plesiosaurus. Five years later, she found a nearly complete specimen of the pterosaur or 'winged lizard' dimorphodon. Buckland described and named the gliding reptile from Anning's specimen. She also found the type specimen of a peculiar fossil fish with a long snout and spine on its head, a chimaera ultimately named Squaloraja polyspondyla.

But you won't normally find her name on the labels of any of these fossils, now housed in the world's leading collections. The donor, not the finder, is remembered. The history of science, says Torrens, is the history of patronage and power, not of discovery. Today, another woman is doing her best to put Anning back in the picture. Liz-Anne Bawden, honorary curator of Lyme's museum, gave up teaching film at the Slade in London and running the academics' union, the Association of University Teachers, to open an art gallery in Lyme with her partner Di Coley. She spent several years on the town council, and in 1988 took over as curator from John Fowles, who had filled the post for 10 years. With the job comes an enormous amount of work, but no pay. Bawden's energy and enthusiasm is a force to be reckoned with.

The museum has 'the greatest potential in our region', says Sam Hunt, in charge of museums for the south-west, 'not only because of its collections, but really thanks to Liz-Anne Bawden – she's a very energetic curator.' Her plan is to use some of the funds raised to restore the fossil gallery to its original condition. There will be no quaint tableau of a dummy Anning with rich customer poring over a plastic ichthyosaur skeleton – this is not heritage territory. Instead, the museum's fossils and rocks will be displayed in wooden cabinets as if it were a Victorian fossil collector's study. Visitors can pull out the drawers and have a look.

Anning would have approved of such an arrangement – as befits a museum on the very site of the house where Anning was born in 1799, and which became her first fossil shop. With luck, the museum will be able to borrow back from Oxford and the Natural History Museum some of the Philpot fossils, and 'beg, borrow or have facsimilied Mary Anning's correspondence,' says Bawden. It's all good news for Lyme and its history, but why should outsiders support the museum?

'It is impossible for a museum like Lyme to conserve its collections and find funds for major redevelopments from income from visitors,' says Hunt. 'It's not the Roman Bath or the Jorvick Viking Centre – it's much smaller, much more delicate. You can't pack millions through it; it's the quality of the experience that's important.' Places such as Lyme's museum have a role in our lives that is difficult to put into words. Perhaps in the ideal world, we wouldn't need them – if we all knew and celebrated the past and present of the places we live. But as it is, a visit to Lyme's museum can help to give us back a sense of ourselves located in history, and in a landscape.

Sue Clifford of Common Ground puts it more eloquently. The museum at Lyme, she says, 'helps to introduce people – visitors and locals alike – to local distinctiveness, to what richness there is in a place that is usually taken for granted.' It makes 'the link between the place and strands of time, with the present as centre of the web.' Fowles says: 'Occasionally I find ichthyosaur vertebrae in my garden. Suddenly you are hurtled back through time.'

Gail Vines

Sun, sand, sea and sensibilities
June 7 1993

Tucked into the sand dunes on Studland Bay in Dorset is a wooden sign. It declares that this wide expanse of sandy beach, and the land stretching back behind it for a good half mile, is a nature reserve, owned by the National Trust. According to the sign, the area is fair bursting with rare and exotic sights: 'Snakes and lizards in the heathlands and dunes, nightingales in the woods, dragonflies in the lakes, ducks and wading birds in the tidal area and insect-eating plants in boggy ground.'

The inventory fails, however, to list one other rare and exotic sight that, according to many locals, can also be found here among the grasses and bracken and scrub. The omission is not particularly surprising; the National Trust is hardly likely to want to advertise the fact that there may be a number of naked people scattered throughout the dunes having sex. While the Trust may not wish to draw attention to the situation, it is not one they can easily ignore. Each year they receive complaints from members of the public, some saying they have witnessed people having sex in the dunes, others saying they have been propositioned. There are reports of heterosexual couples indulging on the beach, but most complaints are about gay men who, it is said, treat the dunes as a pick-up point. According to the locals, most of them come from Bournemouth and Poole.

To the residents of the Purbeck Isle, the peninsula on whose eastern edge Studland sits, both towns are brash and ugly – urban sprawls compared with their rural idyll. Any mucky business on their beaches, they say, is bound to be caused by the people who live just over the water. At the beginning of May, the Dorset constabulary announced that, in co-operation with National Trust wardens, it would once more this year be patrolling the relevant stretch of Studland Bay, starting from Whitsun bank holiday week, the traditional start of the summer season. So the battle for the beach has begun.

Some of the officers will be in uniform, they say, others will be in plain clothes. Of course, this operation presents its own special problems; after all how do you patrol a nudist beach in plain clothes? The northern quarter of the four-mile Studland Bay, a rare expanse of clear sand, is commonly regarded as the first public place in Britain to have been frequented by nudists; people have been taking their clothes off there since well before the second world war. Today, at the height of summer, there can be as many as 5,000 people spread across the sand and throughout the dunes, sans clothing. Only the dressed are out of place.

Most people will have seen the Studland dunes on their television screens at one time or another, even if they didn't know their name. For cash-strapped producers in the seventies it was as close as they could come to a real location. Sometimes they were used by the Goodies if they needed a desert to walk across; at other times it was the *Carry On* films or Benny Hill crews who came to stick their tripods in the sand. But the dunes are out of fashion with film people these days; the nudists have the beach to themselves once more.

Real Studland regulars don't worry about the weather. The greyer the better. That way the voyeurs and the fickle sun-worshipers and the exhibitionists stay away and they can have the beach to themselves. Even on the dullest of winter days you will find them there, sheltering in the same dunes which first made the beach popular with the pioneering nudists in the 30s. Hundreds of people can hide within their hollows and ridges, shaded by the long grasses, without being aware of each other's presence.

In 1935, Purbeck district council did attempt to ban nudism here by introducing a bylaw which made it illegal for men – it made no reference to women – to bathe within 200 yards of a public place while naked. But because it only referred to bathing it was easy for any determined nudist to get around the law. All he had to do was walk naked to the water's edge, slip on a pair of trunks and step into the sea. He could take them off again when he came out. Today there are no such worries. There have been no prosecutions for nudisim since the 1950s, when a small number of men – again, only men – were charged with indecent exposure.

Until the mid-70s, the nudists stayed well back in the dunes, only venturing out to trip down to the sea for a swim. Then, in the broiling summer of 1976, it became far too hot back there, sheltered from the breeze off the sea, and the nudists moved out front. Following complaints from a few people who stumbled across naked day trippers unexpectedly, the boundaries of the nudist beach are now marked out firmly with small, low-slung National Trust signs. On one side, they tell people that nudists can be seen from beyond this point; on the other, the nudists are asked to put their clothes on if they are intending to go past it.

On one gloomy if warm day last month there were very few people sitting on the dunes' outer slopes. Most of the beach down to the water's edge was deserted. It wasn't hot enough to be out there yet. Beyond the first ridge, however, about a dozen men stood on their separate hillocks, 30 or 40 yards apart, some completely naked, others wearing a T-shirt but nothing else. They were watching each other. 'Sure, this is the gay beach,' said one thin, sun-tanned man who was as bald as he was naked. 'We meet each other here,' said another. 'And if the chemistry's right, well then you may go further back.' He waved to where the trees and bushes started another 100 metres back. 'But it's all hidden away.'

None of the nudists I spoke to said the gay men bothered them. 'If you actually saw anything going on then you would have to have been way back in the bushes over there, looking for it,' said one middle-aged woman who has been coming to the beach for 12 years. 'And in any case gay men don't ever bother me. It's the straights who are the perverts.' Ronnie, another Studland regular, agreed. While he did believe it sometimes got out of hand, he could not understand why the police bother to come. 'The most terrible thing that's happening here is that some boys are playing with each other's willies,' he said. 'And then over in Bournemouth and Poole there are people being mugged and houses being broken into. The police only come down here because they can get some easy arrests. What's more, by being so noisy about it, all the police do is attract the kind of people who cause the problems in the first place. It's a self-fulfilling prophecy.'

Inspector Bob Worsdale, based four miles down the coast in Swanage, whose job it is to police the bay, denied they were being bloody-minded. He said they were only responding to complaints. 'The complaints are usually in response to overt homosexual behaviour and flashing,' he said. 'As a result of that, and very much to put people's minds at rest, we will patrol the beach. These patrols will be both overt and covert.'

Asked what form a plain clothes patrol would take on a nudist beach he would only say that they would be in 'suitable attire'. Pushed, he said they would be in bathing costumes – which is one way to make your presence known on Studland Bay beach. 'It isn't isolated to homosexuals of course,' he said. 'We do charge women with offences.' Of the 20 or so cases of gross indecency prosecuted each year, however, only one or two involve women. Liz Roberts, spokeswoman for the Wessex region of the National Trust, was almost apologetic about the patrols. 'Look, it wasn't really a huge number of complaints,' she said, 'really it wasn't. But we didn't feel we could ignore them. We do have to be responsible land owners. So we've co-operated with the vice squad because we've had people indulging in activities which are against the law. Basically, bonking in public is illegal.'

How many cases were pursued last year? 'Nine, I think.' So how many people were charged? 'Well, 18 I would imagine. No hang on, I think one of them was a threesome.' She went off to get the file. 'Oh, actually there were 10 cases last year and none of them were women, though we did have a woman the year before. One thing I must say is that we are not concerned with whether it's men having sex with men or men having sex with women. It's nothing to do with preference, just activity.'

The intention this year, she said, was to keep it low key. In 1984, the year after the beach was given to the National Trust as part of the Kingston Lacy and Corfe Castle Estate, the largest bequest in the history of the organisation, the Dorset police borrowed a few lorry loads of horses from the Avon force. They then swamped the dunes on horseback in an attempt to scare people away, swishing their whips through the grass as they went. 'There will,' said Liz Roberts, 'be no repeat of 1984.' The real problem, she said, is that certain elements in the trust membership have put pressure on the organisation to act against nudism.

'We've had quite a campaign from local people to ban naturism on the beach,' she said. 'They try to claim that all the problems are caused by the nudists, but we don't have any proof of that whatsoever. Some of the people who complain may be the same ones, so this year we'll be keeping a tight log of complainants.' One of those who has made no secret of his opposition to the nudism on Studland Beach is Rowland Hitchcott, a trust member who lives in Bournemouth. Twice in the late 80s he tried to bring resolutions to the National Trust AGM calling for the banning of nudism on its property. Both failed.

His objection, he says, is that it can be uncomfortable down there for people who are not nudists. 'A friend of mine who's a teacher took some children down there and he didn't know it was a nudist beach,' he said. 'And he was really worried because he thought parents might write to him complaining.' Why? I asked. What happened? 'Well nothing actually happened but you know, it is embarrassing. And people can't walk their dogs down there any more. Families can't go down there.' Had Mr Hitchcott ever been naked on a beach? 'Eh, I'm not going to answer that.'

As far as the nudists are concerned, Rowland Hitchcott's complaints are bogus: the movement, they say, is all about families. 'The bona fide naturists on Studland Beach abide by all the rules,' said Ken Tullett the local spokesman for the central council for British naturism. 'Nudism is not the problem.' He is also unconcerned by the reports of people having sex with each other at the back of the dunes. 'Whichever free beach you go to anywhere in Europe, if you want to find strange things going on you will find it,' he said. 'I've even seen it on Brighton beach.'

Back in the dunes sits Colin James, stark naked in his little open-fronted tent. He stares up at the slate grey sky and listens to the sea breaking against the shore over the ridge behind him. Colin has been coming here to shed his clothes for 14 years now. Though only in his 40s he is no longer able to work because of ill health. Instead he comes here to sit on the beach. He has left his body to Southampton university when he dies; he says he wants his corpse to have a nice tan when they get it. Last year he managed 274 days at Studland Bay. He was here on January 2 this year, utterly naked as ever. That's the way he likes it.

He was here in 1984 when the police came with their horses. 'It was ludicrous. I was lying there and all of a sudden I look up and there's this bloody great horse snorting over me. What did they hope to achieve?' He does not have much time for the police. 'They should bugger off and catch some criminals,' he says. He maintains he can always spot the policemen now because they've replaced one uniform for another. Apparently they always wear the same sort of torn off T-shirts and shorts. There were none there on this particular day. 'Do you know, in all the time I've been coming here, all those years, I've only seen something going on between men maybe half a dozen times and really that's nothing. The real troublemakers are the straight couples. Some of these dunes are like amphitheatres. I've seen men and women going at it with audiences of 20 or more.'

Gay men tended to keep to the back dunes, out of the way where they wouldn't be hassled. I was, he said, far more likely to see a heterosexual couple playing with each other than a gay couple. He was absolutely right. Over the ridge on the sand, a naked man and a naked woman are standing up, embracing. This is not at the back of the dunes, nor in a hollow nor behind a tree. But right on the beach. Well, I suppose it beats volleyball.

Jay Rayner

Treasure: Five go mad in Cornwall
August 17 1993

Treasure and her friends are an exuberant bunch. To this quiet corner of Cornwall they have brought the flavour of Holloway. Pop music booms from their bedrooms, the television roars, lights blare, the meter runs out. The bathroom is in constant use and the hairdryer whirs for ever. The picturesque floorboards of our farmhouse resound with the clumping of Doc Martens and clogs; the peaceful village air is rent with squeals. Down here, Treasure's urban language rather grates on the sensibilities.

The word 'horny' is in constant use. I am assured this now merely means attractive. It is applied to the surf board and wetsuit vendor and his chums. Treasure is apt to call it out of the car window at passing youths, rather lowering the tone of our group, I feel. The dog has taken to hiding under the kitchen table. Its nerves are in shreds. So are mine. We wander the cliffs together, breathing deeply and trying to regain our composure. I am fearful that the villagers may rebel en masse and cast us out, just as Mr and Mrs Landlord did. Luckily our farmhouse is slightly isolated and I transport the girls to the beach as often as possible, where they may shriek freely.

Multiple periods and wretched dull weather have rather put paid to surfing, but no one seems to mind very much. Treasure and friends are rather keen on sitting about. They sit on the beach, in the beach cafe, on the harbour wall, outside the Tate. I cannot induce them to look inside. My suggestion of a bracing walk along the coastal path has been ignored. All five Treasures prefer to rest until midday, aiming to leave the house at two. They have shown interest only in a disco and a local cider and wine farm where tasting is encouraged.

Luckily, my friend Mrs H is staying up the road. I have a grown-up to talk to. In her house, the silence is almost absolute. Her son reads quietly and they visit churches and exhibitions, chatting in a cultivated way, taking healthy walks and swims. Mrs H is loving her holiday. Inspired by her example, I suggest to the girls that we all visit the Tate. There is little response. I will treat them. Still no response. Treasure has other, more pressing plans. 'I've got to Sun-In my hair tomorrow,' she says. 'We've been planning it for ages.' This means more intensive showering, hairdrying and clomping. Eventually she swans into the kitchen, her hair the colour of a banana. Hair slightly lightened by sun and a healthy complexion would have been my choice, but there is no sun and Treasure never was one for moderation.

She has, however, helped with the cooking, assuming the role of head prefect and becoming rather authoritative. We have had cream teas, crab, fresh mackerel, picnics and non-stop mass catering. Our holiday is almost at an end. I have a final stab at mustering up enthusiasm for the Tate. The girls agree to go. They seem almost keen. Perhaps the countryside has had a slightly beneficial effect after all. Daisy is making a large sandwich in the kitchen. 'It's so relaxing here,' she says, dreamily. 'I could stay here for ever.'

Michele Hanson

A Country Diary
June 10 1994

ROSELAND, CORNWALL: The family convened here for what used to be known as Whit week. Under its new title, the spring bank holiday, Monday heralded a week of welcome sunshine, light airs and gentle seas and a marked contrast to the climatic regime of the previous week. With five little grandchildren eager for the excitements of a bucket and spade week, we were indeed blessed that conditions permitted such activities. Picking the rising tide on Porthcurnick beach even a swim was possible most mornings though

I concede that the water temperature attracted only small numbers to share this pleasure with me. Rock pools produced excitements up to the level of a baby dogfish, and our twin handle controlled kite flew bravely in the on-shore wind. The lanes around were a riot of wildflowers in which foxgloves, valerian, and campion starred.

Only a few yards from our accommodation, the sound of bat on ball caught my ear on Wednesday evening. I hastened along to find Gerrans engaged in a 20 over knock out round of the Hawkey Cup against St Columb. This is good village cricket. The ground has a gradient from west to east of over four feet. The backdrop, a pewter sea framing Gull Rock and the distant Nare Head, is irrelevant to the on-field action but adds to the charm. But the wicket, certainly no worse than many I played on in cricketing days, and the tight boundaries, make for a high scoring match. And so it proved. Gerrans made 128 off their 20 overs and set the visitors a demanding rate of over six and over from the off. The tension built as the light faded. Much verbal encouragement in the rich dialects of rural Cornwall echoed across the verdant greensward. 'Ow wozzer?' is the local version of the appeal for dismissal. A tractor driver broke his homeward journey from the farm to draw in to the gate and the rich odours of the byre swept before him on the breeze. St Columb fell as they pursued the total in what was inevitably a thrash.

Colin Luckhurst

Box of delights
June 24 1995

It's cold, it's wet, your jelly shoes have cracked under the relentless assault from the round, hard shingle they call sand and you are pretending to have a good time. It's sad. What you want more than anything else is to go home. Yes, you've guessed it. You are doing the undo-able, you are attempting to sun worship without boarding a plane. You are on the south coast and your parents have made you come.

More than any other shared experience, the annual family holiday is the one memory most of us prefer to forget. A bit like going to the brownies – as soon as we reach relative maturity, we stop going. But it's not just the weather that causes us to wince at the idea of a week in the British Isles, it's the complete lack of beach culture. Pamela Anderson's magnificent mammaries may encourage high viewing figures for the Californian soap Baywatch, and clearly we'd be lost without them, but it's the aspirational element of the free 'n' easy, suntanned, surfing beach life that skinny white English teenagers yearn for.

Let's face it, as a nation we don't do beach. Well, not in any recognisable way. Or so I thought until I went to Sussex and met Phyllis Saunders. Phyllis has been doing beach since she was barely bigger than a pebble, and now, at a sprightly 83 years old, she is somewhat of an expert. The secret of Phyllis' success? An eight foot by six foot white wooden construction known as a beach hut. Lined up along the foreshore like a group of synchronised swimmers, the 285 privately-owned beach huts at Goring-by-Sea cut a fine figure on the coastal landscape. Every morning, from the beginning of spring, Phyllis and her fellow hutters decamp down to the beach and don't put up the shutters again until late autumn, thereby following a quintessentially English tradition that started in the early 18th century with the invention of bathing machines by a Quaker named Benjamin Beale.

In 1793, George III took the first royal splash from one of these contraptions and his son, the Prince of Wales, got so hooked he had the Pavilion at Brighton built so that he could indulge every day. The bathing machine was basically a beach hut on wheels, with a door and steps for access. It enabled aristocratic gentlewomen to bathe without fear of proto-paparazzi sneaking up on them. They would undress in the hut while a horse pulled it down to the beach and into the sea until the floor was just above the waves. To make doubly sure no one could see anything, when the horse stopped, a canopy was let down over the door and only then would the bather slip out for a modest splash around. It was an elaborate business that also involved wearing copious clothing and being led into the sea by a female 'dipper'.

Thankfully, things loosened up a little. By Victorian times it was possible to be on the same beach at the same time as a member of the opposite sex without a horse and cart. This was due in part to middle-class people travelling to Dieppe and Boulogne in search of fun and discovering the firmly-rooted huts that Phyllis and her friends enjoy today. The excitement of the beach hut is in part due to the domestic comforts it affords the user. Inside Phyllis's hut, for instance, are all the accoutrements needed for a scene from a Merchant-Ivory production. She has recently installed a new carpet and is keen to point out that tea-making facilities are available all day. There is also a collection of pre-war flip-flops and swimming costumes for the occasional guest caught short: 'We're not worried about fashion down here.' But hut interiors can generate stiff competition. 'One of my friends has her best china in there and is constantly painting the inside,' she says. 'All she needs is a front doorknocker and she could live in there. Some people can get too carried away.'

Phyllis goes on to explain the other uses of her hut: 'Having it means you can be on the beach all day and let the family get on with things while you keep a quiet eye.' And there have been unexpected bonuses, as her late husband David discovered. 'One summer we were down on the beach and he was swimming. When he came out of the water the tide had been so strong his false teeth had been yanked out. He was distraught as you can imagine. Then, five hours later, I was sitting outside the hut having a cup of tea and what should I notice being washed up? His teeth. I don't know where they'd been, but we certainly wouldn't have found them again if we hadn't had the hut.'

According to Mike Collis, the foreshore manager for Worthing and Goring council, demand for beach huts ebbs and flows over the years. He believes they are just the thing for stressed-out urbanites clamouring for their own piece of beachy nirvana: 'On a warm summer day the atmosphere on the foreshore is just like a small village. Some of the huts have been in the same family for decades and they all know each other. People from the city would love it.'

There are the endless possibilities for the designer age in these strange garden-shed constructions. Imagine a Philippe Starck hut, or a Terence Conran self-assembly version. Surely it can only be a matter of time before owning a beach hut on the south coast becomes as impressive as a private box at Wimbledon or a house in the same street as Tony Blair. And now that suntans are verboten, the lack of UV rays should be a positive asset. As for beach culture, Phyllis has this to offer: 'When my son Nigel was a boy, he used to love it at the hut. It meant he could stare at the nudist bathers through his binoculars.' Who needs Baywatch?

Sam Taylor

A Country Diary
June 5 1996

HARTLAND TO BUDE: Pink thrift and dazzling yellow gorse are intermixed on the cliff edge, high above a roaring sea. Creamy spume is driven on to boulder beaches and wisps of it whirl up the cliffs in eddies. This stretch of coast, running south from Hartland Point, takes the full brunt of westerly winds. Hedgerow trees in the sparsely-populated hinterland are severely stunted, shrinking away from prevailing weather and, along the coast, natural vegetation hugs the ground. Short streams, with headwaters rising just west of those flowing to the Tamar and Torridge, have cut out deep valleys, often with rocky gorges and waterfalls before the shore. The coastal path climbs and plunges precipitately up and down between cliffs, many looming more than 400 feet above the narrow valley mouths. After a bus ride to Hartland, we walk through bluebell woods on a muddy path strewn with hawthorn petals, past the landmark of Stoke's tall church tower to an isolated ruin, and then on the coastal path to Bude, more than 12 miles south. Clifftop fields are green after a fortnight's rain, contrasting with the bald cliffs of folded strata, sheer rock slabs and crumbling, slipping earth. Coastal valleys have remarkable flowery turfs carpeted with pale blue vernal squill, yellow vetch, daisies and silvery-pink thrift. White bladder campions, fragrant burnet roses and tussocks of thrift cling to rocky outcrops and, on damp sites, primroses and violets are still flowering after an exceptionally late cold spring. Drifts of bluebells and uncurling ferns grow amongst dwarf thickets of sloe, bramble, ivy and honeysuckle, which harbour boisterous wrens and blackcaps. On the last lap, south from Morwenstow, we are overlooked by the huge, white dishes and spheres of the incongruous listening station.

Virginia Spiers

The steel in the waves
June 29 1996

Madame Rene, 'whose knowledge is not the study of books but nature's gift', looks up from her mail order catalogue. The granddaughter of Gypsy Smith, Blackpool's world-famous palmist, is about to be set a stiff little test. This sea cruise on the *MV Princess Pocahontas* ('View shipping in the estuary, Isle of Grain and wartime wrecks – full commentary, tea, coffee and bar on board') ... would she happen to know if it's running today? Or did someone just omit to wipe the blackboard?

I am certain that the clairvoyant will deny all knowledge of the vessel's movements, thereby making a nonsense of her claims to read the future. But I am wrong. 'It were here yesterday,' she says in an accent so unquestionably Blackpudlian that it could be Gypsy Smith herself speaking. 'But no. I don't think it's coming today.' Not that I approached Madame Rene in order to catch her out. But who else is there to ask about the boat trips? The woman who sells ices has a bit of a crisis on. The pier has lost its power supply, and her freezer has been hooked up to a raucous petrol generator. Conversation is tiring. 'Pocahontas! PocaHONtas! P-O-C-A-H-O-N-T-A-S. Look, just forget it, right?' And apart from the chap in the Jolly Fisherman pub (all canned drinks 70p) and a girl who seems overly preoccupied with her hot dogs, there is nobody much besides me and a sunhatted coach-party from Chelmsford. Out here, at the business end of the world's longest pleasure pier, one-and-a-third miles from anywhere and well on the way to Kent – out here, in what seems like the very middle of the Thames estuary, and with a power failure that might take a week to fix, times are lean.

'The Pier is Southend,' wrote Sir John Betjeman, adding wittily: 'Southend is the Pier.' And today, one of the dinky diesels that haul trains out over the mud carries the poet's name. On the front of the engine, a peeling sticker bears the borough's coat of arms and the motto: 'Per ecclesiam, per mare' (By the church, by the sea). On the driver's window is another sticker. It says: 'Lifeboatmen go after two bangs.' He was right, of course, old Sir John. This horizontal Blackpool Tower, thrust into London's river at the point where it finally makes up its mind to become the North Sea, has done for Southend what George Orwell did for Wigan.

Today, though, any stranger who has seen the faded filigree delights of Brighton's Palace and West piers (the latter now romantically cut off from the shore) might tread these bare Essex boards and ask what the fuss was about. Two fires – the first, in 1976, was so spectacular that it appeared on all the world's front pages – have left Southend with little to swank about but its length in this, the year of the pier. The once Xanadudlian superstructures at either end of the great steel spine are reduced to flailing girders and charcoal beams. Even the single-track railway is but a pastiche of its former self. At the seaward end, where now is but a smattering of benches and a selection of kiosks, a small town once rose from the waves. Sleek electric trains travelled to and fro on double tracks, and 25 ships called most days of the week.

Where Mme Rene practises in a lonely yellow shed, where plastic sheeting flaps around a makeshift bandstand, there once stood a fantastical complex of buildings on four levels, one above the other. Amid a labyrinth of streets and grand stairways were arcades and shops and bars of different sizes. There was a proper theatre. There were halls of slot machines. And somewhere at the heart of it all, hard to find twice among the chasing lights and distorting mirrors, there was a restaurant devoted entirely to the consumption of bacon and eggs. What began 110 years ago as a simple if ambitious landing stage for ships at low tide had become an attraction in its own right – glittering and exhilarating, an ever-so-slightly dangerous item of play equipment. At its peak, before the advent of cheap foreign holidays in resorts where the sun was always up and the tide was never out, five-and-a-half million people played on Southend Pier each year. Slightly dangerous? Well, imagine if you were seven ... It was the idea of it, you see – the knowledge that this was the longest pier in the world.

Sure, the Russians had some sort of jetty for bringing oil ashore. And no doubt the military had things that no one knew about. But these weren't really piers in the accepted sense. And they certainly didn't have a railway on them. And what a railway! To begin with, it would bang and clank like a ghost train through an echoing zone of grimy lattice girders and mysterious pipes, and all the while you knew that beneath you, unseen, was the beach. Then, with a clatter, you were out into the open air, over the sea. Except that the water, invariably, was playing hard to get. A mile out, even beyond the point where the two trains passed each other, you would still see men in waders digging for lugworms. Then, always at the last minute, the sea would make its presence known, at first barely distinguishable from the rippled mud, but ultimately brown and hostile. And wherever you walked in that crazy town on stilts, the heavy waves churned underneath your feet. Occasionally, you would glimpse them unexpectedly – through a crack, perhaps, in a make-believe street. And then they would seem all the more dangerous, because you had forgotten for a moment that you were one-and-a-third miles out on a limb, and the sea had caught you unawares.

On those rare occasions when the tide was in and the waves ran all the way back to the shore, the pier head resembled a collection of ocean liners, water up to their Plimsoll lines, moored together at odd angles. But when the water was low, it was the spooky, sploshing substructure that drew the eye downward. Sometimes, I would see anglers down there – older boys who seemed somehow free both from fear and from parental control. That was the underworld where I was not allowed to go – in truth, would not have dared to go. This afternoon, I rather fancied the *Princess Pocahontas*. But if Mme Rene is correct, she will not grace us with her presence. This is doubly disappointing, since boarding a boat at low tide would have enabled me to glimpse the bowels of this great charred hulk. As it is, a variety of signs warn me of the slippery dangers below, and the stairways are closed off. 'No access unless accompanied by pier staff,' says a notice. And, as if to reinforce the point, a woman is barking repeatedly to her son as he creeps mollusc-like down an old slipway: 'Eddie, get back up here! Get here this minute!'

So, for a while, I content myself with a tour of the upper deck, trying to figure out exactly where the slot-machine hall had stood – the proper theatre and that half-remembered bacon-and-eggery. Was it here, amid this burnt forest of olympian piles, where foot-thick timber balks still carry rusted iron collars around their necks? Or here, where a dozen concrete stanchions have been amputated at the ankle? How could something surrounded by water have burned so fiercely? At the far end, behind a window, is a delicate device of floats and pulleys. 'From this tide gauge,' reads a notice, 'tidal heights are telemetered to the Port of London Authority Thames Navigation Service and to the National Rivers Authority Thames Barrier Control Room.' And then I spot the angler. He is down by the waterline, clambering among the barnacled supports, his carbon-fibre rod flexing like a whiplash aerial. Suddenly, I am seven again.

Barriers seal off the grandest double stairway. But around the back, next to the tide gauge, I discover a narrow flight of steps leading down the outside of the pier. Seaweed the texture of doll's hair and the colour of bottled mint sauce coats every surface, and a skein of orange fishing line hangs from a severed coachbolt. And then I am on a concrete floor. I expected it to be slippery, like the sign said. But underfoot, barnacles and mussels form a gravel carpet. Every yard or so are translucent blobs of melted candle-wax. These are the hundreds of moon jellyfish which, stranded by the falling tide, are now drying out on this unnatural strainer. Septuagenarian concrete arches support this section of the pier-head. These survived the fire, but here and there the cement surface is abscessed, and marine creatures with toothbrush legs scuttle in and out of the ruptured blisters. At three points of the compass, vertebral vistas recede to the horizon. If this is a drowned cathedral, then the oil-refinery flare that burns at the end of one aisle is a smoky candle.

This would all be rather poetic and not at all unnerving if there were another living soul around. But the mysterious angler has vanished, and it occurs to me that, should I take one wrong step, perhaps drop through the floor and into the churning brown water below, nobody would be there to fish me out. My cries would be taken for the shrieks of some herring gull. Come to think of it, I could swear Mme Rene gave me a troubled look when I asked her about the boat earlier ... If I go up that stairway quicker than I came down it, I compensate for this unseemly haste by returning to the shore five times more slowly than I left it.

The train is no TGV, but walking back on the footway is a good way of finding out just how long a mile-and-a-third is. Anyway, it makes sense these days to ride out and saunter home. Ever since the pier-head fire, there's been more to look at on the return journey. In a year or two, it might be a different story. Southend borough council, the pier's owner, has high hopes. A private firm wants to rebuild the huge bowling alley at the shore end that was destroyed by fire last year, and a second company will begin work replacing some of the pier-head buildings this winter. There are even tentative plans to construct a £14m rollercoaster, out there over the water, a mile-and-a-third from dry land. They reckon it will scare the pants off a million-and-a-half customers each year. I reckon they could be right. Personally, I've had enough frights for one day. No chance of rebuilding that bacon-and-egg restaurant, I suppose? I thought not. Oh, well. Some things are best left as memories.

David Newnham

Wight watch
August 17 1996

On a balmy Sunday evening in June, with pale sunshine spilling across wet sands, the woman from the shore-side caff at Forelands dashed out to watch the QE2 cut a swathe through the Solent boating crowd as it swept on towards Southampton. The woman did not need her binoculars to observe another set piece – in the foreground was one of those English watercolour scenes from a more certain time: of children throwing balls to wet dogs, families trawling through shallow water for crabs, and chaps with their trousers rolled up, sitting outside beach-huts beneath cliffs smudged with red valerian.

Sunshine makes the English seaside feel better about itself, and there was a hazy serenity about that seascape. With more sunshine than most other places around these shores, the Isle of Wight should be doing a good trade. After all, its deckchairs now have matching striped awnings as protection against the sun and global warming, and elderly ladies in socks and sandals clutch Ambre Solaire as well as handbags. But along the most well-trodden stretch of coast (between Shanklin and Sandown), with its bay-windowed hotels smothered in chintz upholstery and boasting 'Macaroni cheese and crusty bread, £2.75', Mr Hooper was selling up. Amid rows of cosy bathing huts (£26 a week to hire), Hooper's (boat builders and longshoremen) had flourished for nearly 150 years, providing trips on white launches to see the Needles. But no more. So Mr Hooper had put out his collection of stout, shoe-brown china tea-pots for sale, alongside vintage deckchairs (sans awnings) of golden beech wood. The recent rumblings that the Isle of Wight could be seeking some sort of Manx-like status indicate that all is not well (next month's opinion poll on devolution will reveal the islanders' leanings).

Perhaps it's because the place does not know whether it's coming or going; perhaps it's because it got there first. On the side of a bus was painted 'Blackgang Chine – arguably the oldest theme park in the world'. That's not necessarily a prize-winning slogan for an 'attraction' whose offerings of 'enchanted wood and rumpus mansion' and 'Sleeping Beauty's Castle' can scarcely match the techno-flash of Futuroscope parks. At Ventnor, I asked an elderly couple for directions. I thought they might live there. No, they said, they were 'overners' (from the mainland) too, adding, 'You only asked us because we're old, didn't you?' Which, in a way, was true. They were Londoners and delighted with the island. 'We just didn't know there were so many beautiful places here.' Which is also true. Ventnor has a certain sense of itself, and plans to become the island's antique centre.

With its great green swirling backdrop of holm oaks, Ventnor looks faintly Mediterranean, while the botanic gardens at the nearby Undercliff make a good job of sub-tropical planting. Even the houses have fantasy names, like Montecello and Curaçao (the rest of the island has rows of Seaviews, Seahavens and Seabreezes). At the Ventnor Heritage museum, there are photographs that illustrate the town's links with its most grandiose – and economically significant – past: the magnificent Royal National Hospital for Diseases of the Chest, opened in 1868 and closed in 1964. Its patients recuperated in a half-mile-long terrace of buildings, each of its 162 balconied rooms facing south towards the sea and all linked by an underground service corridor.

Indeed, the island enjoyed its most flourishing times in the 19th century, a beneficiary of that era's initiative (roads, ferries, railway) and creativity. Ventnor boasts its celeb line-up – Marx holidayed here, while the doctor/writer Henry de Vere Stacpoole donated a pond to the nearby village of Bonchurch. He wrote, in forthright manner: 'On this rock each year a moorhen makes her nest, a model of neatness and propriety. May you who enjoy this place emulate her admirable example.' Which couldn't be said for another Bonchurch lad, the poet Swinburne, even if his parents did have Dickens (another summer visitor) for tea. Like many others, Swinburne made his way to the island's west end – along what is now part of the Tennyson Heritage Coast – past the Undercliff, the pretty village of Niton, and the straight military road, built in the Napoleonic wars, over the downs to Freshwater. There, for almost 40 years, Alfred Lord Tennyson (then Poet Laureate) settled, luring crowds of literati to the island. He wrote – not, perhaps, on one of his better days: '... Come to the Isle of Wight; / Where far from noise and smoke of town, / I watch the twilight falling brown / All round a careless order'd garden / Close to the ridge of a noble down.' One gets the picture, and the chalk Afton Down (air worth 'sixpence a pint', said Lord T), for example, is still magnificent.

But, these days, there's not much of a literary feel to Freshwater, although both Lynne Truss's new comic novel, *Tennyson's Gift* (based on the Freshwater folk), and the reopening of Dimbola Lodge (the home of photographer Julia Margaret Cameron) may help to revive those apparently heady days. Tennyson's house, Farringford, is now a not-so-posh hotel, and Freshwater itself sprawls this way and that, a suburban melange. Much better to take the well-marked trail from Dimbola to under-stated Yarmouth (Regency architecture, no beaches, and the last working wooden pier in Britain) through the River Yar valley. For cyclists and walkers the island is a pleasure, the result of much hard graft by the council and environmental groups: masses of signposts and leaflets, special cycling routes, nature trails and walks to fit all moods and occasions.

The coastal path, for example, is a 60-mile round-trip of beaches and cliffs, geology and archaeology; or try the inland Bembridge trail, through wetlands, forest, medieval villages and Roman villas. The Bembridge trail goes through Brading. Forget its Wax museum ('You Won't See Anything Better Throughout The World') with its photograph of David Dimbleby on holiday there in 1980, and remember that it was once a port. Indeed, its town houses expectantly face all in a row, as if the sea were lapping at their foundations. Nowadays, from Brading, you can explore inland along Brading down, or northwards towards the sea along the East Yar valley, an important wetlands area. Another stretch of wetlands, and perhaps the real find of rural Isle of Wight, is Newtown. A national nature reserve, managed by the National Trust (as is one-tenth of the island) in the most low-key sort of way, Newtown estuary lies beside meadow and ancient woodlands that were once part of a now-lost townscape – and the island's main port. Established by the Bishop of Winchester in 1254, Newtown was just that: a place where, in a radical development, the plot-owners, known as burgesses, paid a rent for their land instead of manorial tithes. There is little left: the Newtown Old Town Hall stands alone in a meadow, while Gold Street and Silver Street are now grassy pathways.

There are walks too, through coppiced woodland where you can find the butterfly orchid, the richly named corky-fruited water dropwort and the golden samphire. Newtown estuary has a remote, lost feel. The salt marsh, mud flats and tides are breeding and migratory grounds for colonies of birds – and the bird-watchers come, too. Like Phyl, who helps look after the hides and – besides her birding interests – cooks puddings for red squirrels to forage for in her back garden. The island has a new initiative, called Red Watch, to help conserve the red squirrel, which, although protected from the presence of the predatory grey, needs a helping hand to flourish. Perhaps the whole place needs a Wight Watch – an imaginative eye to stimulate its own survival and wellbeing. On the ferry back from Ryde (robust, Victorian good looks – well, at least from the sea) to the mainland, a teenage girl was avidly studying a pile of brochures for Turkish holidays. At that moment, I was thinking fondly of the Isle of Wight, and despite the brochure pictures – empty beaches, a sun-dried landscape and an occasional camel – I thought: personally, I'd rather be in Ventnor.

Polly Pattullo

Eco Soundings
November 13 1996

Campaigners take heart: Surfers Against Sewage is celebrating South West Water's plans for full treatment works for Newquay's beaches. This will include ultra violet light disinfection, which kills off the viruses that make people on Britain's premier surfing beach sick. The scheme will be finished years before the deadline of 2000 set by Europe. SAS was even moved to this tribute to its old enemy: 'Instead of trying to get away with the bare legal minimum, they have grasped the nettle and gone for the best option for all.'

It may be inconvenient for the residents of Pevensey Bay and Seaford in Sussex, but we salute the forces of nature. The Environment Agency reports that in 24 hours 100,000 tonnes of shingle disappeared from Pevensey and a similar quantity from Seaford during the recent storms. The agency is to replenish the losses, but to show how puny man's efforts are it takes 5,000 lorry loads, at 20 tonnes a time, just to replace the losses on one beach.

Paul Brown

A Country Diary
January 10 1997

NORTHUMBERLAND: Billy Shiel, a native of Seahouses, has spent much of his life in a coble, a flat-bottomed fishing boat. A third-generation fisherman, he tended lobster pots at dawn from an early age. Twenty years ago tourism changed his life and he has since taken thousands of visitors to see the prolific bird life and the grey seal colony on the Farne Islands. A fine naturalist with a wealth of ornithological knowledge, it was Billy who explained to me the salient differences between the terns. Now his expertise and contribution to the tourist industry has been recognised by the award of an MBE in the New Year's Honours list. 'Grace Darling was our heroine in the last century,' said one village resident. 'Mr Shiel is our local hero now.' Their achievements were different but were both earned on the water in a fishing coble. Grace Darling rowed out from the Longstone lighthouse to rescue crew members of a steamer which had been wrecked on the rocks. Every morning, all the year round, Billy goes down to the harbour before breakfast to take a look at the weather. 'I listen to the shipping forecast but I can tell what it's going to do myself by looking at the sea and the sky.' Had he ever had a boatload of visitors stranded on the islands because treacherous tides and strong winds are common here? He admitted there had been one or two occasions when he had seen the elements turn nasty and had cut short a visit to head back to the mainland. He has a huge responsibility to the public. He used to carry up to

12 visitors; now the boats are licensed for 70 and there are a lot of school parties. 'My favourite time of year is late April and May,' he said, 'when the birds start arriving. Every trip is an adventure and I'll never lose interest in the place.' The Farnes are a group of rocky stacks and islands covering 236 acres formed from erosion-resistant quartz doloerite, the most easterly outcrop of the Great Whin Sill.

Veronica Heath

A Country Diary
July 12 1997

MACHYNLLETH: How much do you know about sea spleenwort? Probably not a lot because it lives mostly on sea cliffs and is often inaccessible. It is an attractive fern with shining green leaves and because it seems so full of sea-longing, we might reasonably assume that it needs the spray of the salty waves. Certainly it fears the kiss of Jack Frost and therefore does far better along Britain's western coasts than down the eastern side. This endearing fern has been much in my mind since a fortnight ago, when three friends and I spent a week on Ynys Enlli, the little Welsh island the Vikings called Bardsey, when they lived there. The island is much visited for its birds but we looked at ferns as well. We found the sea spleenwort abundant on rocks sheltered from the prevailing winds and we censused its population along a specimen stretch of the shore, so that future fern enthusiasts will know whether it is holding its own or not. We also thought how interesting it would have been if only the Vikings had done the same for us. Remembering how delirious the Victorians were about ferns, I checked on what a couple of 19th century fern buffs wrote about sea spleenwort. First, Edward Newman, who said: 'It is a most difficult fern to deal with in cultivation unless carefully protected from exposure.' He grew it luxuriantly in a greenhouse, thereby showing that it does not really need salt in the air. Then, in a book by Edward Lowe, I was amazed to learn what stature it can achieve. While on Bardsey, its fronds are mostly a very few inches long, yet in the deep fissures in Co Clare they can be a yard long and must look magnificent. What better reason for making a trip to that botanically sacred region?

William Condry

Surfers lift seaside town on the crest of a wave
August 23 1997

Usually, it is the sea which is angry and the surfers who ride it who are laid back. This weekend, however, it is the other way around. Among the surfers gathered in Newquay, Cornwall, the country's surfing capital, there is a noticeable mood of resentment. It is not caused by the weather – although the still, dull skies means still, duller water and waves – but by the beach bum stereotypes of the sport. In recent years, tens of thousands of people have taken to boards to try to emulate the top performers. Thousands have fallen in love with riding the waves. But, with its image of California cool, surfing is often portrayed as a cross between Baywatch and Blind Date; the equivalent of polo, with barrel-chested hunks and pouting pin-up supporters.

One recent report packed all the cliches in one sentence: 'It's a world of blond-streaked hair, firm jaws and even firmer stomachs, where no bikini is too small and no surfboard – or surfer's ego – is too large.' It focused on 'sun (sometimes), sea (always) and sex (too much say the locals)' – and it really 'pissed off' Barrie Hall, a surfer for 15 years. 'That kind of thing is just crap,' he said yesterday. 'This is a sport and you simply can't get wrecked and perform the next day.'

Colin Wilson agrees. The head of the British Surfing Association, himself a surfer for more than 30 years, says: 'If you took away the commercialism now and all the trappings, you would still have the surfers because that's what it's all about – surfing. They're not really poseurs. They just love what they do.' But commercialism is unavoidable as you walk through the streets of Newquay, as this formerly typical British seaside resort hosts surfing's biggest domestic event, the British Open. Where there were once sweeps of souvenir shops and restaurants, there is now surf shop after surf shop. In all, 20 are dotted throughout the town, many in the most expensive locations. Adding in the five local surf board manufacturers, the distribution centres for the exclusive leisure wear stocked in the shops, and spin-offs such as surf schools, it is estimated that surfing employs up to 2,000 people in the area. This weekend 120,000 people are expected in town – generating business worth more than £300m a year – and up to a quarter of them will be surfers or fans.

Many do conform to the stereotypes; boasting elderly VW camper vans, accents more Bondi beach than Cornish burr, and ridiculously lightened blond hair. With pubs and nightclubs doing a roaring trade off the hip young community, it is easy to see how the beach bum image sticks. Especially when many other visitors to the town are the more typical family holidaymakers, replica football tops, sunburns and all. But even the VW vans have a purpose: the first surfers used them as cheap, makeshift homes in which they could travel abroad.

The nomadic, scruffy lifestyle was what put many in Newquay off surfing when it first began to become popular in the mid-1980s. Now, however, the town boasts of its surfing status. There are even plans to build a £5m surfing centre on Fistral beach, the main surfing beach. Bob Morgan, tourism officer with the local council, said: 'There was a time when some of the hotels refused to have surfers, now several of them have surfing schools. 'That's how it's changed – and that's why it's so important, especially as families are now getting into it. Mums and dads want to see what it is that keeps their children occupied for hours at time. They have a go and get hooked.' The proof was in the sea just further along Fistral beach from the championships, where family groups mingled with teenagers and the occasional blond bombshell. Civil servant Jill Bateson, aged 50, of Huntingdon, there with her son Richard, aged 15, was converted years ago. She repeated the refrain of all surfers trying to explain their passion: 'It's just getting in the water and the waves ...' For Mr Wilson, a fortysomething from Penzance who was among the original 1960s devotees, that enthusiasm remains the most important thing. 'All the shops and everything, that's just commercialism gone mad really. But it brings money into the sport as well,' he said. 'Surfers don't give a stuff if it's fashionable or trendy. They love doing it just for the sake of it. Simple as that.' And, in a world of multi-million pound sports stars, the proof is that the first prize for winning the surfing open is not a huge cheque or even a small bundle of cash but just a small silver trophy – and the glory.

Nick Varley

Wild rover
April 16 1998

Having a dog can rather blight your holidays. Leave it behind and you feel wretched, take it along and you are welcome almost nowhere. But the White Lodge hotel, between Newquay and Padstow, Cornwall, is heaven for dog owners. You know the minute you get there. The entrance hall is crammed with dog information: dog (and saucy) postcards, dog pamphlets. The walls are ablaze with fluorescent dog notices: 'Dogs are welcome on the beach all the year round', 'Please pick up their excrement'; 'Pooper scoopers are available at the desk'; 'Dogs die in hot cars.' And, of course, 'Dogs are welcome in the hotel' – in the bar, lounge, bedroom, bathroom, on the lawn, everywhere, except for the dining room while people are eating.

In we go with the dog. Staff and guests coo over it, like a chubby baby in Italy. Doggie chews and biscuits and several brands of dog food are sold in the bar. And, what luxury, the dog has her very own divan bed in our room. Would we please just spread her own cloth over it? The hotel overlooks the bay of Mawgan Porth, with its two large headlands and wide sandy beach, to which there is a five-minute shortcut over the dunes. No lead necessary. The dog is in paradise.

She bounds freely about the hotel, out across the dunes and down to the beach, from which there is direct access to the coastal path, where you are advised to keep your dog on a lead. But at meal-times, we must leave her alone in our room. Walking along the corridors, we hear the odd whimper or snuffle behind closed doors from other dogs, briefly abandoned during breakfast or dinner. In the early mornings, the occasional bark can be heard as residents go for walkies, otherwise you'd hardly know there are 14 dogs staying here. You might expect trouble, what with the proprietor's two dalmatians, the wine waitress's wild but charming mongrel puppy, the next door builder's sheltie, my boxer, two yorkies, three cocker spaniels and the rest, but there were no fights, no mess; everything was perfectly clean and tidy.

The kitchen staff provided boiled eggs for a pregnant cocker spaniel, which would eat nothing else. They also kept my darling dog's boiled chicken in the fridge (she has particular dietary requirements) – nothing was too much trouble. Clientele is mainly dog-owners and the odd couple of golfers. Naturally, the talk is of dogs – their age, little habits, state of health – fairly sickening for the non-dog-owner, but then they can easily go somewhere else. For the golfing dog-owner, the hotel has a list of golf-courses which allow dogs. And using this dog's haven as a base, you can visit several 'great gardens of Cornwall', a short drive away, which also allow dogs – Heligan, Trewithen, the Japanese garden and Trebah, where the dog was even allowed to visit the restaurant (lovely home-made soup and fruit crumble).

This was down on the south coast, where the beaches are stonier but the bread is sometimes wholemeal. I did desert my dog for a couple of hours to ride across the dunes and gallop along the four miles of Porranporth surfing beach, 20 minutes' drive away and my idea of heaven. 'Watch out for surfers, dogs and potholes.' (In the summer, horses are only allowed on the beach after 6pm). Then back to our room, where the dog and I are reunited. Together we watch *Vets In Practice*, to general approval.

Michelle Hanson

The wages of song are death
September 12 1998

Rousing songs have been echoing over Hull docks to celebrate an era when management was sweating as much labour out of workers as quickly as possible. Sea shanties are taught at schools as a reminder of the quaint past. But as the organisers of the International sea shanty festival will tell you, they were designed as carefully as any Industrial Revolution mill to get fewer people to do more work.

'They were part of an age of ferocious competition,' said Peter Hayselden, co-organiser of the festival. 'Few types of music have been so closely associated with specific jobs of hard, physical labour.' The songs' rhythms and cadences are tailored precisely to hauling ropes, turning capstans and other essential work on clippers plying the routes to America and the Far East. 'A good shantyman's worth six more hands on the rope,' was the saying, and some lines even paid more to a singer who could weld a group together to raise anchor, load cargo and put on more sail. 'Short drag shanties' developed for quick tasks needing a few powerful heaves, and 'halyard shanties' were created for prolonged and heavier work. 'If the rhythm's there, though, and you need a few less people to do a job, you can see the attraction for management in music to help you work.'

Martin Wainwright

National Trust enters the jazz age
May 12 1999

There were cocktails and jazz on the lawn yesterday to herald the return of the good old days at Coleton Fishacre, a remote country house in Devon which is first cousin to the glamorous ballroom wing of Claridge's in London. Having opened Paul McCartney's childhood home in Liverpool last summer, the National Trust has moved back several musical decades and opened its first jazz age house, the 1920s home of the D'Oyly Carte family, owners of the opera company and the Savoy and Claridge's hotels.

Alan Powers, the 20th century architectural historian who has worked with the trust on the house, has a theory that the stark interiors of Coleton Fishacre and other houses of the period are due to the cocktails. The inhabitants were permanently unsteady on their pins and didn't want too much furniture to bump into. The trust has accepted his theory with enthusiasm. Almost every room has its tray of cocktail glasses and shaker – except the bathrooms, which instead offer sumptuously hand-blown crystal sponge and soap dishes, recreated for the house by Dartington glass.

The trust has owned Coleton Fishacre, on a headland near Dartmouth, since 1982, but it has never been open to the public. The estate was mainly acquired for the sake of the coastal path passing the garden gate, as the trust sought to acquire hundreds of miles of coastline. The house has been restored partly in response to 15 years of visitors to the spectacular garden pressing noses to the windows trying to see in. 'The whole point of this house was to look out and admire the views of the garden and the sea,' said Ceri Johnson, the trust's historic buildings officer, who has spent two years researching the history of the house. It was built in 1926 for Rupert D'Oyly Carte – whose father, Richard, founded the opera company and forged the partnership with Gilbert and Sullivan – and

Lady Dorothy Gathorne-Hardy, daughter of the Earl of Cranbrook. The architect was Rupert Milne, who also designed the ballroom wing for Claridge's. A painted map shows a little sunlit kingdom full of escapist happiness, Rupert seated on the headland with his dalmatian. In fact the marriage did not survive the death of their only son in a car accident. Lady Dorothy left in 1936, and Rupert remained until his death in 1948, when the house was sold by his daughter.

Maev Kennedy

Shiverers in the deep
June 5 1999

Waterlog: A Swimmer's Journey by Roger Deakin 320pp, Chatto & Windus, £15.99

I've nothing against swimming – except, perhaps, that it gets you wet. Fortunately, Roger Deakin is made of sterner stuff. He has to be. There are many different ways to travel around Britain, but if I had to rank them from hair-shirt austerity at one end of the scale to pampered luxury at the other, I know where I'd place swimming.

Like all good travel books, *Waterlog* is a record of parallel journeys. First, the standard one through time and space. This starts in the Scilly Isles, in April, from 'a makeshift planked jetty known as Anneka's Quay, after Anneka Rice, who built it (with a little help from the Parachute Regiment) for one of those television programmes in which she performs the impossible before breakfast'. It finishes eight months later, on New Year's Day, in the moat of the author's home in Suffolk. Along the way, he breast-strokes his way through rivers, lakes and seas, with the odd canal, pond and Lubetkin's Penguin Pool at London Zoo thrown in for good measure. (Not that he actually joins the penguins for a dip – though you can tell he's itching to do so.)

Secondly, Deakin writes about the journey through life. No contemporary non-fiction work would be complete without this quasi-confessional, Nick Hornby-style autobiography. *Waterlog* begins with nostalgic recollections of filling in I-Spy books during the 1950s, and ends with the ascetic activities of the Walberswick Shiverers, a group of friends who exercise their right to insanity by plunging into the North Sea each Christmas Day.

So far, so what, you might be tempted to think. But there is a third journey here too: a social history of our obsession with water. This is mainly told through encounters with people Deakin meets on his travels, from Sid, the fenland eel-trapper, to Denis, the skipper of a Medway fishing-boat. Each of these very British eccentrics has his tale to tell, and highly entertaining they are too. During these conversations, Deakin carefully balances the roles of spectator and participant. He has the swimmer's ability to be immersed in and yet somehow apart from his medium, revealed in his ambivalence towards the wetsuit: 'The problem about wearing a wetsuit is sensory deprivation; it is a species of whole-body condom... There is no getting away from the fact that a wetsuit is an anaesthetic to prevent you experiencing the full force of your physical encounter with cold water, and in that sense it is against nature and something of a killjoy.'

It is the fact that the wetsuit is somehow 'against nature' that really causes him to dislike it. For a man whose forensically accurate observations of aquatic wildlife are peppered throughout the book, this is the ultimate sin. Once he strips off and towels himself down, Deakin's next project must surely be an anthology of water-related literature. All the classic names are here, from Izaak Walton to Henry Williamson. Among those less well-known for their love of swimming are Daphne du Maurier, D H Lawrence and Bruce Grobbelaar, who makes a brief cameo appearance at Winchester Crown Court during one of Deakin's rare diversions from the water. But you can't help feeling that Deakin prefers being immersed in the wet stuff to writing about it, even if he does do so uncommonly well. *Waterlog* is a book about a cold, wet subject written with a warmth and passion it surely deserves, but has rarely had before.

Stephen Moss

A Country Diary
July 9 1999

NORTHUMBERLAND: A thousand years ago, Coquet Island offered refuge to monks and hermits. Now a nature reserve, it is owned by the Duke of Northumberland and leased to the RSPB. Twenty thousand pairs of nesting birds come here during the breeding season. Sandstone was quarried during the 17th century and the low cliffs are the result of this activity; coal was mined and sent to Newcastle. Until the lighthouse was automated in 1990, the keepers were guardians of the island, now watched over by RSPB wardens and Dave Gray, a naturalist who skippers puffin cruises around this ornithologist's paradise. As we head out of Amble harbour, tossing in a stiff breeze on the swell of the North Sea, Dave tells us: 'On March 15, the first puffins arrived, a week later than last year, and now 13,000 pairs are on the island.' The noise of the birds is deafening and we can see the numerous puffin families, jostling shoulder to shoulder on the rocks. A forlorn, sickly chick has been abandoned on a rock and Dave remarks that the black-headed gulls will have it by nightfall. Four species of tern nest here, with 15 pairs of roseate terns recorded this year. This is the southernmost breeding site for eider duck on the east coast; male eiders can be seen consorting in chatty groups in Amble harbour.

One family came alongside our boat. 'As soon as they are born the eider now make for the estuary,' Dave says. 'There must be something in the feed there.' From autumn to spring, redshank, curlew and wigeon regularly feed here. The saltmarsh and sand dunes surrounding the estuary are rich in the colourful flowers of sea thrift and bloody cranesbill. Boat owners now use a special pad to absorb oil in their boats' sump so that they do not pollute the estuary when the bilges are emptied. Grey seals surface around our craft, the bulls with black heads and the females with spots, rather like dalmations yet of being near humans. The Sea Mammal research unit are now surveying the survival of grey seal pups from the Isle of May in the Firth of Forth; 215 have been tagged with small green and yellow hats which will fall off when the animals moult next season.

Veronica Heath

Sand and Surf,
and Maybe Sun:
2000-2009

A Country Diary
February 5 2000

YORKSHIRE: Even on a still day the wind blows hard over the exposed chalk cliffs above Flamborough. The day of our visit was not still. Following the coastal footpath along the cliff top of Flamborough Head we were entertained by fulmars and kittiwakes gliding on the air currents rising up from the face of the sheer chalk cliffs. In spring, the few winter tenants of the cliffs and stacks are joined by thousands of others and the species range widens to include puffins, guillemots and razorbills.

At sea level, the pounding of the North Sea has created sea caves and arches in the soft chalk, evolving into blowholes when the sea finally bursts through the cliff slope. In places, the thin soils have slipped, taking the coastal path with them. Elsewhere, there are stretches where the path feels dangerously close to the edge and it is a long way down. At Briel Nook a solitary chalk stack stands a hundred feet clear of the water, yet someone has managed to place an old car tyre on the top. We speculated as to whether they had climbed up from a boat, dragging the tyre behind them, or thrown it, like a hoop-la contestant, from the cliff top. Either way would be exceedingly dangerous. The tyre may look odd, but a herring gull family has made good use of it as a ready made nest container. The pressure on today's farmers means that the fields inland reach as close to the edge as a tractor dare drive. Intensive arable has pushed the coarse coastal grass and chalk loving orchids, cowslips and vetches into an ever-narrowing strip. Skylarks nest in this shrinking habitat, under increasing disturbance from the footpath traffic. It is hoped that some of the inland arable and improved grazing pastures will be allowed to drift back to nature, letting the old grassland provide a seed bank to recolonise the fields. If this happens, skylarks will be able to nest under less pressure, perhaps in greater numbers. In a landscape where every possible inch goes under the plough, it would be a real turnaround if just some could be returned to the wild.

Pete Bowler

A Country Diary
April 6 2000

HOLKHAM BEACH: During our visit to the coast there were two seasons in evidence – one on either side of the belt of Corsican pines that stretches for about three miles from Wells towards the village of Burnham Overy Staithe. To the south of the wood it was sunny and spring-like. The open track formed a warm corridor of still air and there were knots of yellow coltsfoot at the path edge, and in the trees overhead a number of chiffchaffs were performing their unmistakable two-note song. Yet once we crossed to the seaward edge through the dense barrier of the trees the climate changed dramatically. A north wind swept in across the open expanse of sandy flats and we were grateful for our gloves, hats and coats. Amongst the groups of people walking there we could see just one small summer tableau, where a family had stripped down to bare legs and were playing at the water's edge. The moment you looked beyond them, towards the North Sea, their game appeared like a rather desperate optimism. The surface was a cold glassy blue and every few seconds the swell pitched up several hundred common scoter. These sea duck, which form a customary winter flock along this stretch of coast, were involved in a much more serious kind of game, because a horde of gulls roved amongst them as the ducks dived under the water for food. Intermittently a scoter would bob to the surface with its catch, only to be chased incessantly by the predatory seabirds. Once the duck released its morsel one of the gulls would seize it. Having done so, the gull too faced the risk of assault as the rest of the tribe squabbled for the prize. It was a brutal form of piracy but it also produced a dramatic scene of pure winter: the great black slick of seaduck shattering and condensing in response to the harassment, while among them roved the graceful band of gulls, their underwings shining as brilliant blades of white against the dark water. All passed in and out of sight as they rolled on the endless swell.

Mark Cocker

The secret diary of a provincial man
by Adrian Mole, aged 33
August 12 2000

Saturday, Ashby-de-la-Zouch

Ivan Braithwaite continues to be fascinated by what he calls 'working-class culture'. He has suggested that our family go to Skegness on what he calls a 'bucket-and-spade holiday'. He drivelled on about candyfloss, donkeys and 'the glorious vulgarity of the amusement arcade'. I had no choice but to say yes. I can't afford my preferred holiday – visiting literary shrines throughout the world. In fact, so far I have only visited one: Julian Barnes's house in Leicester. Though he left there when he was six weeks old.

Sunday

A boarding house has been booked: the Utopia. Bed, breakfast and evening meal will cost Ivan £13.50 per adult per night – half-price for William. Rosie has refused to go: she said she has got to attend Mad Dog Jackson's graduation ceremony. He is now an MA, and his dissertation, *Socialism, Necrophilia and Other Taboos*, has provoked interest from the *Spectator*.

Monday, the Utopia

Talk about a major infringement of the Trades Description Act! The Dystopia would be a more accurate title for this Draylon hell-hole. I share a draughty attic room with William and Glenn. There is no space in which to swing a dead vole, let alone a cat. The view from the skylight is of mournful-looking seagulls with morsels of chips in their beaks. The owners, Barry and Yvonne Windermere, are ex-variety performers. I shall go mad if Barry tells me another 'joke'. Ivan and my mother think this raddled old duo are 'fabulous characters'. Personally, whenever I hear the fabulous characters phrase, I want to run – into the sea, until the cold waves close over my head.

Wednesday, wind shelter, Skegness

Glenn is sulking in the attic, he has already spent all his pocket money on the slot machines in the arcade where we were forced to take shelter from the cruel wind that blows unchecked from the Urals across the North Sea. Ivan and my mother struggled to construct a windbreak, and William, dressed in an anorak, sheltered behind it and tried to make a sandcastle, but his fingers turned blue and I had to take him into a cafe to thaw out. The place was full of shivering families eating terrible food. Ivan went on saying to my mother, 'This is an authentic working-class experience, isn't it, Pauline?' His eyes were shining with excitement. He is turned on by vulgarity. It is why he fell in love and married my mother. My mother drew heavily on her St Moritz menthol fag with the gold-rimmed filter and said, 'Ivan, I'm no longer working class. I read the *Guardian* and buy coffee beans now, or hadn't you noticed?'

Thursday
The sun came out today. Ivan bought a kiss-me-quick-and-shag-me-slow sunhat. I saw my mother wince when he put it on, but she kept her mouth shut and feigned interest in a stick of rock shaped like a penis.

Friday, Queen Mother's birthday
Barry and Yvonne have decorated the dining room with union jack bunting. The little table where the condiments are normally kept has been turned into a shrine to the Queen Mother. Two candles burn either side of a lurid photograph of the aged one. Barry met her once, back-stage at the Palladium. 'What did she say to you?' I asked. 'She asked me how long I'd been waiting,' he said, his slobbery lips trembling with emotion. 'And what did you reply?' I asked. 'Not long, ma'am,' he said, and almost broke down. Unfortunately, Glen knocked over one of the candles at dinner time and set fire to the Queen Mother's photograph. I threw a cup of tea over it, but the damage was considerable. We have been asked to leave. Proof, perhaps, that there is a God.

Sue Townsend

A Country Diary
August 17 2000

NORTHUMBERLAND: Ahead, the sea sparkled in the sunlight all the way to the horizon. Behind, goldfinches tugged seeds from thistle heads and the warm, blustery wind carried a steady stream of thistledown over our heads and out across the waves. This uncultivated margin between newly cut hay fields and the rocky foreshore – a broad strip of truly wild land – is a refuge for birds, insects and wild flowers at any time of the year. In early summer it was a natural rock garden of sea pinks, silverweed, bird's foot trefoil, cowslips and sea plantain. Now, in high summer, they've given way to purple knapweed, hawkweeds, drifts of pink rest harrow and tall spikes of mallow and russet brown dock seeds. There are uncommon plants too, higher up the slope – such as hound's tongue, whose dull purple flowers produce clusters of hooked fruits that have an astonishingly tenacious grip on walkers' socks. Today a few sea pinks were still in bloom in the crevices just above the rock pools on the upper shore, alongside a patch of late sea campion flowers where a family of pied wagtails hawked for insects. The aeshna dragonfly that rattled past my head was hunting insects too, catching seaweed flies. These breed in vast numbers in natural compost heaps of seaweed left by spring tides, hatching in tens of thousands in the August heat, just in time to feed swallows as they congregate along the coastline before migration. Inland butterflies seem to be having a poor summer but here on the coast scores of meadow browns and common blues danced among the golden yellow grasses as they bent in the breeze. Swarms of metallic green and crimson six-spot burnet moths, recently emerged from papery cocoons on the grass stems, crawled over the knapweed flowers. These burnets are among the most lethargic of moths, never making long flights, merely fluttering from flower to flower. Just as well for this population, as the next landfall if they were to blow out to sea would be the Dutch coast.

Phil Gates

A word in your shell-like: get that monstrosity off our beach
November 3 2003

The woman jabbed an angry forefinger at the map and snapped: 'There! That's where it's going! If it's going anywhere!' If sculptor Maggi Hambling's gift were a horse, its jaw would be aching from the number of people looking it in the mouth. Her giant scallop shell sculpture in honour of the composer Benjamin Britten, a gift to the town of Aldeburgh, Suffolk, which they both loved, is indeed going somewhere: it will be installed on the shingly beach and the former culture secretary, Chris Smith, will unveil it on the beach next Saturday. If the town wanted to buy the piece, it probably could not afford it. Hambling gave her time free, and the cost of construction was raised through hundreds of private subscriptions, a small amount of Arts Council money, and through a special sale of her paintings.

'Mixed' is the polite word for the town's reaction. 'Bloody awful-looking thing, we're going to have to take our walks in the opposite direction now,' one dog walker snapped. At one point the Aldeburgh's blameless Snooks was dragged into the row, when a rumour spread that the town would get the Hambling sculpture rather than a replacement for the little bronze terrier which was stolen last year. The statue was given in memory of much loved husband and wife team of doctors, and even though Snooks is safely back on his plinth, the row rumbles on. 'Much more suitable at Snape Maltings' – the civil version of the dog walker's reaction, and the view of several of the local and county councillors who eventually gave the sculpture planning permission – can be taken as code for 'get that hideous thing off our doorstep'. Snape, several miles inland, is where the annual music festival in Britten's memory is held.

In Aldeburgh itself only a window in the local church commemorates the fact that Britten spent most of his life in the town, which inspired some of his best-loved work including the opera *Peter Grimes*. On an information panel on the seafront, he comes third after the Victorian doctor Elizabeth Garrett Anderson and the Georgian poet George Crabbe. Maggi Hambling sighed deeply. 'I know, I know. It never crossed my mind that it would be in any way controversial. I thought that people might come up and say thank you – more fool me. My own newsagent just said to me, "Hello, how's the eyesore coming along?"'

The eyesore is a glorious thing, four tonnes of steel cut and shaped into giant scallop shells, which will rear up from the beach. From the shore the cut-out letters against the sky will read as a line from Peter Grimes: 'I hear those voices that will not be drowned.' It was made 100 metres inland, by Sam and Dennis Pegg, a father and son team who run a foundry and are usually busy building and repairing boats. They have never made anything remotely like the sculpture before, and are bursting with pride over it. 'Simple really – we had the model, and we just had to scale it up by 37 times, nothing to it,' Sam said. 'We've had a tonne weight hanging off that top bit, and it didn't budge – it'll stand up to anything.' The work has been built to cope with anything the sea can throw at it – on a beach where winter winds can reach 100mph. Hambling – whose equally debated memorial in London to Oscar Wilde was conceived as the poet sitting up in his coffin, inviting visitors to sit down for a chat – has also designed the scallop to be a grandstand view of the waves, and a shelter.

'When somebody climbs up on it to sit down and watch the sea, or when a couple creeps in underneath it to make love, then it will be complete,' she said.

Janet McCarthy looked out at *Silver Harvest*, her partner's fishing boat, coming in on a glittering tide with a haul of dover sole. Her fish shop is the last in the row of timber shacks on the beach, preserved by faith and regular coats of tar. If she looks along the shore instead of out to sea, her view is of virgin shingle beyond the seaside shelters and Edwardian villas. Ms McCarthy tried to be polite about the new view from her shop. 'I don't know much about it but it is a bit of a monstrosity ... I think it would be more suitable at Snape.'

Maev Kennedy

Country diary
December 11 2004

NORTH PEMBROKESHIRE: Walking through this mild November looking at foxgloves and dandelions in bloom around me, I saw buzzards soaring and calling. Then two days running there was a peregrine looking down. A clear sign to go to the sea. Next day was fine in the hills, then wet on the coastal path. At the Parrog we looked up to a strong but truncated rainbow. It shone from a mixture of grey cloud with streaks of duck-egg blue which strengthened as it approached the horizon. The grey was breaking into azure. A small flock of starlings whirled in a stab and search before settling on a wire. The tide was coming in. A lone curlew called across the bay. The coastal path was pocked by badgers digging for worms or bulbs. Clumps of gorse and blackthorn had been tunnelled into. In one section there was a bank of gorse above the sea on one side and a gorse hedge on the other. The shelter this provided was noticeable. We stood still to watch the cormorants fan their wings, to listen to herring gulls challenge those they flew over, to give a rendition of the sound that haunts me still from childhood, but no peregrine. A raven appeared on the piece of cliff which usually has a nest in spring. We scanned the sea for dolphins, nothing. It was a quiet, damp day. An elder bush that had been trimmed back gleamed from the bank: moss had covered it apart from the new tight brown buds, one of which had opened into a floral turn of green leaves. Throughout the walk, bands of mist and grey cloud moved over the countryside, at times broken by a blue gleam. Carn Ingli was always visible.

Returning to the car we were scolded by a noisy silhouette sitting on a blackthorn. The sky was clearing, allowing the sun to deepen the green blue colour of the water and pick out the astonishing variety of autumn colours this season has provided. We arrived home in time to help decorate the village Christmas tree.

Audrey Insch

Last night's TV: The coast is toast
July 30 2005

Those people who cut the crust off their bread are missing out on the best bit – the goodness. It's the same with Britain: the best bits are round the edges. So *Coast* (BBC1) is a bit like toast, and it's wonderful. We've reached the Severn estuary, where the best action actually takes place away from the sea. But it's worth making a little journey inland to see the Severn bore. Nicholas Crane waits in the moonlight, by a glassy smooth river. It seems that nothing could disturb this peace, but then out of the darkness it comes, an impossible wave, heading upstream. 'My God, huge breaking waves, fantastic,' shouts Crane before leaping on his bike and peddling off into the night to catch the wave. Bespectacled, cagouled, rucksacked, overflowing with breathless enthusiasm, he's like your favourite geography teacher. Or Dan Cruikshank without a passport. From there we head out along the estuary of the Severn, whose massive tidal ranges cause that wave upstream. And we end up round the corner in Aberystwyth.

I like this programme because it's not about history, natural history, geography, geology or tourism. It's about all of those things. So we see the footprints of children who walked the mudflats of the estuary 7,000 years ago. We visit Cardiff with its early Tiger Bay multiculturalism, then carry on to the towering limestone cliffs of South Glamorgan, and Dylan Thomas's Laugharne. We find Honeycomb worms, sea mice, an amazing dogfish embryo swimming around inside its pod, and the cave where the Red Lady of Paviland, who wasn't a lady at all, was found. We see the huge water harbour of Milford haven, where the *Sea Empress* spilled her evil cargo; we walk along Pembrokeshire's coastal path; and we make a 20-mile deviation to visit the Smalls lighthouse, with its history of madness and death. See what I mean about the crust being the best bit? It's full of richness. The only thing I don't approve of are the blue BBC Discover Your Coast signs they're putting up to advertise the programme's tie-in interactive walks. Don't ruin it all with your horrible signs. Oh, and I was upset that Charlotte Church didn't get a look in. How can you pass through Cardiff and not pay homage to the cultural contribution of Charlotte Church?

Sam Wollaston

To the edge of the canvas
July 14 2007

Margate. Twinned, in a step-sisterly way, with St Ives. A pair of seaside peninsulas. England's two big toes. Waning fishing ports. Both blinded by light, blessed by Turner, and contemporised by strong female artists, Tracey Emin and Barbara Hepworth. But why? After a life in St Ives and a day in Margate, my eye tells me it's not all down to light. Yes, logically, the day has nowhere to hide as half of each town is sea, so the rays bounce off the water and sand, making the day feel brighter and longer. But, and this is a big fat 'but', it's overrated, overwritten and not the primary pull of each place. Theorists, gallerists and hoteliers use the 'light' as currency to fuel their keep, but there is a more potent force at work here. The sea, the sea.

We come to the sea to get away from the land. It's about the removal of something. The greatest artists work towards subtraction and simplicity all their lives until what is left is so pure, so raw, it can only be art. Dark, bare and elemental. Barbara Hepworth first came to St Ives one midnight in torrid rain, with weary triplets. Her spirits zero. The next day the beauty hit her. 'At high tide, the waves thumped the house and spray fell all around us. I crept down at dawn to collect stones, seaweed and paint, and draw by myself.'

The sea sieves the mind of urban cholesterol. It's the edge – where land stops and ocean starts. Solid, static matter versus a fluid, saline animal that always wins. The beach makes us happy, but if land only met sand, it would be a desert. Artists need friction. The coast is the most dynamic threshold on earth. It begs bravery. Yet much of our seaside art is clumsy or, worse still, dull. The smarter artists find a way around this provincial myopia. The landscape art pioneer Richard Long uses the coast as a material, transposing a Norfolk pebble to a Welsh beach. He then reverses the 'sculpture' by walking an Aberystwyth pebble to Aldeburgh beach. We recently collaborated on a synchronised walk and talk at Tate St Ives. He spoke of the shape of a walk: 'You're tracing a natural form. I sometimes measure my walks by tides rather than days. They differ around the coast and can dictate when to start and end a walk. The tide is the sea breathing.' It makes you think of the moon as lungs. Artists help us see the world from the inside out.

For Antony Gormley, the sea is a springboard for scale. Havmann, a 10-metre tall, black body mass 46 metres from shore in a fjord, 'reads as a black hole, like a void or a keyhole … Because there's an indeterminacy of scale in relation to the landscape, it is difficult to judge its actual size.'

Peter Lanyon, who once taught Long, told his students to 'lie on your back, look at the sky, and feel …' To which I would add, 'the salt'. Lie close to a cliff, as DH Lawrence did when he wrote of Zennor in Cornwall: 'I lie looking down at a cove where the waves come white under a low black headland, which slopes up in bare green-brown, bare and sad under a level sky.'

Mother Ocean is one strange old magnet. Ions and ethers do things that science tries to explain, only to give up and gulp the salt air instead. Recently I was whipped by a wave on Margate pier. Just three days off June, the town shut (a bank holiday) and the once-great lido in mid-suicide, its mouth ajar, drowned with sand. The town is on its knees. But a beacon beckons. Three years from now, David Chipperfield's radical £29m Turner Contemporary will crowbar Margate into the 21st century. It's a salute to Turner's lifelong love of the sea, the town and 'his darling', *The Fighting Temeraire*, sketched from a steamer as she was towed to her Rotherhithe grave.

Yet the story here is an upper. Last year's Artangel-backed 'The Margate Exodus', with Gormley's magnificent *Waste Man* in flames, is setting the tone. Culture resuscitates communities. The Glasgow Business School called it 'the Tate effect', which reunites us with St Ives. Post-Tate, my home town got its 1960s swagger back and it radiated through the town, from sewage-free beaches to hollandaise-free fish. Let's hope Margate is fully flaunting its mojo come 2010.

Peter Kirby

Country diary
January 12 2008

ABERDARON: From long habit, at epiphany I take myself down to the furthest end of Lleyn and walk round the coastal path from Porth Meudwy to visit the most redolent and inaccessible of all the holy wells in Wales – Ffynnon Fair, in the cliffs below Braich y Pwll. At the parking place on the common of Mynydd y Gwyddel, Barbour-clad couples emerge from 4WD behemoths to strike poses and brandish binoculars. I slip away down the stepped descent to sea level and traverse to the triangular, rock-girt pool, dip my face into clear water and drink, open my eyes and see small fish clinging to its viridian-weed-lined walls, copper pence greening in the sandy bottom. The sea in the cove is a thick, muttering impasto, in the flecked texture of which I catch sight of a small bird before she dives. She comes up near the mouth of the cove, rises briefly in the water to shake her wings, then takes off in scudding flight between the waves and heads for offshore Bardsey. She's a Manx shearwater, her presence here and now reminding of the strange and changing nature of the seasons. As I search the tide-race for glimpses of her, from overhead comes the whistling high call of a pair of choughs. As though connected by elastic, they stretch and rebound in playful flight before landing with that lovely corvid bounce on the open greensward where imposing ruins of the great pilgrims' church and hospice still stood in Thomas Pennant's day. They probe the grassed banks and dykes of former walls, red curved bills seeking for ants. On the road above, the Barbour-wearers are still by their vehicles, webcams recording proprietorialism. A lone raven grates out its harsh and minimal commentary as I follow the banked lane back towards Aberdaron, and a flock of lapwings 50-strong drifts by, their plangent cries like elegies.

Jim Perrin

Lives & letters: 'A raft on the sea'
February 23 2008

Heading into south-east London via docklands in early spring last year, I passed a spray of flowers propped against a wall to commemorate the anniversary of the death of Derek Jarman. The artist lived in various riverside warehouses in the 1970s, arriving at the third floor of block B, Butler's Wharf, in 1973. During his first summer there, he wrote in his diary: 'The studio is a forest of emerald-green columns, at sunrise, the ducks float in on the driftwood over a glacial river which reflects orange and vermilion, while the sun pours through the doors.' By 1979 , however, he had jettisoned the old grain warehouse, having tired of lording it over a 'gay Butlins'.

I've never been a fan of Jarman's art or even his films, many of which feature in a new exhibition at the Serpentine Gallery. As a native Londoner with a link to the neighbourhood that Jarman made his home in the 1970s, and with a passion for the Kent coast around Dungeness where he lived in the years before his death in 1994, I prefer his diaries (*Modern Nature, Dancing Ledge, Smiling in Slow Motion*) and the early Super 8 footage in which he documents his impressions of these landscapes. The bleakness of the redundant docks in the 1970s appealed to Jarman much as the shingle beach at Dungeness did in the following decade. His relationship with the Thames was succeeded by a passion for the English coast.

His writings are dotted with sketches from his childhood holidays at the English seaside: Bexhill, where his mother grew up; travelling to Bournemouth and being rewarded with sixpence for spotting Corfe Castle before his sister; Southend, the week before graduating; sketching the landscape at Seaview, the Isle of Wight, during the summer England won the football world cup. His most cherished coastal memories were of the holiday his family took at Kilve on the Somerset coast, creating driftwood sculptures on the beach: '*Oklahoma!* on the gramophone, maidenhair ferns watered with cold tea, a cat and a boxer puppy. Bulb catalogues, scented balsam poplars, a vegetable garden . . .'

Long after Kilve, Jarman discovered a personal heaven at the final stop on the diminutive Romney, Hythe and Dymchurch railway, where the 15 mile coastal journey comes to a halt. His affinity with this landscape was first hinted at years before – squinted at in the 1970s, on a day away from the docklands. He had no idea then it would be his final home. Jarman described the marshy peninsula of Dungeness, with its expansive shingle and its headland dwellings scattered like shrubs, as the 'ivory fang of a prehistoric shark'. His name has become synonymous with the place, and his later diaries are dominated by it. It is a terrain that has captured the imagination of other writers, notably HG Wells and E Nesbit. In *The First Men in the Moon*, written from the author's home at Sandgate, using Romney Sands and Dungeness as the setting, Wells likened it to a 'raft on the sea'. It is on the marsh that the protagonist, Bedford, meets the eccentric Cavor, who has discovered the means to transport men to the moon. When they eventually arrive on the moon, the landscape is not too dissimilar from that of Dungeness, as viewed from his bungalow at Lympne: 'bulging masses of a cactus form, and scarlet and purple lichens that grew so fast they seemed to crawl over the rocks'. When Bedford returns to earth, it is to the exact spot from which he was dispatched weeks before: 'Away to the right curved the land, a shingle bank with little hovels, and at last a lighthouse . . .'

Wells moved to Sandgate in 1898, and built his home – Spade House – in 1900, the year he wrote *The First Men in the Moon*. With his wife, he used to visit the children's writer Edith Nesbit and her husband Hubert Bland in Dymchurch when they were taking their summer holidays in Kent. Nesbit first visited Dymchurch during the drought of 1893. Two years before her death in 1924, and having married again, she settled permanently on Romney Sands. Home was two huts joined by a passage the couple referred to as the 'Suez canal', which had previously served as a storehouse and a laboratory for the military. This set-up struck some visitors as bizarre, as did Jarman's later choice of home, only minutes away in Dungeness – a run-down cottage built in 1900 for a local fishing family.

For Nesbit, the landscape more than matched those of the idyllic summers of her childhood, spent in Dieppe, Paris and Bordeaux. At home, in her final days, she lay propped up in her four-poster bed, with a panoramic view of the marsh and 'the little lovely hills of Kent'. For Jarman, too, this stretch of coast outshone the foreign settings of earlier summers: 'Never in my sleepless nights had I witnessed a spectacle like this. Not the antique bells of the flocks moving up a Sardinian hillside, the barking dogs and the sharp cries of shepherd boys, nor moonlit nights sailing the Aegean, nor the scented nights and fireflies of Fire Island, smashed glass star-strewn through the piers of the Hudson – nothing can equal this.' Echoing Bedford's description of the landscape as 'the most uneventful place in the world', Jarman wrote of how he had rediscovered his 'boredom' at Dungeness. 'The train could carry me to London,' he wrote in *Modern Nature* ... 'But I resist.'

Prospect Cottage, the exterior of which Jarman painted black with sherbet-yellow window frames, was bought in 1986 with money he inherited after his father's death. It was the first and last home he owned. Soon he was aware that Aids was circling him 'like a deadly cobra'. In his attitude to this subject, too, his elitism and sense of superiority were evident. There was no death greater than that of the gay auteur with Aids, according to Jarman: 'all the brightest and the best trampled to death – surely even the great war brought no more loss into one life in just 12 months, and all this as we made love not war'.

Even at Dungeness he could not escape the ugliness of the modern world: on a day out from Bart's hospital, sick, tired, with his hands in soil or shingle up to the plastic identity band on his wrist, he observed of neighbouring Greatstone, where many working-class Londoners had retired: 'Can you find in these four miles of houses one constructed with love or care? This is not covered up by their names: Ben Venue, Costa Lotta, Seadrift. Behind them, Hopeville: a scatter of concrete and caravans.' Snobbery permeates Jarman's writings, almost as much as sex and travel. In his view, only an artist has the ability to transform debris, found objects and a dilapidated seaside home into a thing of beauty. Both Jarman and Nesbit chose to end their days living on a coastal stretch that could not be further removed from the London landscape of their youth. Both had thrived in the cultural margins of the capital. Nesbit was an author steeped in the politics of class and gender; Jarman was preoccupied with the politics of sexuality. Nesbit is buried beneath a spreading elm in the churchyard of St Mary's-in-the-Marsh, Jarman in the grounds of St Clement's at nearby Old Romney.

Jarman began the garden at Prospect Cottage when he found a piece of flint on the beach at low tide, some driftwood and a dog rose. He was a boy again on the beach at Kilve, creating sculptures, but this time the tide would not wash them away. In a neighbour's garden, along the road at Windrift, Jarman created an artwork from a piece of slate on which he carved the words: 'The timeless sadness of childhood.' (These works now appear on the pages of books and glossy newspaper supplements with features targeted at those scouting for a second home on the coast.) On the day he first visited the cottage, Jarman left Dungeness with thoughts of Matthew Arnold's 'Dover Beach': 'Down the vast edges drear / and naked shingles of the world.'

He asked the previous owner if the sound of the wind ever ceased at Dungeness. It was a soundtrack, a tinnitus, a hum to which the residents became immune. When the wind rose on an October night in 1987 heralding the storm that swept across England, it was reminiscent of that created by Cavor in *The First Men in the Moon* for launching himself and Bedford into outer space: 'A large fragment of fencing came sailing past me, dropped edgeways ... In that instant the whole face of the world had changed. The tranquil sunset had vanished, the sky was dark with scurrying clouds, everything was flattened and swaying with the gale.' Prospect Cottage was severely shaken by the storm, and Dungeness was left without electricity. 'I stared at the glittering power plant on the horizon,' Jarman wrote, 'and wondered if, like the Emerald City and the great Oz himself, my life and this cottage had been dreamt all those years ago . . .' Twilight here, according to Jarman, was like twilight nowhere else in England, or even the world: 'You feel as you stand here that tired time is having a snooze.'

Michael Collins

Magical moments as Folkestone emerges from the waves
June 20 2008

Witty, thoughtful and definitely worth a day at the seaside, the inaugural Folkestone Triennial, curated by Andrea Schlieker, reflects both the town's past and its run-down present. A fashionable Victorian and Edwardian resort, Folkestone declined following the first world war, when thousands of young men embarked from here to the Flanders trenches, many never to return. Mark Wallinger has lain out a square of numbered beach pebbles on the grassy clifftop, one for each life lost on the first day of battle on the Somme. Close to a number of public benches facing Boulogne and the distant French hills, Christian Boltanski broadcasts readings of letters exchanged between lovers on the brink of war, and from a soldier longing for his family – all donated by local families. The words float on the wind.

In the public library, a film by Tacita Dean records a dawn crossing from Boulogne to Folkestone; the camera's alternating views from port to starboard have an increasingly queasy and soporific effect. In a coastal lookout on the cliffs, another film, by Langlands and Bell, contrasts the tough determination of France's busiest fishing port to Folkestone's demoralised quiet. At low tide in the harbour, the old buildings of a fish market appear on the mud – a drowned world constructed by Polish artist Robert Kusmirowski. This is magical. Unexpectedly, so too are Tracey Emin's small, bronze casts of abandoned plimsoles and other bits of infant clothing, dotted casually about the town like so much flotsam. A bronze mitten spiked on a railing waves to no one. All are reminders of the teenage pregnancies and lost kids in south-coast towns.

Richard Wentworth's similarly discrete interventions around the town describe nearby local flora on a number of blue plaques – privet, the plane tree, a weeping ash in the graveyard – none of which were originally indigenous species. As with Emin's work, there is a subtext in a town with its share of asylum seekers and its mistrust of outsiders. But the art rarely strays from the more picturesque parts of Folkestone. Up on the cliff, Ayse Erkmen has covered a local Martello tower with camouflage. It is like trying to hide an elephant. American Mark Dion has built a giant fibreglass replica gull, which doubles as a travelling 'gull appreciation unit', doing a bit of PR for these maligned creatures, liberally spattering the town and filling the air with their cries.

Even Dion's kiosk is not immune. Sometimes there is no gratitude.

Adrian Searle

We do like to be beside
August 19 2008

In *Waterlog*, an account of his wild swimmer's journey through Britain, the late Roger Deakin observes the 'hairless apes squealing with pleasure in the sea' at Porthcurno in Cornwall, and wonders why people are so playful and carefree on the beach. He concludes that our species emerged from the sea, and our dry-land existence is a recent phenomenon, so we simply feel more at home on the shore. The resurgent interest in 'wildness' among contemporary nature writers, such as Deakin, Robert Macfarlane and Kathleen Jamie, has often gravitated towards the beach. This is partly because many of our beaches, on the Jurassic coast of Devon and Dorset or the great shingle peninsulas in the south-east, are such strange, otherworldly places. But it's also because the beach is a point of accommodation between humans and nature. Deakin may have felt the call of the wild, but he was also a dedicated beach anthropologist, wandering Monsieur Hulot-like among the tame holidaymakers with their windbreakers and Primus stoves.

The ideal of the beach in western culture is of a beautiful tabula rasa, a deserted landscape of virgin sand and transluscent sea where you can escape from the stresses of modern life – which is presumably why you can now buy a 'beach in a box' for your office desktop, with a miniature deckchair, sea shells and sand. But as the BBC series *Coast* showed – once you got beyond its self-consciously stirring music and sweeping aerial views – the British beach is a case study in cultural history. Our beaches have had all sorts of uses, including land speed record attempts at Pendine Sands in Carmarthen Bay, improvised airstrips at Southport and D-day dummy runs at Slapton Sands in Devon. More recently, beaches have become highly artificial environments, as tidal changes and coastal erosion force resorts such as Minehead and Lyme Regis to import or dredge sand from the seabed. The beach is a frontier not only between water and solid ground, but also between the wild and the domestic. It is where sand-yachters and kite-buggyers share space with picnickers and sunbathers, in states of proximity and undress they would never tolerate in their ordinary lives. As a self-policing community, the beach also condones a certain amount of low-level lawlessness, from nicking boulders for garden water features to scavenging for Nike trainers in the cargo ship containers that occasionally wash up. Even Ian McEwan admitted to liberating a few pebbles from Chesil beach, although he later returned them at the invitation of Weymouth and Portland borough council.

Deakin admired beaches as places where social hierarchies are temporarily suspended. So I imagine he would have disliked the current fashion, in newspaper travel supplements, for listing our 'best' beaches. This trend for grading beaches began with conservation societies worrying about pollution. But it has become a beauty contest, as resorts compete over things like wave size and sandcastle buildability. Some of this is less to do with the beaches themselves than the accident of location. Resorts that are within second-home distance of London's middle classes tend to emphasise the clean minimalism of their beaches, because that is what appeals to busy professionals and downshifters. The struggling resorts in my own area of the north-west, such as Blackpool, Morecambe and New Brighton, rely instead on council-led regeneration plans for casinos, lidos and refurbished art deco hotels, and don't go on about their beaches so much.

Contrary to some reports, the Policy Exchange publication *Cities Unlimited* does not write off all the regeneration schemes in the north. It is fairly optimistic about inland cities and gloomiest about coastal towns. In a motorway-based economy, it argues, these places are literally at the end of the road. It is an anti-coast manifesto. All the places it commends for being well connected – Corby, Daventry and Oxford – are miles from a beach. Fortunately, the beach has no truck with neoliberal economics, or indeed beauty contests. Almost everywhere on the coast has a serviceable beach nearby. And I will happily trade living in a motorway hub for living as I do within 10 minutes' drive of Crosby beach. On late summer evenings when the day-trippers have gone, there is no one else about except some naked, cast-iron men staring out across Liverpool Bay. Anthony Gormley's rusty artwork, *Another Place*, is a reminder that, even on a deserted beach, people have left their mark.

Joe Moran

Designing the Seaside: Architecture, Society and Nature, by Fred Gray
March 28 2009

John Cowper Powys vividly recalled ogling girls' ankles on Brighton beach, as well as the 'smells of seaweed and fish and tar and sweat and sandwiches and rope and paint and cheap perfumes and foam drenched petticoats and bilge-water and beer'. A professor at Sussex University, Fred Gray's study of seaside architecture is rooted in his knowledge of Brighton, 'Britain's greatest seaside resort'. In the 1730s, the Rev William Clarke and his wife more or less invented the seaside holiday when they told their friends of lazy days spent sunning themselves on the beach, bathing and listening to the 'plashing of the waves against the cliffs'. They stayed at Brighthelmstone, later renamed Brighton. Although *Designing the Seaside* is dry at times, the wonderful illustrations (including McGill's saucy postcards) more than compensate. From pavilions and piers (including the scandalous demise of Brighton's West Pier), to bungalows, beach huts and bathing machines ('the first purpose-designed form of seaside architecture'), this is a fine celebration of a very English invention.

PD Smith

Resurgent British resorts braced for bumper Easter
April 9 2009

For many people around Britain who recall the 1970s the scene will appear eerily familiar: a car packed full of luggage and already fractious children, about to set off to a seaside resort or campsite for a few days of wholesome fun in reliably tepid weather. There may even be a caravan involved.

After a period in which spring sunshine breaks in the Canaries or even Florida became increasingly common, this year's Easter holiday season, which begins in earnest today, has taken on a decidedly retro flavour. A combination of financial worries, a weak pound and a general, longer-term trend towards domestic breaks, will see millions eschew foreign destinations in favour of relaxation closer to home.

While many will still pack the airports, around 10m cars are taking to the roads while the rail network will handle 1 million more passengers than this time last year. Bookings to classic British holiday destinations such as Blackpool, Windermere and Scarborough have doubled from 2008, according to rail operators, while many camping and caravan sites are already booked out. Bournemouth, meanwhile, has seen a sudden upsurge in inquiries about beach huts.

Peter Walker and Dan Milmo

Index

SCOTTISH BORDERS COUNCIL

LIBRARY &

INFORMATION SERVICES